# RAISING UP A FAMILY
## TO THE LORD

Other publications by Elder Gene R. Cook:

*Living by the Power of Faith*
*Fathers Are Forever*
*Faith in the Lord Jesus Christ* (audio tape)
*Receiving Answers to Our Prayers* (audio tape)
*13 Lines of Defense: Living the Law of Chastity* (audio tape)

# RAISING UP A FAMILY TO THE LORD

## GENE R. COOK

Deseret Book Company
Salt Lake City, Utah

*To faithful parents*
*who are striving with all their hearts*
*to raise up their families to the Lord*

**Library of Congress Cataloging-in-Publication Data**

Cook, Gene R.
   Raising up a family to the Lord / Gene R. Cook.
     p.   cm.
   Includes index.
   ISBN 0-87579-713-X   3/12  47717987
   1. Family—Religious life. 2. Church of Jesus Christ of Latter-day Saints—Doctrines. 3. Mormon Church—Doctrines. I. Title.
BX8643.F3C66
248.8'45—dc20                    93-8928
                              CIP

Printed in the United States of America    72082-4677
10  9  8  7

# CONTENTS

# CHILDREN OF THE NOBLE BIRTHRIGHT

When we consider what it means to raise up a family to the Lord, we must ask ourselves a few questions: Who is this generation that we are attempting to raise up to the Lord? Are they really the children of the noble birthright? What part will they play in this final dispensation of time? Let me illustrate in part the answer to those questions with something that happened in our family a few years ago.

One of our older sons was working in a cemetery, and my younger sons and I used to go there in the evening and scare him. That was probably not the thing to do, but we all enjoyed it, including the son who worked there. Once when we were kidding about it at supper, I told him, "Son, if you have any spare time up there, why don't you dig a big hole for your father. It ought to be about six and a half feet long and six feet deep. You may as well get it ready." One of my other boys said, "Yeah, do one for me, too. When the day comes for me to be called home, I'll be ready." We all laughed about it.

However, another son very seriously said, "Well, you won't need one for me."

"Why not?" we asked.

"Because I'm not going to die."

We all laughed and said, "Surely you're going to die. Everybody's going to die. Nobody escapes death."

He said, "Well, I'm not planning on it."

I could tell he meant what he had said, so I pursued it further. "What do you mean?" I asked.

"After hearing about my friend's patriarchal blessing and some other things, I hope I'll be here when the Savior comes," he replied. "I hope I'll be caught up and changed in the twinkling of an eye, so I won't need some cemetery plot."

We could see he was very serious about the idea, and who were we to say otherwise? Perhaps what he said will come to pass. It was a serious thought that reminded me of the inspired question, "Who is this generation we are raising up to the Lord?"

My wife and I were somewhat sobered some days later to see our six-year-old son come home with a T-shirt they'd given him at school. Across the front of this beautiful green shirt were the words *The Class of 2000*. We were quite taken aback to think that one of our own would be graduating in that year. Of course, no one knows when the Lord will come but our Father in heaven. But certainly the time is drawing closer. It may well be that this generation we are attempting to raise up to the Lord will be the generation to meet him when he comes. At any rate, we must give our best effort to prepare this generation to receive him, either in this life or the next.

# ACKNOWLEDGMENTS

What a blessing to have been raised in a good family with parents, brothers, and a sister who taught me much about wholesome family life! I am also profoundly indebted to my own good wife and children for having patience with me as their husband and father in allowing me to learn while serving my own family. Most of what we have learned about raising up families to the Lord has surely come from the Lord through these wonderful spirits whom he has entrusted to our care.

Particular appreciation is expressed to my wife and children who helped organize the scriptures, stories, and other material in this book, and who also helped edit the manuscript. My daughter-in-law Ashlee Ethington Cook supplied the illustrations, for which I am grateful. I would like to thank Kristine Buchanan, Deon Saunders, Rebecca Day, and Christa Whitaker, who did much of the typing and editing of the manuscript. Thanks also goes to Jack M. Lyon, managing editor of Deseret Book Company, who edited the manuscript and greatly assisted in its compilation.

May I especially express my deepest gratitude to the Lord for his guidance in assisting us in our attempts to raise up a family to him and for the direct inspiration that has come in compiling this book.

Lastly, may I say that this book is not in any way an official publication of The Church of Jesus Christ of Latter-day Saints, and any shortcomings, omissions, or deficiencies are clearly mine. May the Lord bless all who read this material to better raise up their families to the Lord.

# RAISING UP A FAMILY
# TO THE LORD

A couple of years ago while on a plane to a stake conference, I sat by a couple in their sixties, both of whom were faithful members of the Church. After we had discussed the gospel a little, the woman began to pour out her heart to me about her six children. She felt that she and her husband had been fairly successful with four of them, but two had turned completely away from the Church, rebelling at everything that was good.

Through her tears she said, "What did we do wrong? They went through the Young Men and Young Women programs, through Boy Scouts, through all the activities the Church provided. We made sure they were active in the Church, believing that would keep them on the right track.

"We also believed that if we fulfilled all of our Church callings, which we did, our children would be blessed and protected. Now we're confused—we don't know what we could have done differently."

This good woman nearly begged me to explain to her and her husband what they had done wrong or to tell them if they had misplaced their faith in the "systems" of the Church. She was brokenhearted and desperate for an answer. She also expressed great concern about the upcoming generation and what she should do to influence her active children and grandchildren. All in all, it was a touching, heartbreaking discussion with her and her husband.

As I listened to this good couple, I lamented with them about what had happened to their family. My heart was drawn out in sympathy, and I wanted somehow to help them. I've thought many times since that day about some of the hard questions they asked. For example, "If you do your duty, will the Lord take care of your family?" "If you fulfill your callings faithfully, to what degree will the Lord help with your family and 'take up the slack'?" "What influence can we have on our children and grandchildren when they're not living daily under our tutelage in our own home?"

Is it natural that some children are just going to rebel? After all, a third of the hosts of heaven did. Also, some of Adam's children and some of Lehi's did. Are there things we can do to ensure, to some degree, that none of our children will be lost and that none will rebel? Why do things seem to go fairly smoothly in some families while others seem to have all kinds of difficulties? Why is it that in some families some of the children have turned out all right and others, at least so far, have not? Why do children rebel? Are children, in the beginning, all good and holy and wholesome? Does responsibility for their rebellion rest with the parents, with the children, or with both?

The prophets have given some specific hope and counsel about such questions as came from this good couple. Elder Boyd K. Packer has said, "It is a great challenge to raise a family in the darkening mists of our moral environment" ("Our Moral Environment," *Ensign,* May 1992, p. 68). President Harold B. Lee said, "We emphasize that the greatest work you will do will be within the walls of your home" (*Ensign,* July 1973, p. 98). President David O. McKay said, "No other success can compensate for failure in the home" (*Improvement Era,* June 1964, p. 445).

The measure of our success as parents, however, will not rest solely on how our children turn out. That judgment might be just if we could raise our families in a perfectly moral environment, but that is not now possible. And even if it were, they would still have the agency to choose for themselves. Were not the lost third of the hosts of heaven raised in our heavenly home?

Even good and responsible parents sometimes lose children to influences over which they have no control. They agonize over rebellious sons or daughters. They are puzzled about why they feel so helpless when they have tried so hard to do what they should. It is my conviction that those wicked influences will one day be overruled.

Elder Orson F. Whitney, a member of the Quorum of the Twelve, once said:

> The Prophet Joseph Smith declared—and he never taught more comforting doctrine—that the eternal sealings of faithful parents and the divine promises made to them for valiant service in the Cause of Truth, would save not only themselves, but likewise their posterity. Though some of the sheep may wander, the eye of the Shepherd is upon them, and sooner or later they will feel the tentacles of Divine Providence reaching out after them and drawing them back to the fold. Either in this life or the life to come, they will return. They will have to pay their debt to justice; they will suffer for their sins; and may tread a thorny path; but if it leads them at last, like the penitent Prodigal, to a loving and forgiving father's heart and home, the painful experience will not have been in vain. Pray for your careless and disobedient children; hold on to them with your faith. Hope on, trust on, till you see the salvation of God. (*Conference Report*, April 1929, p. 110.)

This promise gives hope to all of us. The real purpose of this book will be to try to describe what the role of parents is and what they can do to be as faithful as possible and thereby assist in the redemption of their children, particularly for those who go astray. Thus this book will try to deal with some of the hard realities, such as:

• What do you do when a child does not want to pray?

• Are all family prayers spiritual ones, or at times are they somewhat routine or even, on occasion, humorous?

• What can you expect from family home evenings?

• How do you handle difficult problems when children do not want to read the scriptures with the family?

• Do you get children up in the morning to read the scriptures, or do you read at night?

• What do you do to keep children from rebelling against what is right?

• How do you handle children who don't want to get a job in their teen years?

• What do you do with a child who may want to have an undesirable friend?

• How do you teach your children to be self-reliant?

• What kinds of family activities help develop spiritual maturity?

• How do you handle discipline?

• Are family rules necessary?

• How important is the content of family prayers?

• What can be done to make routine experiences into spiritual ones?

I salute all of the parents of Zion. I salute the active parents, the less-active parents, the part-member families, and the single-adult parents, for raising a family is one of the greatest challenges of life.

After my mission, I thought, "If I can just get married, all of my problems will be solved." How naive I was! I knew nothing of the challenges that naturally come with marriage and children. I repeat, I salute the families of the Church for the challenges they face and the countless decisions they must make as they faithfully lead their children to do what is right.

## A NOTE ON MARRIAGE AND SINGLE PARENTS

By design, this book centers upon the relationship of parents and children. I have purposely not written about the relationship of husbands and wives. However, in stressing the relationship between parents and children, I have assumed that the relationship between husband and wife is healthy, viable, and strong.

I recognize that many homes have only one parent. I am convinced that they, too, can employ the practices described in this book and be successful, even though it may be more difficult than if there were two parents. Sometimes a family has just one parent because of death or divorce. Sometimes only one parent is a member of the Church. Sometimes one is less active than the other. Just the same, one spiritually motivated parent can successfully raise up a family to the Lord. Some of the best men and women I have known have come from such families. May the Lord always bless those good mothers and fathers who may think they have to do it "on their own" but actually bring up their children under the direction of the Lord.

In families with two parents, the husband and wife must always keep in mind that their relationship is more important than the relationship between parents and children. In time, the children will grow up and start their own homes and families, and the tie to their own children will probably be stronger than that to their parents. But the husband and wife will be together always. If they are faithful, their marriage will be eternal.

Thus, from the time a husband and wife are married, they must continue to strengthen their relationship. They must be particularly careful during and after the years they have children at home. Often husbands go off to work while wives become involved with their children's problems and perhaps schooling or employment after the children have left home. Couples must be careful not to invest so much time in their children, work, and other activities that they lose touch with each other. After the children are gone, some parents sit and look at each other, not knowing what to do. Many marriages have broken up after the children have gone because the husband and wife no longer knew each other. Over the years they have grown apart. Thus, as couples bring up their families, they must also take time for each other.

The purpose of this book is to help parents, no matter what their marital status, raise up their children to the Lord. In it I have tried to teach true principles and then give scores of stories, illustrations, and examples so the principles can

be clearly understood and applied by anyone. I hope and
pray that this effort will help thousands of parents to better
raise up their children to the Lord.

## NORMAL FAMILY CHALLENGES

To emphasize the everyday challenges families face, let
me list some of the challenges we shared with our eight
children over a two-week period—sort of a "snapshot" of
their lives:

*Returned missionary, age twenty-one:* How can he find
a wife? Should he enroll in college? Will his grades be good
enough? Will he have to work while going to school? Will he
be able to get a job? How can he use his faith to find a job
when "there are none"? How can he live while he has no
money to draw upon? What financial assistance should he
expect from his parents? How can the parents help him
while still allowing him to be self-reliant? Should he buy a
car? If he buys one, should he pay cash or buy it on credit?
Should his parents co-sign with him or not be liable? How
does he adjust to life when he has lived in a protected environment and must now return to "the world"?

*Boy on a mission, age nineteen:* Who finances his mission? If his parents finance it, how will they make ends
meet? Who writes letters to him week after week? Do all the
family take turns, or does one person do most of it? How can
we encourage him when he is down? What principles should
we try to teach him in our letters? How can we more effectively pray for him and his investigators? How can we better convey our love to him? How do we help him when his
companion is discouraged or uncooperative? How do we tell
him about what is happening at home without making him
homesick? How do we deal with his girlfriend who likes to
visit us regularly?

*Boy, age eighteen:* Girls, girls, girls! Do parents get him
up early to go to work, or does he get up on his own? Prob-

lems with friends; difficulties with girlfriends. Who decides what time he comes home at night from a date? How many dates should he have? Whom should he date? Who decides his bedtime and his time to get up? How do we manage sharing and use of the car? Who puts gas in the car? Who pays for the gas? How much time should he spend with the family? How much with friends? How do we let him spread his wings and leave the nest without knocking the nest down? How often can he go skiing? How much money should he save? How much should he spend? Does he pay his tithing promptly? How much should he save for his mission? How much time should he study? How much time should he have fun? How many ball games should he go to? How many games should he watch on TV? How can we help him have more initiative?

*Girl, age sixteen:* Boys, boys, boys! Who decides on dress standards? How short is too short? How stylish is too stylish? Is she overweight? Is she underweight? How can we counteract the influence of peers? Should she go to the dance? Will she be asked to go? How often can she use the car? Where can she go? Should she put gas in the car? Does she eat properly, or does she eat too much junk food? Does she fast too much or not enough? Piano lessons. Flute lessons. Who sets the standard on television shows, especially those that are questionable but that "everyone else at school watches"? Who handles the ups and downs of her emotions? Who handles the stresses of sensitivity between allegiance to friends and allegiance to family? How can she handle the pressure of a Church calling? How can she help a friend in trouble? How can she deal with hurt feelings? Who will go with her to the swim meet, the school play, the a capella choir presentation? Who provides the needed priesthood blessings? Who provides the long talks that always come late at night? Who helps her build her self-esteem?

*Girl, age thirteen:* Telephone calls, telephone calls, telephone calls! How can we have patience to answer the phone (again) when we know the call will be for her? Who handles the emotional roller-coaster ride of puberty? Who handles the talks about exercise and weight? What do we do about flute lessons and piano lessons? How can she handle challenges with grades and school work? Friends, friends, friends! If she needs to go to the store or to school or to various activities, who will drive? Since she is too young to get a job, how can she earn money? How much should she spend? How much should she save? What if her financial needs are greater than the family can provide? What movies can she watch? What videos? How many, how often, and with whom? What music can she listen to? Can she have a tape player? What radio stations are allowed? How can she handle problems with a teacher? Can she wear big earrings, little earrings, or no earrings at all? Can she wear makeup? How much? Who decides? How often should she baby-sit? What if she has agreed to baby-sit but now doesn't want to? How do we handle the dozens of school activities, plays, concerts, Church activities, and so on?

*Boy, age eleven:* Friends, friends, friends! Awakening feelings for a girlfriend. Doors left open. Bed left unmade. Messy room. Face needs washing. Hair needs combing. Shirt needs to be tucked in. Tennis shoes need to be tied. Needs to learn gentleness with girls. "I'm bored." Is he proficient in division and multiplication? Who makes sure? Who takes him through the flashcards? Piano lessons. Reading assignments. Who helps with science? With English? Do we just accept handwriting as a total loss? What can he cook? He focuses mainly on brownies, cookies, cakes, and pies—but how often is too often? Who helps him with cookie sales to the neighborhood? Who decides what TV shows are appropriate? Who assigns chores? Who will play chess and checkers with him? Who will go walking with him? Who will make sure he writes in his journal and reads the scriptures? Who will drive him to the store? Who will get him to bed on time?

*Boy, age seven:* Who will help him practice his reading? Who will help with his handwriting? Who will help with arithmetic? Who helps him clean his room? What do we do about pajamas in the bathroom, bedspread on the floor, tennis shoes on the pillow, gum on the bedpost, and marbles in the shower? Dog to be fed? "It's not my turn." "Chores are for girls." "Housework, especially, is for girls." "Girls are dumb." Who teaches him to clean the kitchen? Who will take him to the store, to school, to activities? Mud on the carpet; toys in the garage; bike on the front porch. Broken collarbone from falling from a tree. Short prayers. Very little clean-up and hang-up but lots of mess-up. How can we be more loving and tolerant?

*Girl, age four:* Love, love, love! Games, games, games! Wants to be involved with the older kids but is left out of most things: "She's too little." Struggles in conversations to get in her "two bits." Time to go to bed; time to get up. Time to learn her ABCs, to draw, to write the alphabet. Problems with friends. Problems in not having friends. "Mommy, can I play?" "Can so-and-so come over?" "Guess what? Guess what?" Excitement about telephone calls. Dirty face, messy hair. Forgot to brush her teeth. Learning to work around the house. Talk, talk, talk! "Mom, what can I do?" "Do I have to?" "Tell me just one more story." "You forgot to come in and pray with me."

Seeing this brief snapshot of typical family life should make us humbly salute all parents, especially those who in dedication respond to the needs of their children. Parents all over the Church face such challenges every day of their lives. Even when many of the responsibilities belong to the children, who has to teach the children to accept them? Good old Mom and Dad. The numbers of decisions to be made, the judgment required, the sensitivity, love, inspiration, diligence, and hard work needed to raise children are beyond anyone's ability to describe. Even after the children have left home, the responsibilities of parents do not end.

Instead, they expand as children marry and begin raising children of their own.

### RAISING A FAMILY WITH
### THE SPIRIT OF THE LORD

I bear testimony that parents cannot adequately raise their children without direction from the Lord. The challenge is too great, and the consequences are eternal.

President Ezra Taft Benson often said that his goal was to have "no empty chairs" in heaven. He wanted every member of his family to be there. He has counseled:

> Make it a family objective to all be together in the celestial kingdom. Strive to make your home a little bit of heaven on earth so that after this life is over, you may be able to say:
>
> > We are all here!
> > Father, mother, sister, brother,
> > All who hold each other dear.
> > Each chair is filled—
> > We're all at home. . . .
> > We're all—all here
> > (*Ensign*, November 1981, p. 107).

Is that not the objective of all good parents? Was this not the concern of the good couple I spoke with on the plane? There are no perfect families. There are no families without problems. There are no families who "have everything together." Part of the purpose of life is to learn how to raise a family in the face of the adversities and trials that come in mortality.

President Spencer W. Kimball, in providing comfort to some who had lost their children to unfaithfulness, commented on the proverb "Train up a child in the way he should go: and when he is old, he will not depart from it" (Proverbs 22:6). He said, "As a prophet, perhaps I would say that the scripture could very well read, 'Train up a child in the way he should go, and if it even be that he is old, he will ultimately return to it.' " Above all else, parents must never give up hope. There *are* things they can do to bring back family members who have strayed, many of which will be discussed in this book.

This book was not intended to provide an academic approach to raising families. In it you will find very little theory and no high-sounding words, flowery concepts, or beautifully organized plans. Instead, I have tried to emphasize the hard realities of raising a family from the point of view of a father, a mother, and their children. I have used many stories and examples to illustrate key elements of how to help children pray, read the scriptures, have faith, and repent. I have tried to show the impact of love, discipline, work, and the Spirit of the Lord upon a family. I apologize for all of the personal examples about our family or people close to us, but I know no way to write such a book without such stories. As you read these stories and examples, please try to overlook the personalities and watch for the principles that made an experience a success or, because of our weakness, made it go not so smoothly.

Although the principles of how to raise a family to the Lord never change, the personality of each father, mother, and child is unique, and how they apply those principles will also be unique. Thus we should never critique one another in our skill as parents. Situations and circumstances vary widely from family to family, and only the Lord, in his ultimate wisdom, can properly render any such judgment. I have a feeling that even then, most of the judgments will be our own, as we may have a clearer view of what we have done or not done in raising our families.

Those who feel they have all the answers about raising a family may still have a lot to learn. The very idea of something so challenging will humble all good parents, leaving them with more questions than answers. On the other hand, in raising a family, particularly a large family, parents do learn much, and by sharing the principles they have learned, they may help others. That is the purpose of this book.

If we would follow the counsel of the Lord more directly,

more of the true fruits we desire in raising a family would be ours. Alma said it beautifully: "My son, I trust that I shall have great joy in you, because of your steadiness and your faithfulness unto God; . . . I say unto you, my son, that I have had great joy in thee already, because of thy faithfulness" (Alma 38:2–3). John also said it well: "I have no greater joy than to hear that my children walk in truth" (3 John 1:4).

## MARRIAGE AND ATTEMPTS TO HAVE A FAMILY

Let me share a personal experience that taught us to better trust in the Lord even in the face of challenges and trials. Perhaps this example will start us at the beginning, before children arrive in a family on earth.

After my mission, I had a great desire to be married. Part of that feeling came from a young lady who waited two and a half years for me. More importantly, though, I had studied the scriptures enough to know, in some measure, the great value of being married and raising a family.

When I returned home, things did not work out with the young lady who had waited for me. Seven months later, though, I married Janelle Schlink in the Mesa Arizona Temple. We both had great desires to have a family and were pleased and delighted that at last the time had come when we could do so. Our friends began to have their families—a boy here, a girl there. Nine months passed, a year, a year and a half, two years of waiting. Still no children came.

I gave my wife priesthood blessings two or three times during those years, promising that she would conceive and bear children. Still nothing happened. Three years, then three and a half years went by, and then four. During this time, my wife had a miscarriage that was very traumatic. That was the only time I saw her discouraged. I suppose our desires and expectations were so high that to finally conceive and then to lose the baby was devastating.

Finally five years passed by. We determined to seriously

consider adoption. I spent a number of occasions alone over a period of weeks praying about it, as my wife felt better about adopting than I did. Finally, I definitely received an answer that we should adopt. It helped me when I recalled that Jesus was adopted by Joseph, the husband of Mary; that Joseph Smith had two adopted children; and that one of my best friends had just adopted a baby girl. All in all, it felt like the right thing to do.

We put our names in for adoption through the Relief Society and were informed that it would be perhaps a year or more until we would be able to have a baby. The wait began.

## A PRIESTHOOD BLESSING

About this same time, we went to the Arizona Temple. After the session, we were visiting with a good brother, a longtime family friend. As we visited, it was determined that he ought to provide a blessing to my wife. We were overjoyed, as we knew that he was very close to the Lord. We told him we would be glad to have the blessing but thought we should fast and pray about it. We set a date for a few days later when we would all fast and come together for the blessing.

The appointed day arrived. We went to this good brother's home in the spirit of fasting and prayer. He gave my wife a beautiful blessing, very similar to those I had given her. He promised her that she would have natural children.

We left his home filled with the Spirit. To our great delight, about six weeks later the doctor confirmed that she was pregnant. We surely thanked the Lord in prayer and in fasting for the blessing we had received, trying to put as much effort into giving thanks as we had in asking for the blessing. We also called the adoption agency and had our names taken off the list, saying, "We're going to have our own baby now. Adoption won't be necessary." Our joy increased as the months passed by.

## ADDED TRIALS

About four months into the pregnancy, I arrived home from work one day to find my wife weeping. She had just arrived home from the doctor's office; the doctor had found that the fetus was dead and would have to be removed immediately.

This was one of the only times I have hardened my heart against the Lord. "What more can we do?" I thought. "We're trying to keep the commandments. Thou hast commanded us to multiply and replenish the earth. We've fasted. We've prayed. We've had blessings. We've waited for five years. Thou hast not answered our prayers. And now we have to go through another miscarriage."

My wife said, "We've got to go right now. The hospital is waiting for us." Her bag was packed, and we went to the car to leave. As we drove out, she told me we ought to go by and tell this good brother and his wife about it. I said, "No, absolutely not." Feeling as I did at that moment, the last person I wanted to talk to was this spiritual priesthood holder who had given her the blessing. I refused to go.

As we drove off, my wife persisted. I continued to tell her no, that we wouldn't stop. Fortunately, this good brother's home was on the way to the hospital. She continued to persist. Finally I said, "Well, you go in. I'll just wait in the car." But that would not do; she thought I should be the one to tell them. I finally consented to briefly go in.

We knocked on the door. As soon as the man's wife saw us, she knew something was wrong. I emotionally blurted out what had happened, asked her to tell her husband, and then turned to leave. However, this faithful brother was in the next room and heard what was said. He immediately walked into the living room, fell to his knees, and said, "Let's pray." His wife knelt down, and my wife went over and knelt down. I was left standing there with no desire whatsoever to pray. Finally, probably from the pressure, I knelt down as well.

Then I learned a great lesson that has helped me with

others on many occasions since that time. I heard a servant of the Lord pray with all of his soul. He poured out his heart, telling the Lord we didn't know why this had happened but that the priesthood blessing was still in full force. He said that we would humbly submit to this trial in spite of the apparent problems and difficulties and our strong feelings about them. He said that we knew the Lord loved us, and that we loved the Lord and would do whatever he commanded us to do. He confirmed with the Lord that we would *humbly* submit to this trial and to any other that might come—that we would trust in God.

This great leader in the priesthood, in that brief prayer, softened my heart. He removed, by the Spirit, all of my anger. He invited the Spirit of the Lord to return to me and humbled me, for which I will be ever grateful. We then left, humbled in spirit even though still saddened. We went to the hospital, where the surgery was performed.

## ADOPTION

A few days later I was again alone in prayer. I felt a strong impression that my wife and I should *immediately* call the Relief Society adoption agency and put our names back on the list for adoptions. "Do it now," the Spirit whispered. "Right now!"

My wife and I immediately called them. They said, "We're glad to reinstate your name on the list. However, because you canceled out, it will take about a year and a half wait now."

We said, "Well, that's all right. We just want our names back on the list."

About three weeks later, I received a phone call at work. The Relief Society sister on the other end of the line said, "Would you like to have a baby son? If so, come and get him right now." I called my wife and rushed home. We could hardly believe our good fortune! We ran to the store to buy some diapers. We didn't even have any place to put the baby.

When we got to the adoption agency, they left the baby in a room with us and said, "We'll give you a few minutes to look him over and decide whether you really want him." He was unclothed. We checked him over from head to foot and found him in perfect condition. We just wept for joy.

We told them we would be very pleased to have him. We signed the papers, and the caseworker said, "As you know, there were many, many people before you on the list. You would have had a long time yet to wait, even if you had not taken your name off the list the first time. But as we went through the pictures of the families, we tried to place the baby but couldn't. We went over and over the pictures of people who were on the list way ahead of you. None of them felt right. We finally got down to some of the relatively new applicants, namely the Cooks, and felt the Spirit tell us, 'Place the boy there.' For that reason we called you."

We were overjoyed as we took the baby home. He ended up sleeping in a chest of drawers for the first few nights. We didn't have furniture, clothing, blankets, or anything for him as he was totally unexpected.

What a great joy to us to finally have a son! I'm sure we must have been the happiest parents in all of Mesa, Arizona. He was our boy. About a year and a half later, after the adoption was final, we had the great joy of taking him to the Arizona Temple to have him sealed to us for time and all eternity. At last we had a son. At last we were on our way to fulfilling the injunction of the Lord to multiply and replenish the earth.

## PROMISES FULFILLED

About a year and a half later, six and a half years into our marriage, our first natural son arrived. A year and a half later another son came. Then a daughter arrived less than two years later. Another daughter graced our home three years after that. Then another son came less than two years later. He was followed by another son four years after that.

Three years later another beautiful daughter arrived. How blessed we have been with our children!

Truly the Lord answers prayers and fulfills all of his promises. He has said, "Whatsoever ye shall ask the Father in my name, which is right, believing that ye shall receive, behold it shall be given unto you" (3 Nephi 18:20).

How true also are the words of Moroni, "I would show unto the world that faith is things which are hoped for and not seen; wherefore, dispute not because ye see not, for ye receive no witness until after the trial of your faith" (Ether 12:6).

True it is that "after much tribulation come the blessings" (D&C 58:4).

It is easy to see, after the fact, the involvement of the Lord in an experience such as this one. I'm sure having had that challenge of no children for so many years caused us to do our best to be prepared when the children did come. We thank the Lord for a good family, as I'm sure you do as you think of your family.

I bear testimony that the Lord fulfills his promises. If we will do our part, be patient, and keep the commandments, the Lord will answer our prayers concerning our families. He will bless us in our *sacred duty* to raise up our children unto him.

# CHAPTER ONE

# THE INDIVIDUAL, THE FAMILY, AND THE CHURCH

Some years ago a fire erupted in the middle of the night, completely destroying a family's residence. A neighbor tried to console the family's seven-year-old, not knowing that he was about to be taught a great principle. "Johnny, it's sure too bad your home burned down," he said.

Johnny thought a moment and then said, "Oh, that's where you're mistaken. That wasn't our home; that was just our house. We still have our home; we just don't have any-place to put it right now."

What a great principle that child taught about home. What does the word *home* bring to your mind? To some, it means a place to eat, a place to sleep, a place where worldly goods are stored. To others more spiritually inclined, it means a place where family is, where the heart is, a sacred place, a peaceful place, an escape from a wicked world.

The still, small voice whispers yet a deeper meaning: home is heaven. We are strangers here on earth. My real home is not here but there. My challenge is to learn how to make a home here on earth similar to the one I left in heaven. The Lord says we were taught "even before [we] were born." We "received [our] first lessons in the world of spirits and were prepared to come forth . . . to labor in his vineyard for the salvation of the souls of men" (D&C 138:56).

A good part of this teaching—perhaps the most impor-tant part—may have been to know how to labor at home. We were taught by the Lord, by the best of all teachers, and our task during mortality may be to relearn in the flesh what we once knew in the spirit.

How might I remember and rediscover what I once knew? The Lord answers, "Pray and I will make 'known

1

unto [you things] . . . from the foundation of the world . . . according to [your] faith and . . . holy works' " (see Alma 12:30). "I will 'bring all things [back] to your remembrance, whatsoever I have said unto you' " (see John 14:26; Alma 12:30) "and [will enlarge] the memory of this people" (see Alma 37:8).

## THE CONSTITUTION OF FAMILY LIFE

This chapter is one of the most important chapters in the whole book as it attempts to lay a constitution or doctrinal base from which all the responsibilities of individuals, families, and the Church flow. It discusses in some detail the eternal view of family and home held by the Lord coming from the scriptures themselves. If we can clearly understand that divine role and the relationship that exists between us as individuals, the family, and the Church, we will have a much better understanding of what the Lord expects of us, of the things for which we will ultimately be held accountable with respect to ourselves and our families. You might be tempted to read through this chapter quickly or perhaps even skip over some of the material, as considerable emphasis is given to doctrinal matters. Please do not do so, and you will find the information of great benefit later in the book.

## ALL ARE MEMBERS OF A FAMILY

At times when we speak of home and family, some who are single or widowed might feel that these teachings don't apply to them. But when the Lord sent us here for our individual growth, he sent us to live with and be nurtured spiritually and temporally by a family. The Lord organized the whole earth this way. There is no other way to enter mortality.

You still may say, "I don't have a family. I'm all alone." May I remind you that you always were and ever will be a member of the family of God. You are his son or his daughter. It doesn't matter if your parents or spouse or brothers or sisters or children are members or nonmembers, living or dead; they are still your family. And if you are righteous and faithful to the end, no matter what your present status, you will ultimately be blessed as part of a family unit. Remember also that when the scriptures use the word *family*, they may be speaking not just of one's immediate family but also of an extended family—grandparents, great-grandparents, and so on. We must keep this extended view of family in mind in order to understand the instructions the Lord has given to families (particularly those instructions dealing with self-reliance).

Whether we are parents, grandparents, brothers, sisters, uncles, cousins, or children—whether we're married or single—we must understand that in the Lord's view, we are part of a family. Regardless of our family situation, we must learn and live, to the degree we can, the principles governing family life in preparation for exaltation.

## THE PREMORTAL FAMILY COUNCIL

When I try to explain the eternal principles governing family life, the Spirit witnesses that we lived as a family before we came here, and that these principles are "burned into" our souls. "You're on the right track," it whispers. "Keep moving forward. Discover and live these principles related to families, and in time you will create a home on earth similar to the one you experienced in heaven."

If we are willing to listen, the Lord will teach us of the sacredness of that heavenly organization called family, called home.

For just a moment, imagine that you are in the premortal existence, in that council in heaven, yes, even a council of the Father's own family. Could not the Father have given us counsel like this: "My children, my children, marriage on earth will be ordained of God unto men [see D&C 49:15–16; 131:14].

"By divine decree, you will be copartners with God in

bringing children to earth [see Genesis 1:22, 28; 2 Nephi 2:22–23; D&C 132:56–63].

"The family will be the principal agency for the spiritual and temporal nurturing of the individual [see Mosiah 4:14–15; D&C 68:25, 28].

"When you go to earth, teach your children to love the Lord thy God with all their hearts [see Deuteronomy 6:5–7] and to love and serve one another [see Mosiah 4:15].

"Pray in your families both morning, mid-day, and evening, and I will quicken your memory of these teachings [see 3 Nephi 18:21; Alma 34:21, 27; D&C 68:28].

"Teach your children repentance, faith in Christ, baptism, the gift of the Holy Ghost, priesthood covenants, and temple ordinances [see D&C 68:25, 27; 132:19]. Grandparents, uncles, and aunts, you can help.

"Consecrate your family resources to the Lord. Be free with your substance [see D&C 42:30–31; Jacob 2:17; D&C 119:1–7].

"Provoke not your children to wrath [see Ephesians 6:4], neither suffer that they fight and quarrel one with another, thus sowing seeds of contention [see Mosiah 4:14].

"Fathers-to-be, you will learn that true spiritual leadership is mostly at home, not so much in the world. Mothers-to-be, yours will be a sacred calling unlike any other, to raise these little children so they will someday be as I am. And unless all of you become as little children, you will not be able to return home to me.

"Learn your duty from living prophets and from the scriptures.

"Lastly, because of the sacred nature of parenthood, I will personally teach you, through the Holy Ghost, those things that matter most. Stay close to me; humbly ask for help."

## CAUTIONS FROM THE FATHER

Perhaps the Father cautioned us in words like these:
"My children, the influence of the world will be strong,

and there will be heavy influence to keep your families small. However, remember, 'As arrows are in the hand of a mighty man; so are children. . . . Happy is the man that hath his quiver full of them' [Psalm 127:4–5].

"Remember to keep your family responsibilities as a priority. There will be many who will want to encroach upon your responsibility to teach and provide activities for your family. Never forget that yours is the primary responsibility, and that your ultimate success in all other endeavors will be in direct proportion to the attention you give these divinely appointed relationships [see D&C 88:119].

"Strive to be together. Avoid activities that would pull you apart. Remember, where love runs deep, so too do feelings and frictions, as love may become frustrated [see 2 Nephi 1:14, 21].

"As children, be sure to give heed to your father and mother, remembering that I, the Lord, have placed them over you. Honor them [see Exodus 20:12].

"Remember that once you are a parent, you will always be a parent, whether a grandparent, a great-grandparent, or a parent as I am. Your responsibilities to preside go on through the generations to help turn the hearts of the children to their fathers. Resist the temptation to be uninvolved, to retire from your family, and to follow only your own interests. As grandparents, your wisdom and vision will allow you to draw together your whole family, which I, the Lord, have given you [see Mosiah 2:5]."

Perhaps he concluded:

"My children, don't be too concerned about remembering all these things. When they are taught to you, they will seem wonderfully familiar, as if you had always known them. You will have, because you learned them here in your heavenly home [see 1 Nephi 15:8, 11].

"You will suffer affliction with your children in allowing them to grow and develop, just as I have suffered affliction with you [see D&C 133:52–53]. But don't be afraid; I have given my angels charge concerning you. I will send them from my very presence to be with you, to bear you up [see D&C 84:42, 88; 133:53]. This is your opportunity to experience what I have taught you. Follow the promptings of my Spirit. Remember that I love you."

## THE EXALTED CONCEPT OF HOME

Parents, whatever you are doing, return home.

Children, wherever you are, no matter what your failure, problem, or sin, you will always be loved by your family. Go home.

Grandparents, brothers, sisters, uncles, aunts, draw your families together. Return home. May the concept of home be exalted, for the Lord so organized it in the beginning.

I pay tribute to my grandparents, to my parents, especially to my wife, and to my children in having made my home the best place in all the world. There's no place I would rather be than home.

And lastly, may the day come when together we will sing this praise of home and family:

> O my Father, thou that dwellest
> In the high and glorious place,
> When shall I regain thy presence
> And again behold thy face?
> . . . . . . . . . . . .
> In the heav'ns are parents single?
> No, the thought makes reason stare!
> Truth is reason; truth eternal
> Tells me I've a mother there.
>
> When I leave this frail existence,
> When I lay this mortal by,
> Father, Mother, may I meet you
> In your royal courts on high?
> Then, at length, when I've completed
> All you sent me forth to do,
> With your mutual approbation
> Let me come [home] and dwell with you
> ("O My Father," *Hymns of The Church of Jesus Christ of*

*Latter-day Saints* [Salt Lake City: The Church of Jesus
Christ of Latter-day Saints, 1985], no. 292).

## THE ROLE OF THE INDIVIDUAL, THE FAMILY, AND THE CHURCH

Even with this divine understanding of home, some people become confused as they struggle to balance what they should do at home, as individuals, and in the Church. To be successful with our families, we must clearly understand our roles as individuals, the role the family plays in support of individuals, and the role the Church plays in supporting the individual and the family.

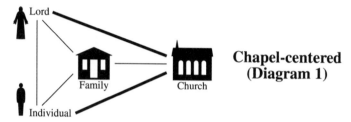

**Chapel-centered
(Diagram 1)**

Diagram 1 illustrates the way some might incorrectly direct their families. You will notice the dark lines indicating that the Church is connected to and directed by the Lord and that the Church bypasses the family and is well connected to the individuals in the Church.

In this diagram, the relationship of the family to the individual and the family to the Lord is weak. The link from the individual to the family and to the Lord is also weak, the individual perhaps not having a proper understanding of the value of the Lord in his or her life and of the support the family can be. This approach is more chapel centered, meaning that the person's approach to a spiritual life is centered around the Church.

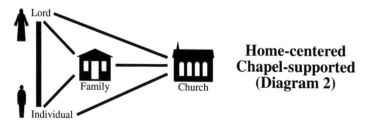

**Home-centered
Chapel-supported
(Diagram 2)**

Diagram 2 shows the relationship that should properly exist between the Lord, the individual, the family, and the Church. The link is strongest between the individual and the Lord, for every person is saved individually, not as a member of a group. The family has a strong relationship with the Lord and with the individual, whom it supports in the quest for exaltation. Individuals are not exalted as singles but within a family unit. The Church appropriately makes available all the priesthood keys and necessary ordinances for the salvation of man. It is also directed by the Lord in its proper role as a *support* to the family and as a *support* to the individual.

Following are some specific principles that outline the roles of the individual, the family, and the Church. You might be tempted to read over them quickly, but I believe it is essential to understand them before reading what follows in this book. Please consider them carefully; you may also want to look up some of the scriptural references to broaden your understanding.

**THE INDIVIDUAL**

1. Our Father in Heaven is an individual (D&C 130:22).
2. Each of us, as one of his children, is an individual (Moses 2:27; Abraham 3:22–23).
3. Each of us has certain godly capacities and gifts that are necessary attributes for exaltation (Abraham 3:24–26; Moses 1:6, 13).
4. The greatest of all the gifts of God is eternal life (D&C 14:7).
5. The gift of eternal life is made possible through the atonement of Jesus Christ (Mosiah 5:7, 15).
6. The following are *unconditional gifts* of God given freely to all:
   a. The capacity to know good from evil through the Light of Christ (D&C 84:46; 93:2; Moroni 7:15–16).
   b. The capacity to choose (free agency) (2 Nephi 2:15–16).

- The ability to resist temptation (1 Corinthians 10:13).
- The ability to live the commandments (1 Nephi 3:7).

c. Mortality (2 Nephi 2:22–25).
- A physical body (D&C 93:33–35).
- The opportunity to prove ourselves (Abraham 3:25).
- The ability to procreate (Moses 2:28).
- The ability to die (1 Corinthians 15:21–22).

d. Resurrection (Alma 11:42–44; 2 Nephi 9:22; 3 Nephi 26:4–5).

7. Because we are endowed with these capacities and gifts, we have within us, in embryo, the ability to be exalted (D&C 132:19–20; Moses 1:39).

8. To be exalted, we must use these godly capacities and gifts in such a way that additional gifts, privileges, and capacities may be given us. Some of the most important *conditional gifts* we attain through personal effort are:

a. Faith in the Lord Jesus Christ (3 Nephi 27:19).

b. Forgiveness (through personal repentance) (3 Nephi 27:20; D&C 19:15–19).

c. Personal direction from God (revelation) (D&C 42:61; 43:16).

d. Gifts of the Spirit (Moroni 10:8, 17).

e. Priesthood (Alma 13:1–9; D&C 84:17–21).
- Men—hold the power of the priesthood (D&C 113:7–8).
- Women—enjoy the blessings and influence of the priesthood.

9. We *must* receive specific ordinances to be exalted:

a. Baptism by immersion for the remission of sins by one having authority (3 Nephi 11:33–34).

b. Confirmation as a member of the true Church of

Jesus Christ and reception of the gift of the Holy
Ghost (D&C 33:15; John 3:5).

c. The temple endowment (D&C 105:11–12, 33;
110:9).

d. Marriage for time and all eternity (D&C 131:1–4).

10. In addition to required ordinances, there are many
commandments we must obey to qualify for
exaltation. Some of the most important are:

a. Exercise faith in the Lord Jesus Christ (Alma 5:15).

b. Repent of personal sins (D&C 29:49; 19:16–17).

c. Pray (3 Nephi 13:6; 2 Nephi 32:8–9; D&C 10:5).

d. Obey the will of the Lord as revealed through the
living prophet (D&C 28:2).

e. Search out, understand, and apply the principles
found in the scriptures, as revealed by the Holy
Ghost (John 5:39; 2 Nephi 32:3).

f. Renew covenants through partaking of the
sacrament (D&C 59:9; 3 Nephi 18:6–7).

g. Share the gospel (Mark 16:15; D&C 133:8–11;
88:81).

h. Keep appropriate personal records and seek out our
kindred dead (Moses 6:5, 8, 45–46).

i. Consecrate our time, talents, and means to the
Lord (D&C 42:30–34; Mosiah 2:34; D&C 58:35, 36;
Omni 1:26).

j. Develop the pure love of Christ (charity) (Moroni
7:47; 10:21).

k. Keep all of the laws of God and endure to the end
(D&C 14:7; Mosiah 2:22, 41).

Clearly the *individual* is the focus and the reason for
the plan of salvation, and *the Savior and his teachings are
the center of all that is done that the individual might be
exalted.*

### THE FAMILY

1. Marriage is ordained of God as the foundation for the

procreative relationship between men and women (D&C 49:15–16).

2. The eternal marriage relationship (sealing) is consecrated by our Father as the basic relationship in the eternal family unit (D&C 131:1–4).

3. By divine decree, men and women are copartners with God in providing bodies for his spirit children (Genesis 1:22, 28; D&C 132:63).

4. The Lord has ordained the family unit as the principal agency for the nurturing (both spiritual and temporal) of the individual (Mosiah 4:14–15; D&C 68:25, 28; Deuteronomy 6:4, 7).

5. Individuals are exalted as members of family units (D&C 132:16–17; 128:18).

6. Our Father in heaven has designed that every family unit, through the priesthood, has the right and the capacity to accomplish:

   a. Marriage for time and all eternity (D&C 131:1–4; 132:19–21).

   b. Being sealed as an eternal family (immediate and extended) (D&C 128:18–19; 131:1–4; 132:19–21).

   c. Exaltation (D&C 132:19–21, 37).

7. Many family responsibilities help individuals qualify for exaltation. Some of the most important are:

   a. Teach gospel ordinances and covenants within the family.

   b. Teach gospel principles within the family (D&C 68:25–28; Ephesians 6:4; Alma 39:12; D&C 93:40–50).

   c. Teach children to pray. Pray as a family. (D&C 68:28; 3 Nephi 18:21).

   d. Provide for the essential needs of the family (D&C 83:2, 4; 75:28; 1 Timothy 5:8).

   e. Share the gospel as a family (Mosiah 18:8–10; D&C 52:36).

   f. Prepare the family to be worthy to be sealed

together for time and all eternity (D&C 88:22;
132:19).

   g. Consecrate family resources to the Lord (D&C
42:30–31; 119:1–7; 51:3).

   h. Strengthen family members in keeping all of the
commandments (D&C 68:25–28; 93:41–43;
Proverbs 22:6).

*The family is the most important unit in time and in
eternity. It is through families that we are exalted.*

## THE CHURCH

1. Just as our Father in heaven designed the family unit
to help exalt the individual, so he organized the
Church to help exalt both individuals and families
(D&C 1:17, 22, 23, 30, 36; 20:1–2, 14).

2. The Church accomplishes this work through two
dimensions, both of which are designed to fulfill a
common goal:

   a. Doctrinal dimension (principles, doctrines,
ordinances).

     • The Lord directs his Church by revealing his will
and doctrine through his prophets (Amos 3:7;
D&C 28:2).

     • Through his living prophet, God provides his
priesthood with the keys of authority to teach
the doctrine and to perform the saving
ordinances (D&C 84:19–21; 107:65, 67).

   b. Institutional dimension (programs, services,
methods, and facilities).

     • The institution helps teach and implement the
doctrine by providing support programs, services,
methods, and facilities (D&C 38:34–36; 55:4;
70:11–12; 94:14–15).

     • The institution provides its members an
opportunity to serve God in an organized way
(D&C 59:5; 75:28–29).

3. The *doctrines* of the Church are based upon revealed
eternal truths. The current application of these

doctrines is revealed from God through his living
prophet (D&C 132:59, 34, 35; 124:39).

4. The *institutions* of the Church are designed to help
teach the doctrines. The institutional programs are
subject to change and adjustment in order to meet the
needs of individuals and families. Then changes are
made through the priesthood line of authority using
prescribed procedures (D&C 61:22; 62:5, 7–8).

*Truly, the Church exists to serve the individual and the
family.*

## POINTS OF FOCUS
## FOR INDIVIDUALS AND FAMILIES

To properly delineate the roles of the individual, the
family, and the Church, you might find helpful the following outline of responsibilities of individuals and families. It
is provided to help individuals and families select goals,
establish priorities, and obey the commandments. Foremost
attention is given to helping families worship, pray, share,
serve, work, and play together. (This information is not
meant to be all inclusive.)

### SPIRITUAL WELFARE

1. Practice basic gospel principles.
   a. Exercise faith in the Lord Jesus Christ.
   b. Repent of personal sins and maintain personal
   worthiness.
   c. Have regular individual and family prayer.
   d. Fast regularly and as needed.
2. Search the scriptures.
   a. Have daily scripture study as individuals and as a
   family.
   b. Study and obey messages of the prophet and other
   General Authorities.
3. Give Christ-like service (sacrifice time, talent, and
means in serving the Lord).
   a. Hold your spouse and family as a sacred priority.

  b. Magnify your callings in the Church.

  c. Help activate, fellowship, and strengthen those in need.

 4. Prepare for and receive priesthood ordinances and blessings.

  a. Blessing of children.

  b. Baptism.

  c. Confirmation.

  d. Ordinations to the priesthood.

  e. Temple endowment.

  f. Marriage for time and all eternity.

  g. Sacrament for the renewing of all covenants.

## TEMPORAL WELFARE

 1. Keep physically fit.

  a. Eat a balanced diet.

  b. Get sufficient sleep.

  c. Get appropriate exercise.

 2. Increase self-reliance (personal and family preparedness).

  a. Maintain financial independence.

   • Pay honest tithes and offerings

   • Avoid unnecessary debt

   • Save regularly

   • Develop employable skills (for example, through educational or vocational training)

  b. Provide for basic needs.

   • Food (plant a family garden)

   • Clothing

   • Fuel

   • Shelter

   • Obtain and maintain a year's supply of food and other necessities

**MISSIONARY WORK**

1. Prepare children for missions.
2. Prepare yourself to serve a mission.
3. Regularly friendship someone to hear the gospel.
4. Give financial support to a missionary and to the Church's general missionary fund.

**FAMILY HISTORY**

1. Complete your family records.

    a. Four-generation family group sheet.

    b. Personal and family history.

2. Participate in family record name extraction as invited.
3. Perform temple ordinances as possible.

One can truly understand the prophetic statement by President Spencer W. Kimball when he said, "Only as we see clearly the responsibilities of each *individual* and the role of *families* and the home can we properly understand that the *priesthood quorums* and the *auxiliary organizations,* even *wards and stakes,* exist primarily to help members live the gospel in the home." President Kimball further said that our success "will largely be determined by how faithfully we focus on living the gospel in the home."

## HELPING FATHERS STAY ON TARGET

Some years ago the Church published a statement of thirteen principles that has always helped me keep my role as a father in focus. These same principles, of course, would generally apply to a single sister who heads her family or to a sister married to a nonmember. The principles should help fathers distinguish their role clearly from the roles of individuals and the Church:

1. The family is an eternal unit and provides the basis for a righteous life.

2. The father is the presiding authority in the home. He is the patriarch, or head of the family.

3. The mother is the helpmate, the counselor.

4. The role of the father is inseparable from the role of the mother—they are one, sealed for time and all eternity.

5. The priesthood quorum is organized to teach, inspire, and strengthen the father in his responsibility; it must let him learn his duty.

6. If the father fails in his responsibility, the priesthood representative (home teacher) must work with him to strengthen and help him do his duty.

7. The father is responsible for the physical, mental, social, and spiritual growth and development of himself, his wife, and each of his children.

8. A father cannot be released from his responsibility.

9. The father is responsible for leading his family through example, prayer, love, and concern.

10. The model for fatherhood is our Heavenly Father. To know how the Lord works with his children, of course, the family head will need to know something about the gospel, the great plan of the Lord.

11. The father must yearn to bless his family. He must go to the Lord, ponder the words of God, and live by the Spirit to know the mind and will of the Lord and what he must do to lead his family. The priesthood quorum can help.

12. The Church exists to assist the father in leading his family back into the presence of our Father in heaven.

13. The father and all leaders will solve their problems in the Lord's way.

## INDIVIDUAL AND FAMILY WORSHIP

The mission of the Church is well explained in the scriptures: to bring all to Christ by proclaiming the gospel (D&C 133:37), perfecting the Saints (Ephesians 4:12), and redeeming the dead (D&C 138:54). The mission of the family is also clearly stated in scripture. The Lord has indicated that a man and woman joined in marriage become one flesh (Genesis 2:24). Then this new eternal unit is to have a family. When that couple is sealed together, the man and woman may eventually become exalted as gods and have a continuation of the family forever (D&C 132:19–20).

Parents, then, help their mortal children come to know the Father and the Son and teach them the road to eternal life. Children begin that process by being born under the covenant or by being sealed to their parents. Thus, the Father's mission is to bring to pass the immortality and eternal life of man. Parents participate in that same mission in a general sense, but specifically in attempting to teach their children to "press forward with a steadfastness in Christ . . . endure to the end . . . [and thus obtain] eternal life" (2 Nephi 31:20).

## THE YOUTH STUDY

As we look at the true meaning of home and the role of the individual, the family, and the Church, we may ask, "Of all the duties, responsibilities, and commandments parents are supposed to teach their children, which have the highest priority?"

Some years ago, the Church conducted what was called "A Youth Study." Found within that study, I believe, is the basic answer to what causes individuals and families to turn to the Lord. The study focused only on young men, but the spiritual principles relating to the worship of the Lord would surely have application for young women as well. The study asked some hard questions about what constitutes success in raising a family, and it found four "gospel outcomes" that indicated, in some measure, that parents had been successful. The four gospel outcomes were:

1. Ordination to the Melchizedek Priesthood.
2. Serving a full-time mission.
3. Receiving the temple endowment.
4. Marrying in the temple.

Perhaps any parents whose son had accomplished those four gospel outcomes could feel, in some measure, successful as parents. At least they would feel that they had launched their son on the road to eternal life. Perhaps no other gospel outcomes outweigh those identified above.

After those outcomes had been determined, hundreds of young men were interviewed throughout the United States to determine if any common factors determined whether a young man would accomplish those outcomes or not. Those who had obtained the priesthood, gone to the temple, and served missions were interviewed, as were others who had not accomplished those things. The results were astounding; the causes were so simple that perhaps some of us have overlooked them.

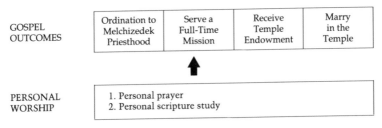

| GOSPEL OUTCOMES | Ordination to Melchizedek Priesthood | Serve a Full-Time Mission | Receive Temple Endowment | Marry in the Temple |
|---|---|---|---|---|

| PERSONAL WORSHIP | 1. Personal prayer 2. Personal scripture study |
|---|---|

The study showed that two factors were at the root of whether young men would attain those gospel outcomes: personal prayer and personal scripture study.

It ought not surprise us that to attain the desired gospel outcomes, individual worship of the Lord would be preeminent. One who has turned fully to the Lord in prayer and searched the words of the Lord to learn what the Lord would have him do would naturally be led to those outcomes. In fact, the correlation between the gospel outcomes and the practices of regular personal prayer and personal scripture study was in the high ninetieth percentile, one of the highest correlations of any study the Church has done.

We can conclude that if children truly pray and read the scriptures on their own, that may be the best insurance of all that the children will ultimately achieve those outcomes.

The next logical question is, "How do you get young people to pray and to read the scriptures?" What was it, in the case of those young men, that influenced them to do what they did? Again, the answer was so simple that some of us have probably been looking beyond the mark. The influencing factors were:

1. Family prayer.
2. Family scripture study and family home evening.
3. Family agreement on values.

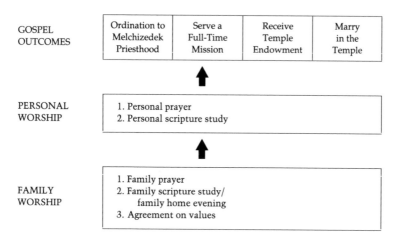

| GOSPEL OUTCOMES | Ordination to Melchizedek Priesthood | Serve a Full-Time Mission | Receive Temple Endowment | Marry in the Temple |
|---|---|---|---|---|

↑

| PERSONAL WORSHIP | 1. Personal prayer<br>2. Personal scripture study |
|---|---|

↑

| FAMILY WORSHIP | 1. Family prayer<br>2. Family scripture study/<br>   family home evening<br>3. Agreement on values |
|---|---|

If we want our children to pray, we must show them by example through family prayer. If we want our children to read the scriptures, they need to see the scriptures being read in the family. The factor that has the greatest effect on private religious behavior is family worship, meaning that the family is having regular family prayer, family scripture study, and family home evening.

## CONVEYING SPIRITUAL VALUES

The third factor in influencing children to pray and read the scriptures is an agreement on values that are transmitted from parents to children. An example might be when your daughter asks, "Why are we the only family in the whole ward that won't ——— on Sunday?" You might be tempted to say, "Because I said so," or "Because the Church says so." But a more inspired parent might say, "Well, you know that keeping the Lord's day holy is not something we just made up. Let me show you something." Then you could

open the Doctrine and Covenants to section 59 and read
these beautiful verses:

> And that thou mayest more fully keep thyself
> unspotted from the world, thou shalt go to the
> house of prayer and offer up thy sacraments upon
> my holy day; for verily this is a day appointed unto
> you to rest from your labors, and to pay thy devo-
> tions unto the Most High; nevertheless thy vows
> shall be offered up in righteousness on all days
> and at all times (vv. 9–11).

Then you could explain, "As you can see, the Lord
teaches us that Sunday is a holy day. It's not a day for us to
do what we want. It's a day to rest from our labors and 'to
pay our devotions to the Most High,' meaning that we
should go to our Church meetings, partake of the sacrament,
do our other Church duties, and visit the sick, the poor, and
the needy. It's a day consecrated to the Lord, and I bear testimony to you, my dear daughter, that this is true and that
the Lord has blessed us greatly for keeping the Sabbath Day.
Here are some of the blessings he promises:

> And inasmuch as ye do these things with
> thanksgiving, with cheerful hearts and counte-
> nances, not with much laughter, for this is sin,
> but with a glad heart and a cheerful counte-
> nance—verily I say, that inasmuch as ye do this,
> the fulness of the earth is yours, the beasts of the
> field and the fowls of the air, and that which
> climbeth upon the trees and walketh upon the
> earth.
> Yea, and the herb, and the good things which
> come of the earth, whether for food or for raiment,
> or for houses, or for barns, or for orchards, or for
> gardens, or for vineyards; yea, all things which
> come of the earth, in the season thereof, are made
> for the benefit and the use of man, both to please
> the eye and to gladden the heart; yea, for food and
> for raiment, for taste and for smell, to strengthen
> the body and to enliven the soul. And it pleaseth
> God that he hath given all these things unto man;

for unto this end were they made to be used, with
judgment, not to excess, neither by extortion (vv.
15–20).

"Can you see, my dear, that the Lord gave us all of these
things for our benefit? These are truly beautiful promises
about the Sabbath Day, aren't they?"

After that, you might bear testimony, saying, "I know
that these blessings from keeping the Sabbath Day are real,
and that's why we do it."

Perhaps then the daughter might say, "I never quite
understood it that way. I do believe that's true. Thank you.
I can see why I should keep the Sabbath Day holy."

Through such interaction, a value is transferred from
one generation to another. Such values are often "caught"
more than they are "taught" as children see them operating
in their family. If family prayer, family scripture reading and
home evening, and the sharing of values are taking place in
the family, they tend to produce young men and women
who will pray and read the scriptures on their own. And
thus they will attain such gospel outcomes as serving missions, receiving their endowments, and being married in the
temple. That should probably not surprise us, as the true
role of the family is as a support and strength to the individual.

## SCRIPTURAL INSTRUCTION
## TO PARENTS

Moses surely had a clear view of the proper role of parents when he conveyed these important instructions to the
house of Israel:

Hear, O Israel: The Lord our God is one Lord:
and thou shalt love the Lord thy God with all
thine heart, and with all thy soul, and with all thy
might. And these words, which I command thee
this day, shall be in thine heart: and thou shalt
teach them diligently unto thy children, and shalt
talk of them when thou sittest in thine house, and

when thou walkest by the way, and when thou
liest down, and when thou risest up.

And thou shalt bind them for a sign upon thine
hand, and they shall be as frontlets between thine
eyes. And thou shalt write them upon the posts of
thy house, and on thy gates. And it shall be, when
the Lord thy God shall have brought thee into the
land which he sware unto thy fathers, to Abraham, to Isaac, and to Jacob, to give thee great and
goodly cities, which thou buildedst not, and
houses full of all good things, which thou filledst
not, and wells digged, which thou diggedst not,
vineyards and olive trees, which thou plantedst
not; when thou shalt have eaten and be full; then
beware lest thou forget the Lord, which brought
thee forth out of the land of Egypt, from the house
of bondage. Thou shalt fear the Lord thy God, and
serve him (Deuteronomy 6:4–13).

Clearly the focus of these verses is upon loving the Lord.
That seems to be the foundation and the secret for raising a
family to the Lord. It also seems evident that parents are to
teach the word of the Lord diligently to their children, not
just in formal settings but, in the words of the scripture,
*"when thou sittest in thine house, and when thou walkest
by the way, and when thou liest down, and when thou risest up."* It also seems evident that in those days the word
was even written down and carried with people (see verse 8)
as they went about their daily affairs. They even put these
writings in a small container at their door or post or gate
(see verse 9) to help them not to forget the Lord.

The Lord described the blessings he gave that he swore
to give Abraham, Isaac, and Jacob; their houses were full of
all good things, and they were prospering with wells, vineyards, and olive trees. Then the Lord gave a great warning:
*"Then beware lest thou forget the Lord, which brought thee
forth out of the land of Egypt . . . Thou shalt fear the Lord
thy God, and serve him, and shalt swear by his name."*

All of us have a tendency to forget the Lord and not have
him be a full partner in our families. The meaning of these

words cannot be misunderstood. Surely an eternal family must have as its foundation the love of God so that the Spirit of the Lord will permeate the family. A celestial family, an eternal family, can be such only if founded upon these principles.

These concepts have been true throughout the ages. We learn of Adam and Eve, "By them their children were taught to read and write, having a language which was pure and undefiled. . . . Therefore I give unto you a commandment, to teach these things freely unto your children" (Moses 6:6, 58).

Isaiah tells us, "All thy children shall be taught of the Lord; and great shall be the peace of thy children" (Isaiah 54:13).

Proverbs contains what is probably the best-known instruction to parents about teaching their children: "Train up a child in the way he should go: and when he is old, he will not depart from it" (Proverbs 22:6).

What a responsibility rests upon parents! If they can teach their children when they are young, inspiring them to be taught of the Lord as Isaiah said, truly when they are old they will not depart from the truth. In ways that are not well understood by us, the Spirit of the Lord is planted into their hearts. Even though they may depart from it for a while, they will return because they are children of the covenant. The Lord has written his word in their hearts, and ultimately it will bring them back to him.

The Book of Mormon teaches a powerful example of the evil influence parents can have upon their children if they teach them incorrectly:

> Ye shall remember your children, how that ye have grieved their hearts because of the example that ye have set before them; and also, remember that ye may, because of your filthiness, bring your children unto destruction, and their sins be heaped upon your heads at the last day (Jacob 3:10).

> Behold, ye have done greater iniquities than the
> Lamanites, our brethren. Ye have broken the
> hearts of your tender wives, and lost the confi-
> dence of your children, because of your bad exam-
> ples before them; and the sobbings of their hearts
> ascend up to God against you. And because of the
> strictness of the word of God, which cometh down
> against you, many hearts died, pierced with deep
> wounds (Jacob 2:35).

The power of example for good or evil can have a lasting
impact on children. Thus the Lord has told us, "I have commanded you to bring up your children in light and truth"
(D&C 93:40).

Inspired General Authorities have also spoken about the
sacred role of parents:

> The Lord organized the family unit in the
> beginning. He intended that the home be the cen-
> ter of learning—that the father and mother be
> teachers.
>
> The Lord fixed families to give parents more
> influence on children than all other agencies com-
> bined. There is safety in this arrangement. It pro-
> vides *parents* the privilege, the awesome privilege,
> of molding the life and character of a child, even
> though outside agencies have influence.
>
> Parenthood imposes a singular responsibility.
> Not only must parents put good things into the
> minds of children, we must keep bad things out.
> That is why we have been cautioned against the
> unrestricted invasion of our homes by the media.
> While some agencies that have influence on our
> children are good, some are not. Parental vigilance
> should be constant. Safeguard your children
> against those who seek to destroy them.
>
> How would you pass the test, parents, if your
> family was isolated from the Church and *you* had
> to supply all religious training? Have you become
> so dependent on others that you do little or noth-

> ing at home? Tell me, how much of the gospel
> would your children know, if all they knew is
> what they had been taught at home? Ponder that.
> I repeat, how much of the gospel would *your* chil-
> dren know if all they knew is what they had been
> taught at home? (Elder A. Theodore Tuttle).

Perhaps all of our responsibilities as parents are best summed up by these last three quotations from modern-day prophets:

"The greatest work you will ever do will be within the walls of your own home" (President Harold B. Lee).

"We should be teaching our people over and over again that the most important leadership position in time and eternity is that of father [and mother]" (President Spencer W. Kimball).

"No other success can compensate for failure in the home" (President David O. McKay).

Thus, as we consider the responsibility the Lord has laid on parents from the beginning, we recognize the awesome nature of attempting to lead a family in righteousness. Could anyone do that without the full direction and partic-ipation of the Lord? We can clearly see the necessity of hav-ing the Spirit of the Lord to guide us, or it could not be effec-tively done.

In summary, private religious behavior (such as private prayer and scripture study) is much more powerful than public religious life (attending meetings, classes, social events, athletics, and so on) in determining whether or not the desired gospel outcomes will be attained.

## THE DIVINE ROLE OF THE CHURCH

What role, then, does the Church play in these gospel outcomes? The Church plays an important role in support-ing the individual and the family. It helps in teaching chil-dren about prayer, scripture reading, and gospel values, but it is much less influential than the family.

| GOSPEL OUTCOMES | Ordination to Melchizedek Priesthood | Serve a Full-Time Mission | Receive Temple Endowment | Marry in the Temple |
|---|---|---|---|---|

⬆

| PERSONAL WORSHIP | 1. Personal prayer<br>2. Personal scripture study | Role of the Church<br>• Classes<br>• Social Activities<br>• Meeting Attendance<br>• Church Athletics |
|---|---|---|

⬆

| FAMILY WORSHIP | 1. Family prayer<br>2. Family scripture study/ family home evening<br>3. Agreement on values | Role of the Church<br>• Classes<br>• Social Activities<br>• Meeting Attendance<br>• Church Athletics |
|---|---|---|

In some families, the Church becomes the only influence in these areas. But we should not assume that the Church alone can teach children to pray and read the scriptures. Do not make the Church the cornerstone of your hope for your children. In doing so, there would be much risk. You have the responsibility to teach them correct principles, with the Church assisting.

Some have asked, "What impact do classes, social activities, meeting attendance, Church athletics, Scouting, and so on have on young people in attaining the gospel outcomes?" The answer is that they do help, but they have much less of an impact than the family itself.

Another important element revealed by the Church's study is that when young men reach age sixteen or so, an adult advisor (normally not the bishop but some other good man) has about as much influence upon them as do their parents. As you probably know, there are times when parents have a hard time getting through to their children or when the children are not able or willing to receive counsel from their parents. A trusted adult advisor who can share the same message as the parents and be a "second witness" can be of great help, especially in the later teen years, in assisting young men to reach those gospel outcomes.

Such adult advisors have much more potential for obtaining the gospel outcomes than do peers, bishops,

Church programs, or maybe even a young man's own family when he is that age. The study found that the advisor's age, education, or occupation didn't matter much. What really mattered was whether the young man felt that the advisor was trusting, respectful, and caring—characteristics of the advisor himself.

We should not underestimate or misunderstand the role of the Church. Participation in the Church really does reinforce the spiritual foundations that are laid at home. But mere attendance at church activities is not an end in and of itself, nor does it guarantee that young men and women are moving toward desired gospel outcomes. However, if an activity is calculated spiritually to move young people toward those outcomes, then the impact is real and is an addition to what is happening at home.

Considering the information from the "youth study," we might now ask, "If all of the above is true, how can families so be taught? Can that not be accomplished through church meetings and activities, and especially through home teachers? Is that not their divine role as they relate to individuals and families?"

| GOSPEL OUTCOMES | Ordination to Melchizedek Priesthood | Serve a Full-Time Mission | Receive Temple Endowment | Marry in the Temple |
|---|---|---|---|---|

↑

| PERSONAL WORSHIP | 1. Personal prayer<br>2. Personal scripture study | Role of the Church<br>• Classes<br>• Social Activities<br>• Meeting Attendance<br>• Church Athletics |
|---|---|---|

↑

| FAMILY WORSHIP | 1. Family prayer<br>2. Family scripture study/ family home evening<br>3. Agreement on values | Role of the Church<br>• Classes<br>• Social Activities<br>• Meeting Attendance<br>• Church Athletics |
|---|---|---|

↑

| VISITS TO HOMES | *"And visit the house of each member, and exhort them to pray vocally and in secret and attend to all family duties"* (D&C 20:47). |
|---|---|

The duty of the home teachers is to "visit the house of each member, and exhort them to pray vocally and in secret and attend to all family duties" (D&C 20:47).

I am always impressed, as I think of this scripture, to recognize that when the Lord talked about priesthood holders visiting the homes of the Saints, he could have given them a long list of commandments. But he simply said, "Visit the house of each member, exhorting them to pray vocally and in secret and attend to all family duties" (D&C 20:51). Note where the primary emphasis lies—to get them to pray. Prayer will draw people to the Lord and inspire them to attend to their family duties.

Some have asked, "What are those family duties?" Some have suggested they may be found in fulfilling the mission of the Church to convert people to the Lord through proclaiming the gospel, perfecting the Saints, and redeeming the dead. That is a teaching worth pondering. Perhaps another good description is found in a booklet published by the Church entitled *Family Guidebook*. You would do well to obtain a copy. A summary of its content is:

- Hold family home evening at least once a week.
- Have family and individual prayers at least twice a day.
- Bless the food you eat (at each meal).
- Make time for family activities.
- Study the scriptures as a family.
- Have meal-time discussions.
- Discuss the gospel while working together.
- Use special holidays and occasions to teach the gospel.
- Teach by example the payment of tithing and other offerings.
- Teach the gospel through bedtime stories.
- Hold private interviews.

All such activities help parents become the true spiritual leaders of the home. If parents were to concentrate on prayer, scripture reading, and these other family duties, surely they would be successful in raising up a family to the Lord.

If home teachers, after counseling with family heads, were to focus on these basics, they would have a much greater impact in helping parents strengthen families. Without question, inspired fathers, mothers, and children would welcome them into the home. Yes, inspired home teachers have a divine role to play in helping turn parents and families more fully to the Lord.

This booklet also describes blessings and ordinances that may be performed in the home:

1. Consecrating the oil
2. Anointings
3. Sealing
4. Special blessings

## THE COUNSEL OF LIVING PROPHETS

I have always been impressed with the teachings of the prophets, for they speak not only to people living at this time but also to the next generation. Their prophetic statements prepare families for the challenges and problems that lie before the Church and the world.

For example, President Heber J. Grant talked so much about the Word of Wisdom that many people wondered, "Is that the only talk he has?" Conference after conference he addressed the Saints on the importance of keeping the Word of Wisdom. In those days, some of the Saints were quite slack in keeping that commandment, and the emphasis was greatly needed. One man wrote to President Grant, saying, "Do you not have some other talk? Please give some other talk other than the Word of Wisdom." President Grant's response to his secretary was, "Well, there's one man that surely needs it," and the next conference he gave another talk on the Word of Wisdom.

How inspired President Grant was! In our day we can clearly see the assault of Satan on the Word of Wisdom, for the world is full of alcohol, tobacco, and drugs. How important it was that a prophet could see a generation ahead and teach the parents to teach their children so that they might be prepared for the onslaught that would come. Had that not been done, a generation of the Church might have been lost.

Think of President David O. McKay. What was his principal teaching? The importance of home, family, and marriage, including the duty of husband and wife to love and cherish one another. What followed in the next generation? Divorce, separation, destruction of the family unit. Once again, had parents not abided by his counsel, a generation of the Church might have been lost.

What about another prophet of the Lord, President Ezra Taft Benson, who, in conference after conference, stressed the importance of reading the Book of Mormon. Surely he spoke not only to the present generation but also to the generation that would follow. If we will follow his counsel, our children will be able to withstand the onslaught that is yet to come. I have a feeling that only young men and women who have been raised on that kind of a spiritual diet will be able to withstand the winds and torrents that will descend upon the world in the generations that will follow ours. How important it is that we make sure our families are being raised on that most inspired counsel.

President Benson once said: "Any man who will not teach his family to read in the scriptures and do that which he has been commanded to do relative to the Book of Mormon is in as much peril as the men who would not enter the ark in the days of Noah." What solemn counsel from a prophet of the Lord.

Thus we can clearly see that if parents will teach their children these basic elements relative to prayer and scripture reading, they will have dealt with two of the great cornerstones of gospel conversion. They will be in good stead for having helped their families become converted to the Lord and to be so converted throughout their lives.

As you now read the rest of the book, please keep in mind these important principles of what home and family really mean and your responsibility before the Lord to raise your family righteously. Keep in mind the true roles of the individual, the family, and the Church, and especially the importance of individual and family worship on the outcomes described in the youth study. On this foundation we can raise up a family to the Lord.

## CONCLUSION

Let us conclude this chapter by turning to the inspired principles directed to parents. These are found in Doctrine and Covenants, section 68, upon which the rest of this book is structured:

### PARENTS ARE TO TEACH THE DOCTRINE OF REPENTANCE, FAITH IN CHRIST, BAPTISM, AND THE GIFT OF THE HOLY GHOST

"Inasmuch as parents have children in Zion, or in any of her stakes which are organized, that teach them not to understand the doctrine of repentance, faith in Christ the Son of the living God, and of baptism and the gift of the Holy Ghost by the laying on of the hands, when eight years old, the sin be upon the heads of the parents. For this shall be a law unto the inhabitants of Zion, or in any of her stakes which are organized" (vv. 25–26).

### CHILDREN ARE TO BE BAPTIZED AND RECEIVE THE LAYING ON OF HANDS

"And their children shall be baptized for the remission of their sins when eight years old, and receive the laying on of the hands" (v. 27).

### PARENTS ARE TO TEACH THEIR CHILDREN TO PRAY AND TO WALK UPRIGHTLY

"And they shall also teach their children to pray, and to walk uprightly before the Lord" (v. 28).

## THE SAINTS (CHILDREN INCLUDED) ARE
## TO BE TAUGHT TO OBSERVE THE
## SABBATH DAY

"And the inhabitants of Zion shall also observe the Sabbath day to keep it holy" (v. 29).

## THE SAINTS (CHILDREN INCLUDED) ARE
## TO LABOR IN ALL FAITHFULNESS AND
## NOT BE IDLE NOR GREEDY

"And the inhabitants of Zion also shall remember their labors, inasmuch as they are appointed to labor, in all faithfulness; for the idler shall be had in remembrance before the Lord. Now, I, the Lord, am not well pleased with the inhabitants of Zion, for there are idlers among them; and their children are also growing up in wickedness; they also seek not earnestly the riches of eternity, but their eyes are full of greediness" (vv. 30–31).

## THESE SAYINGS ARE TO BE TAUGHT
## TO ALL THE SAINTS (INCLUDING
## CHILDREN)

"These things ought not to be, and must be done away from among them; wherefore, let my servant Oliver Cowdery carry these sayings unto the land of Zion" (v. 32).

## THE SAINTS (CHILDREN INCLUDED)
## ARE TO OBSERVE THEIR PRAYERS

"And a commandment I give unto them—that he that observeth not his prayers before the Lord in the season thereof, let him be had in remembrance before the judge of my people" (v. 33).

## THESE SAYINGS ARE TRUE AND FAITHFUL
## FOR ALL (CHILDREN INCLUDED)

"These sayings are true and faithful; wherefore, transgress them not, neither take therefrom. Behold, I am Alpha and Omega, and I come quickly. Amen" (vv. 34–35).

It is interesting that in this commandment the Lord says

that parents are to teach their children a set of doctrines before they are eight years old or the sin will be upon their own heads.

It has always been impressive to me that we are to teach these doctrines to children *before* they reach the age of eight. It is no small matter that Satan cannot tempt children before that age. Perhaps this has more to do with a "divine timing" and parents' opportunity to teach than many have realized. The specific doctrines the Lord mentions are:

- Faith in Christ.
- Repentance.
- Baptism.
- Gift of the Holy Ghost.
- Prayer.
- Walking uprightly before the Lord.
- Observing the Sabbath Day, to keep it holy.
- Laboring in all faithfulness, without being an idler.
- Preventing children from growing up in wickedness or having their eyes full of greediness.
- Seeking for the riches of eternity.

At the conclusion, in verse 34, the Lord indicates that these sayings are true and faithful, referring to the whole section, but I believe also specifically to these verses. He also says that we are not to transgress them or take from them. I believe he is saying that if we will follow those principles and teach them by the Spirit to our children, we will be able to raise up a family to the Lord. Thus, the remainder of this book is largely constructed upon the principles mentioned by the Lord in these key verses.

# CHAPTER TWO

# TEACHING YOUR FAMILY BY THE SPIRIT

One afternoon a few years ago, one of my sons (about sixteen years old at the time) came home from school very upset about things. He was having trouble learning everything he needed to know for some tests the next day, and some friends had been giving him a hard time as well. He really felt down. In his frustration, he began to cause some contention in the family. My wife and I thought, "Should we get involved?" As the night wore on, we thought, "No, we'll let it pass. He'll sleep through this thing and feel better in the morning." We opted not to get involved, which is difficult sometimes, but I think we were wise to stay out of the situation that night.

The next morning, however, the problems started again at breakfast. Because our son was upset, he offended one of his sisters, and she began to cry. When breakfast was over, I took him by the arm and said, "Son, come here for a minute." I took him into my bedroom, shut and locked the door, and knelt down. He knelt down as well, still angry.

I did my best to offer a prayer for him: "Heavenly Father, bless my son. He's hurting today. He's had some problems with the family. He's worried about his tests at school." And I expressed my love to him the best I could in that prayer, exercising my faith that the Lord would help him that day if he would humble his heart.

After a few minutes, his heart was humbled, and as soon as the amen was uttered, he said, "Dad, let me pray." In his prayer he asked for forgiveness. He told the Lord that he loved him and that he loved me. He told the Lord he would ask forgiveness of his sister. He said he was feeling great stress but that he believed the Lord would help him. After that prayer, a father and a son embraced in great love, and, with the Lord as part of the solution, the love between the two of them was enriched a hundredfold.

He went off to school that day, did well in his tests, and came home on cloud nine, thrilled to tell his mother and me about his success and that he *knew* the Lord had intervened and helped him. He had no doubt about that.

About two weeks later, I was feeling the pressure and strain of having to direct some important meetings and give a couple of talks that day. Again we were sitting at breakfast, and I was not as responsive to some of the children as I should have been. I was feeling about the way my son had felt. I even caused a bit of a problem with one of the children.

After breakfast, my son took me by the arm and said, "Dad, come with me a minute." Again we went into the bedroom. He shut the door and locked it. He knelt down and I knelt down. Then I heard a good boy offer a prayer for his dad, saying things like, "My dad's really worried. He's got to do some things that he's not had a chance to prepare for as he would have liked to do. He's concerned about his meetings and his talks. Please help him, Heavenly Father. Please inspire him. I love him."

It didn't take long for a heart that wasn't as humble as it should have been to be rapidly humbled. And then I offered a prayer of thanksgiving for a good son and asked forgiveness of the Lord. After the prayer there was another hug, and again our love multiplied.

I've often wondered why the love multiplies so in such situations. It is because the Lord is in the situation. It is not just a father or mother giving counsel to a child. But the Lord is in it, and when he is in it, revelation flows and love multiplies.

Well, I went off to work that day and did all of the things I had to do. Everything went well. When I pulled into the garage that evening, this same son, who had called ahead to find out what time I had left the office, was waiting for me. When he saw me, he asked, "Well, Dad, how did your

day go?" Then, of course, that morning's experience flashed back into my mind, and in gratitude I replied, "Son, this has been a great day. My concerns were unfounded. The Lord did bless me, and I was able to give my talks."

"I already knew," he said.

"What do you mean?"

"Well, I already knew, Dad. That's the way the Lord does it. I've prayed for you about seventeen times today. I prayed in nearly every class. I prayed when I was at the cafeteria. I even prayed when I was in the bathroom that the Lord would bless you today." And then he added, "I already knew."

I've thought much about this incident in relation to teaching by the Spirit. I suspect that neither I nor anyone else could ever teach in words or doctrine all that can be learned in a *real experience* with the Spirit of the Lord.

## THE POWER OF
## WORSHIPING THE LORD

In teaching and learning by the Spirit, the importance of

individual and family worship cannot be overstated. It may be the most important key in raising up a faithful family to the Lord. We ought not to be surprised that this is so. One day a lawyer asked Jesus, "Master, which is the great commandment in the law?"

Jesus answered:

> Thou shalt love the Lord thy God with all thy heart, and with all thy soul, and with all thy mind. This is the first and great commandment. And the second is like unto it, Thou shalt love thy neighbour as thyself. On these two commandments hang all the law and the prophets (Matthew 22:35–40).

In other words, the first commandment to us as individuals as well as families is to love the Lord with all our heart, might, mind, and strength. After having done so, we are to learn through our families how to serve others in the family and then others beyond the family. That great summary statement of the Lord is so inclusive: all of the scriptures in the Savior's day centered upon those two great commandments. What they do is tie an individual or family to the Lord. And when the Lord is part of something, it will not fail.

Naturally, then, we must learn to become more reliant upon the Lord. We must learn how to teach our families by his Spirit, for if we teach in any other way, it will not have a lasting effect.

If we learn to have the Spirit of the Lord with us and to teach by that Spirit, we will be able to keep the roles of the individual, the family, and the Church in their proper perspective. We will better understand the sacred roles of father, mother, and children. We will receive ample instruction from the Lord because, after all, our children were his children first. He desires even more than we do to see his children saved. Thus, he wants to be a full partner in your marriage, in your family, and in your relationship with yourself. I repeat, he wants to give daily instruction in how to better direct our families in an inspired way.

The Lord has clearly stated, "There is a law, irrevocably decreed in heaven before the foundations of this world, upon which all blessings are predicated—and when we obtain any blessing from God, it is by obedience to that law upon which it is predicated" (D&C 130:20–21).

Clearly, when we desire *any blessing*, it is governed by a law. The secret to working with the Lord is to discover what the law is and obey it; then the Lord will convey that blessing to us. The Lord has also said: "All who will have a blessing at my hands shall abide the law which was appointed for that blessing, and the conditions thereof, as were instituted from before the foundation of the world" (D&C 132:5). Evidently the law includes certain eternal conditions, which, if met, will allow us to obtain the blessing at the Lord's hand. Let us, then, attempt to describe some of those conditions that, if present, will allow the Spirit of the Lord to be with a good father or mother in leading the family.

## LISTENING WITH THE SPIRIT

When we consider what it means to teach by the Spirit, we must recognize clearly that three parties are involved: the one speaking, the one listening, and the Spirit of the Lord. One of the most challenging things for the one speaking is to hear correctly what the Lord would have him or her teach.

President Marion G. Romney once said to some of his associates, "Brethren, I'm really beginning to worry about my wife. Her hearing is going out on her. I'm going home tonight and test it." That evening he sat down in his big chair in the living room and called out, "Ida, please bring me a glass of water." There was dead silence. So he said a little louder, "Ida, please bring me a glass of water." Again nothing. So this time he loudly said, "Ida, please bring me a glass of water!" She arrived at his side and said, "My, my, my,

Marion, I've answered you three times. What do you want?"
He was really embarrassed to finally admit that his own
hearing was going.

In truth, it's one thing to be able to hear and another to
understand. I often think of a time when Brother Romney
followed two young people out of a meeting at which he
had spoken. One boy said, "That was the most boring meeting I've ever attended in my whole life. All Brother Romney
did was quote scriptures. I couldn't stand it. I couldn't wait
to get out of there." The other boy said through his tears,
"That was the most spiritual meeting I've ever attended. I
think I have had my life changed." The difference was in
the attitude of those listening and their reception and
response to the Spirit.

## THE HOLY GHOST IS THE TEACHER

I think one of the greatest things I know about teaching
is that the one taking the role of teacher really is not the
teacher. Be very careful if you see yourself beginning to act
like one who has all the answers, because that would be
getting out of your true role. The Lord has said: "I the Lord
ask you this question—unto what were ye ordained? To
preach my gospel by the Spirit, even the Comforter which
was sent forth to teach the truth" (D&C 50:13–14).

Who was sent forth to teach the truth? The Comforter.
Me? No, the Comforter. I may assist. I may be an instrument in the hands of the Lord to preach and help things
along, but the Comforter is the teacher. I think that is a
truth we would all agree to, but I also think most of us have
a hard time applying it or recognizing it. This boy that
Brother Romney overheard had been taught by the Holy
Ghost. He had heard the Lord's voice to him personally.
Brother Romney did something, but I think he would have
been quick to say it was very little. Perhaps he prepared the
way and did some things to set the stage, but he would
clearly have recognized who it was that had changed the
boy's heart.

If someone asked me, "What is the single greatest thing you know about teaching?" I would be quick to respond that it *must be done by the Spirit*. And I believe I would add, "The thing that has the greatest effect on teaching and learning by the Spirit is that one's heart must be in tune with the Lord, largely through prayer."

Is it not logical, then, to understand that the Lord will teach us? He will, and he can *enlighten* our understandings and *quicken* the light within us until we can see and foresee things we would not otherwise understand.

Remember when the Nephites gathered at the temple in the land Bountiful? The first time the Lord spoke, they understood it not. The second time, they understood it not. The third time, "[they] did open their ears to hear it," and they heard (see 3 Nephi 11:3–5). The Lord explained in Doctrine and Covenants 136:32 *how to open* our ears, our eyes, and our hearts: "Let him that is ignorant learn wisdom by humbling himself and calling upon the Lord his God, that his eyes may be opened that he may see, and his ears opened that he may hear."

Let's look at that verse phrase by phrase: "Let him that is ignorant learn wisdom . . . " Of whom is the Lord speaking when he says this? He's speaking about us.

While reading, I might ask myself, "How does one obtain wisdom?" The world would say by reading, studying, going to college, learning from experience, and so on. Those are pretty good answers, none of which, however, the Lord gives. He says there is another way to do it. It is not that those answers are bad, but that they are secondary. Here's how one gets wisdom: First, "by humbling himself . . . "

Isn't that interesting? If we want to be wise in the Lord, if we want to understand in our hearts what he is saying to us, if we want to be able to hear that voice, the answer, above all others, is to humble ourselves before him.

For example, we must recognize who is who before we stand to teach. We might run through our minds in prayer those feelings of who we are, who the Lord is, and what he must do now—not what *we* must do, but rather what *he* must do to touch the hearts of our children. If you can humble the hearts of your children, they will understand what God says to them.

The second way we learn is by "calling upon the Lord . . . "

If we will pray that the Lord will teach us, after we have humbled ourselves, what will be the result? "[Our] eyes may be opened, that [we] may see, and [our] ears opened that [we] may hear," for, as the Lord says in the next verse, his "Spirit is sent forth into the world to enlighten the humble and contrite."

## THE SPIRIT TEACHES
## THE HUMBLE AND CONTRITE

Whom will the Spirit enlighten? The humble and contrite. How about the prideful? The Spirit of the Lord will not attend them.

Occasionally I have sat in Church classes about how to properly raise children. I have often been amused to see that the younger couples seem to have all the answers. They may have received some training about how to be good parents, so they tend to think they really know how to do it. The more seasoned parents who have been through the experience are not so quick to raise their hands.

If we ever allow pride to enter our hearts, thinking we know all about how to raise a family and that we "are really good parents," in that day the heavens will be sealed to us. But if we will humble ourselves and pray to the Lord as often as we can, the Lord truly will open our eyes that we may see and our ears that we may hear. I bear witness to that principle. Don't be too worried about the details of teaching. Be much more concerned about how to turn to the Lord and receive instruction from the true source. Knowing how to receive an answer from God may be the greatest gift you could ever bequeath to your children.

Some might say, "Well, I don't know how very well

myself." That's all right. If you just have the desire to know more, and if you keep persisting, the Lord will bestow that knowledge upon you little by little until you feel more confident. I bear testimony of that truth.

In most cases, children who have the Spirit of the Lord with them are alert and responsive to brothers and sisters and their parents. Rebellious, disobedient children do not have the Spirit. They look down at their feet, won't look you in the eye, and when asked a question do not respond or do so reluctantly. I bear testimony that if we will teach our children to have the Spirit of the Lord, they will be responsive not only to the Lord but to their parents and brothers and sisters as well. Perhaps that is one of the final measures of the degree to which people have the Spirit—they are responsive to the Lord and to their fellowman.

It is one thing to have the Spirit yourself. It is another to be able to use it with other people. When you are ready to teach, make sure the Spirit is there. As the Lord has said, "If ye receive not the Spirit ye shall not teach" (D&C 42:14). Your teaching won't do any good or make any difference if you don't have the Spirit.

As I watch teachers, sometimes I worry that they're not concerned enough about having the Spirit of the Lord with them *all the time* while they are teaching. Again, if we don't have the Spirit, we shall not teach—at least not in the Lord's way.

Let us teach our children to have a prayer in their hearts as we instruct them. Then they will learn through the Spirit of the Lord. Parents must be praying as well while they're teaching.

A parent might offer a simple prayer, such as: "Please instruct me, Heavenly Father. I'm worried about one of my sons. I don't know what to do to soften his heart. Help me." As she prays with a humble heart, the Lord will speak to her and whisper to her something she can now do that she had not thought of before. And as great as the instruction is, the one thing perhaps greater is that she is learning *how to receive* instruction from the Lord. If we take the Spirit for our guide, we will not be deceived, and we will be enabled to get through these perilous times (see D&C 45:57).

## HOW TO INVITE THE SPIRIT

Think, for a moment, of times when you really need the Spirit. I would like to make some specific suggestions about how you can have that blessing, either for yourself (in times of discouragement, for example) or for those you are teaching. These suggestions will prepare the way for the Spirit; in fact, they will *immediately* invite the Spirit into what you are going to do. I've emphasized the word *immediately* because that's when we usually need it. For example, when we are teaching or counseling someone, we can't wait for help later; we need it right now. Here are the suggestions:

### 1. PRAY

One of the most important things you can do is pray fervently for the Spirit. The Lord tells us so in the scriptures. Sometimes missionaries try to counter the objections of an investigator by giving their opinion or an explanation or some kind of reasoning. And those things are all right. But a more powerful way to deal with an objection is to pray. When someone tries to reason against paying tithing, for example, a missionary might say, "What did the Lord say about tithing when you asked him about it? Come on, Brother Brown, let's kneel down." Then Brother Brown is in the hands of the Lord. Brother Brown's heart will be changed, if he is humble, by the Lord himself.

You may have a child with whom you are struggling. When appropriate, kneeling in prayer with the child could have a much greater impact than anything you might say in reasoning with him or her. Children need to see prayer in action. They need to feel it. Then comes the witness, which is so important.

I have often said something to missionaries that also applies to parents. The primary objective of a missionary is to provide a spiritual experience to the investigator. Similarly, the single greatest thing you can do for your students—for your children—is to give them a spiritual experience. Help them to experience the Spirit *with* you, and then teach them how to have the experience alone. Either way, it's worth more than all the instruction you could provide on the subject. In essence, what we're talking about is showing them a *means* for doing it.

When you have a problem with one of your children, is one of your first inclinations to pray with him or her, or does that come later or not at all? Perhaps that is a measure of your own spirituality. When you are presented with a problem of any kind, is your first inclination to pray? If it is, I would say to you, "Bless you for humbly recognizing that God is in his heaven. He holds all nations in his hands and is surely capable of helping you." If your first inclination is to turn to him, I bear witness in the name of the Lord Jesus Christ that he will speak to you. He will give you revelation. He will change the heart of a child or a student or someone else who is not responding. He can do that. You can't. All you can do, in large measure, is to help set up an environment where that can happen.

Let us remember, then, when teaching that to pray is absolutely essential or understanding will not occur. The Lord said it so well in the Book of Mormon: "And it came to pass that he commanded the multitude that they should cease to pray, and also his disciples. And he commanded them that they should not cease to pray in their hearts" (3 Nephi 20:1).

It's evident that Jesus, wanting to talk to the people, asked them to stop praying vocally. But in order for them *to understand* his teaching, even being the Son of God, it was necessary that they pray in their hearts while being taught. Jesus further illustrated this with the words: "I perceive that ye are weak, that ye cannot understand all my words which I am commanded of the Father to speak unto you at this time. Therefore, go ye unto your homes, and ponder upon the things which I have said, and ask of the Father, in my name, that ye may understand, and prepare your minds for the morrow, and I come unto you again" (3 Nephi 17:2–3).

He seemed to sense when the "students" were filled and tired and knew when to stop teaching. But he counseled them that some of the greatest learning was yet to take place even after they left him, and that in order to bring that learning about, they would need to go to their homes and ponder and ask the Father in prayer that they might understand. If they would do that, then the understanding of what he had taught would rest in their hearts, and they would be prepared for his teachings when he came the next day. If we can understand that principle, we will be much more successful as parents when we're actually teaching our children. They have a very real part to play in learning. The teacher's role is not just to place concepts in someone's mind. It is to help students learn and experience the concepts for themselves. Real learning takes place between the learner and the Lord.

## 2. USE SCRIPTURE

I know when we speak the words the Lord has given us in the holy scriptures, the Spirit of the Lord comes. If you will do it *in humility*, the moment you pick up the passages and start to read them, the Lord will speak through you in power, and the Spirit will be conveyed to those who are listening.

The scriptures are the words of the Lord to us, and the Spirit of the Lord will speak through them to all—both young and old. If we use the scriptures to teach our families, the very words of the Lord will reach their hearts.

I remember once when two of our daughters were coming into their teen years and were beginning to feel pressure from their peers to dress a little more like some of the young women of the world. Some were telling them they should wear more makeup, more jewelry, more worldly clothing. We were reading the scriptures one morning when the subject came up. I think by inspiration we just happened to be reading in the Book of Mormon in the words of Isaiah: "Because the daughters of Zion are haughty, and walk with stretched-forth necks and wanton eyes, walking and mincing as they go, and making a tinkling with their feet—therefore the Lord will smite with a scab the crown of the head of the daughters of Zion, and the Lord will discover their secret parts" (2 Nephi 13:16–17).

We immediately saw that these passages were not directed to daughters of the world but to the daughters of Zion, to faithful female members of the Church. The Lord spoke of how in the last days many would be tempted to do just what some were suggesting to my daughters that they do—namely, to dress in a more worldly way.

Isaiah continues: "In that day the Lord will take away the bravery of their tinkling ornaments, and cauls [hairnets], and round tires like the moon [ornaments like a crescent moon]; the chains and the bracelets, and the mufflers [veils]; the bonnets, and the ornaments of the legs, and the headbands, and the tablets, and the ear-rings; the rings, and nose jewels; the changeable suits of apparel, and the mantles, and the wimples, and the crisping-pins; the glasses [transparent garments], and the fine linen, and hoods, and the veils" (2 Nephi 13:18–23).

Evidently the Lord is not pleased with those who go too far in adorning their bodies. The Lord is surely not suggesting that we go to the extreme of not doing anything to adorn ourselves, but he is giving a great caution about going too far, about beginning to dress in the way of the world.

This underscores a great principle that is taught to the missionaries and that probably applies well to teaching this principle to our sons and daughters: There should never be anything about you—the way you speak or especially your appearance—that comes over stronger than the real you. In other words, we want people to know us and love us for being ourselves, not for external adornments used to attract attention or perhaps even motivate some unrighteous feelings in those who might be influenced by us.

As we read these passages that morning and, as parents, bore testimony to the truthfulness of the principles, we could see that the message reached the hearts of our girls. They asked a number of questions: "What about this? What about that?" As we worked through those questions as a family, a standard evolved about what the Lord expects of a righteous young woman in properly adorning herself. The standard was not our standard, but it was based on a standard given in the scriptures. In other words, it was the Lord's standard.

What made this experience so powerful was the fact that had it been just our standard, we would later have had to enforce it with more specific rules and perhaps to discuss it frequently with our children. (And we have done some of that over the years.) But what impressed us most was the fact that the Lord himself, through his Spirit, reached the hearts of our daughters that morning. He placed in them a value, a standard, a level of expectation, that did not come from their parents. It came from the Lord. Thus, they accepted it as their own and lived it from that day forward.

Thanks be to the scriptures. Thanks be to the Lord for his words that are so imbued with his Spirit. You will face nothing in life for which the basic principles are not found in the scriptures. The key is to understand them and to share them with your family. Nephi taught the value of the scriptures when he said: "Angels speak by the power of the Holy Ghost; wherefore, they speak the words of Christ. Wherefore, I said unto you, feast upon the words of Christ; for behold, the words of Christ will tell you all things what ye should do" (2 Nephi 32:3). It is evident that the Lord does provide the answers in the scriptures if we will but seek them out.

May I restate again that it isn't just the finding of the knowledge or the clarification of the principle in the scriptures. It's the added testimony that goes with it that causes the teaching taught by the Spirit through a good parent to reach the heart of the child and change his heart. Sometimes some of the teaching will not occur as quickly as illustrated above. Sometimes one of your children might really need to prayerfully consider something and weigh it over a period of time in order to gain a true understanding. Yet, once again, if the parent teaches the principle by the Spirit and then the child is taught how to receive an answer from the Lord by praying about it himself, he will then obtain from the Lord the truth in his own heart, which will change his behavior.

I have always loved these words: "They shall give heed to that which is written, and pretend to no other revelation; and they shall pray always that I may unfold the same to their understanding" (D&C 32:4).

This passage has to do with the scriptures. It indicates clearly that if we will pray about them, the Lord will unfold them to our understanding. By that I mean not just an academic understanding but a true understanding of the heart.

In the Book of Mormon, the leaders struggled for some time to teach the Saints of their day how to properly use the scriptures. They were attempting to bring souls to Christ— the nonmembers and the less active—and had used many different means to do it, but they had not been too successful. Then Alma, the great high priest, as they were preparing to go on a mission to reclaim the apostate Zoramites (the less active), received this great understanding from the Lord: "The preaching of the word had a great tendency to lead the people to do that which was just—yea, it had had more powerful effect upon the minds of the people than the sword, or anything else, which had happened unto them— therefore Alma thought it was expedient that they should try the virtue of the word of God" (Alma 31:5).

The preaching of the word of the Lord affected their minds and changed their hearts; nothing had a more powerful effect on the people. If parents can adopt that approach, making sure that their children are exposed regularly to the words of the Lord, many of their problems will be solved in the children's early years and will never come up later. There really aren't any big problems; there are just a lot of little ones that have been allowed to fester and grow. (More specific information on scripture study is given in chapter 4.)

## 3. TESTIFY

Testify frequently while you are teaching. This may even be more important than the thing you are teaching. Testify in the name of the Lord that the things you are teaching are true. If you will do that, it will bring the Spirit of the Lord.

At times parents forget the great power that is found in bearing testimony to their children. Sometimes we're more of a mind to try to convince them logically that something is right, such as paying tithing, keeping the Sabbath Day holy, coming in at a reasonable hour in the evening, being kind to their friends, and so on. At times we can describe things logically and teach them to our family and they are accepted. But many times that is not the case. One of the greatest spiritual tools the Lord has given us for influencing others, including our children, is the power of our own testimony.

Nephi wrote, "I . . . cannot write all the things which were taught among my people; neither am I mighty in writing, like unto speaking; for when a man speaketh by the power of the Holy Ghost the power of the Holy Ghost carrieth it unto the hearts of the children of men" (2 Nephi 33:1). If fathers and mothers will speak by the power of the Holy Ghost in love and testimony to their children, the message will reach their hearts and can change them.

Alma provides a powerful example of this principle. He stepped down from the judgment-seat "that he himself might go forth among his people, or among the people of Nephi, that he might preach the word of God unto them, to stir them up in remembrance of their duty, and that he might pull down, by the word of God, all the pride and craftiness and all the contentions which were among his people, seeing no way that he might reclaim them save it were in bearing down in pure testimony against them" (Alma 4:19).

Children as well as adults can be proud or angry or contentious and thus repel the Spirit of the Lord. But a parent's testimony can help dispel such negative attitudes.

I had an interesting experience with one of my sons when he was about eight years old. He was studying math and had learned nearly all of his pluses and minuses, passing them off with me. But after a while he got discouraged and quit. I let him decide what to do, thinking that after a while he would come back and finish them up. But he never returned. Finally, some days later, I "laid down the law" and told him that we had to solve this problem that had come between us. He was a little hard-hearted and didn't want to do it. I had him sit on a chair for a while, and that still didn't help to humble him.

Finally, I realized I was approaching him in the wrong way, so he and I went into the bedroom and had a word of prayer together. That softened his heart about halfway. Then I told him he ought to stay in the bedroom and pray and find out what the Lord wanted him to do, to listen for the voice of the Lord. Somewhat to my surprise, instead of staying there a minute or two, he stayed there on his knees ten or fifteen minutes. When I finally went back to see how he was doing, he said the Lord had told him by the Spirit that he should do his math and that he would obey that voice and do it even though he didn't want to.

I was thrilled to hear that he had had a real experience with the Lord. He and I went to tell his mother about it. Then we spent some time studying, and he passed off the first of three tests on his pluses. He couldn't pass off his minuses that day, but a couple of days later he did.

Later that same night I had a chat with him to reinforce the importance of what had happened. I asked him how he felt about it, and we reviewed the fact that he had been a little prideful and hard-hearted and mad and that's why things had not been going well in math for him during the past month. I told him I had felt inspired, when I was upset with him, to take him into the bedroom so we could kneel and pray together. I reminded him that the time he had humbled himself was when I had prayed and then he had prayed.

I asked him, before I told him any of the things I have just stated, "Son, have you ever in your life heard the voice of the Lord?" He answered, "Yes, I have."

I said, "When?"

He said, "Today."

I said, "What do you mean?"

He said, "When I went in and knelt and prayed and stayed in the room and asked the Lord what to do, that's when he told me I should do my math."

I said, "How do you know? What was the voice like?"

He said, "Well, it was just a voice that told me it was okay, that it was right to do, and that everything would be all right and that I could do it."

I said, "In other words, it was a peaceful, calm voice?"

He said, "Dad, that's what it was."

He seemed touched by the fact that I reinforced that with him, and I think he learned a good lesson, as did I. I told him he should be careful to remember this time when he prayed and immediately got an answer from the Lord. I told him that he would have other problems when he got older, but that they could all be solved this same way. He seemed very pleased by that.

This whole episode seemed to turn on the impression that I should take my son into our room to pray. The thought was clear that if I could do that and humble his heart, then he would respond and learn his math tables. But it had to be because he wanted to, not just because I wanted him to. The Spirit had to touch him for that to occur—my words were not enough. The whole issue began to turn when, on bended knee, I bore testimony and told him that I knew the Lord would help him if he would have faith. The words were carried from my heart to his, and he humbled himself and stayed there in the room, praying until his heart was fully humbled. If we can remember to use such spiritual tools in dealing with our children, we will have much more of an impact upon them.

Another example that illustrates this principle is how I came to obtain my own testimony. My older brother had always been an inspiration to me. One evening when he was about seventeen, he came home from a Church youth meeting and announced to me that his teacher had told him to gain his own testimony and not to rely on those of others. He said—almost prophetically—"I'm going to gain that personal witness and testimony, no matter how long it takes or what the cost. I will pay the price to know."

He then began fasting, praying, and studying the Book of Mormon. One morning a short time later, he was stricken by paralysis. He could not move his body, and his right side was in terrible pain. He was barely able to whisper to my father that he wanted a blessing. As soon as the blessing was completed, my brother was miraculously healed. He uncoiled his tense body, straightened up, and was free of pain.

When he was later examined by a doctor, the diagnosis was that he had had what appeared to be a ruptured appendix, but no trace of damaged tissue was found in his body. Later, my brother told me of his feelings about being healed, and he told me that he knew the Church was true. However, he said a spiritual witness of the Book of Mormon had come before the healing. He told me how he had studied the book and prayed over every page. He bore his testimony to me. I was very touched by this experience, and I said in my heart, "If the Lord will answer my brother, he will also answer me."

Thus at age twelve I began to read the Book of Mormon. I, too, received a personal confirmation of the truthfulness of the gospel. I knew then and have never doubted since that the Book of Mormon is the word of God and that the gospel is true.

It is now clear to me that my brother's testimony reached my heart and caused me to desire the same thing he had. Many times the teachings parents have given to their children lie dormant in their hearts, waiting for a time to come forth. When problems and challenges surround us, if we will be alert enough to turn them into spiritual experiences through our testimonies, our children will be turned to the Lord. Then the teachings we have planted in their hearts will spring up and bear fruit, and our children will be able to use them to resolve many of their own problems.

## 4. USE SACRED MUSIC

Music has a great impact on the soul. For a long time in our home, we have had a practice of singing when we have family prayer—both in the morning and in the evening. I am not suggesting this as a doctrine of the Church or even suggesting that you ought to do it. I'm just telling you what we do. We have found it to be very helpful with our children, when we kneel down in a circle, to sing a hymn before we pray. We have found that it prepares the way for the Spirit among family members. It calms the little ones who may be punching their neighbor or things like that. It quiets them so that they're thinking of the Lord, and then we pray.

As a child I never really learned the Primary songs because I didn't have many opportunities to go to Primary. However, my children and my good wife have taught me most of the songs as we have sung before family prayer. Singing seems to bring the Spirit. If you ever feel down, get into the habit of singing to yourself. Sing those sacred hymns, and they will fill you with the Spirit of the Lord.

Some time ago in California, we had a meeting of our area council (regional representatives and mission presidents). Instead of talking about the less active, we said, "We want you to go out and be with the less active. We're going to give you half an hour of instruction, and then we'll ask you to go out for two hours and meet with some of them. Your objective is to bring them back to the Lord." We gave them instructions about what to do and discussed the spiritual tools mentioned here—tools that can prepare the way for the Spirit.

The brethren were filing out to make their visits, and, as you can imagine, it was quite a challenge for them to go out and begin reactivating people within an hour or so and try to turn them to the Lord. (We later learned that thirty-seven people were activated that night as a result of these brethren visiting in their homes.)

One of the brethren was walking out without a hymnbook, and I said to him, "You forgot your hymnbook. Take a hymnbook with you in case you want to sing in the home of a less-active member."

He said, "Brother Cook, I'm willing to do six of those things you listed, but one of them I will not do. I couldn't sing in front of anybody. I've never sung in my whole life, and I'm not planning on it."

I said, "I know you're not, but what if the Lord is planning on your singing?"

He kind of stared at me and mumbled, "Oh, I'll take it." He reported to us later that as he took the book, he said in his heart, "I'll never sing, not for anybody."

Well, they went to the home of a less-active member. They prayed with him, read some scriptures, and bore testimony. But the man was hard-hearted and would not respond. This leader sat there praying, "Heavenly Father, what shall we do? How can we humble this man before thee so we can teach him with the Spirit? There's no need for us to go ahead until he's humbled in his heart."

He later recounted, "I was sitting there praying, trying to decide what to do, when all of a sudden my younger companion stood up and said, 'My companion and I are going to sing to you.' I looked at him and thought, 'You've got to be kidding.' But we decided to sing 'As I Have Loved You' because it was the shortest number in the book."

These two men, the one about sixty and the other about forty—two companions who had never sung to an audience before in their lives—stood up in front of this older, less-active fellow, his wife, and an inactive son. They started singing, "As I have loved you, love one another, this new commandment, love one another." They had only got about halfway through when the tears started running down the cheeks of this crusty old fellow. To see and hear these two men singing this sweet song humbled his heart. They then bore testimony and taught him some basic things about how to pray.

I later learned that this man now pays a full tithe and attends some of his sacrament meetings and ward socials. The change in his life is due, at least in part, to someone who knew how to use music to humble the hearts of the people. Use music in your home. Use it for yourself. It will bring the Spirit of the Lord.

Some have asked, "How can I effectively use music in the home to set a spiritual mood?" Several answers come to mind.

• Our family sings before family prayer—usually just a verse or two and almost always from memory.

• We sing before scripture reading and during family home evenings.

• We have a number of tapes of spiritual music that we really like. Many times, especially on Sunday or early in the morning, we'll play them to set the spirit in the home. Sometimes when there has been a little contention or some problems, my wife turns on some of that music, and it seems to calm everyone.

• As parents we have found it most enjoyable for all if Dad or Mom sings to the children after they have prayed and are in bed ready to go to sleep. We've always sung to the younger ones. Our older girls even enjoyed that "special attention" into their teenage years.

• As a young missionary, I had a number of discouraging days, but I learned a great lesson and now I have a lot fewer of those days. What I have learned is that I used to wait until I was discouraged before using music or some of the other spiritual tools. As I got a little older I thought, "Why wait? Why go into the valley of despair before trying to be happy? Why not use those things *every day* and thus avoid discouragement altogether?"

• In a home where music is properly used, you would probably hear good music at many times. For example, you might hear the father singing in the shower on most mornings. He might not be a very good singer, but he would be better than he used to be. Try it! Your voice will sound great when you've got all that tile around you. Singing in the shower certainly helps cheer you up, and it might even help you have a little better day. A family that uses good music might carry a few tapes of spiritual music in the car that the family can listen to if they feel the need. Little things like these can make a real difference and help remove discouragement.

• I believe that parents have a responsibility to set a proper spirit in the morning before people leave for work and school. For some years, each morning we've played music on the stereo. Sometimes we play something lively like "You Are My Sunshine," "Zip-A-Dee-Doo-Dah," "When the Red, Red Robin," or other fun music—something lively to get everyone going. At other times we play spiritual music, such as hymns performed by the Tabernacle Choir, that fill the house and lift everybody's spirits.

Music can have a great impact on our families if we use it appropriately. It was the Lord who said: "My soul delighteth in the song of the heart; yea, the song of the righteous is a prayer unto me, and it shall be answered with a blessing upon their heads" (D&C 25:12).

Thus, if we can use music in the spirit of worship, it will become a prayer to the Lord, helping you, your spouse, and your children to soften your hearts and be taught by the Spirit of the Lord.

I've always been impressed by what Jesus and his apos-

tles did before he went out to suffer in the Garden of Geth-
semane: "When they had sung an hymn, they went out into
the mount of Olives" (Matthew 26:30).

I'm sure the Lord received great comfort from that
hymn. Could not our families obtain the same benefit? Also,
great teaching comes from singing the songs of Zion. It has
been a great blessing for me to learn songs like "I Am a
Child of God" and "Teach Me to Walk in the Light."

If children were to hear the songs of Zion sung at home
and learned themselves to sing while getting dressed or taking a shower, it would surely remove a lot of negativity from
our homes and replace it with the Spirit of the Lord. There
is nothing quite like a good hymn to discourage discouragement. Remember what King Saul did when he felt discouraged? He asked David to play the harp for him, which
seemed to bring the Spirit back to him: "It came to pass,
when the evil spirit which was not of God was upon Saul,
that David took an harp, and played with his hand: so Saul
was refreshed, and was well, and the evil spirit departed
from him" (JST, Samuel 16:23).

Paul also understood the power of good music: "Let the
word of Christ dwell in you richly in all wisdom; teaching
and admonishing one another in psalms and hymns and
spiritual songs, singing with grace in your hearts to the
Lord" (Colossians 3:16). Truly we can teach and admonish
one another through hymns and spiritual songs if we do it in
the right spirit.

Let us, then, let music ring in our homes—good, wholesome music that will lift the spirits of all and lift our hearts
to the Lord. Thereby we will invite the Spirit of the Lord to
be with us.

## 5. EXPRESS LOVE AND GRATITUDE
## TO GOD AND MAN

Express love openly for God and his children, and the
Spirit will be felt profoundly (see John 13:34–35; 1 Nephi
11:21–23; Moroni 7:47–48). It is impossible to stand up and

express love for the Lord and not have the Spirit of the Lord come upon you. If you want to bring the Spirit of the Lord into your home, you must learn yourself and teach your children how to regularly express love and gratitude to God and to one another. It's impossible to humbly count your blessings and not have the Spirit of the Lord come to you. It's impossible to express your love sincerely to one of your family members or to your spouse and not have the Spirit of the Lord come.

Love has tremendous power. No wonder the scriptures say that God is love (see 1 John 4:8). I don't know anything more powerful than throwing your arms around your children every day. At the end of our family prayers, my wife and I throw our arms around every one of our children. We hold them tight and whisper, "I love you." Sometimes harsh words and many other problems can be melted away in an embrace, surpassing anything you could say. Be sure to express your love amply to your family and to the Lord, and the Spirit will be with you in that very instant.

Let me illustrate this principle with an incident that occurred between my daughter and me when I was about to leave for a stake conference. I was talking with her one night, and after she had said her prayers, I asked her what she prayed about.

She said, "What do you mean, Dad?"

"What do you pray about?" I responded. "Now that you're older, you say your prayers silently, and I don't get to hear them anymore."

She replied, "Well, I always tell Heavenly Father how much I love him. Not just sometimes—I always tell him. He's given me so many blessings. I'm very thankful for all my blessings."

Then she said, "Dad, do you have to go to conference again tomorrow?"

I told her I did.

She said, "Oh, it breaks my heart to have you leave. It's

hard for me to see you go every week. Do you have to go again?"

I told her that I did, and I explained why. She threw her arms around my neck and expressed her love to me, telling me how much she would miss me. I found it hard to make her understand why I had to go.

I finally determined that the best way to help her understand was to pray with her. I asked her to offer prayer that I would be safe on the journey, and she did so, expressing love for me and faith in the Lord that I would be protected. Then I offered a prayer in thanksgiving for such a wonderful daughter. The Spirit of the Lord came in abundance, and our love was greatly increased as a result of that small experience together.

The next day as I flew to San Francisco, I thought, "What a power love is, especially the love between a father and a daughter." The Spirit seemed to impress upon me how much I loved my daughter and what a good girl she was. Her heart was always softened to spiritual things. She was always quick to help others. I thought what a wonderful wife and mother she would one day be.

The impression continued. I wondered, "If my daughter ever became inactive as she grew to adulthood, how far would I go to reclaim her?" I answered in my heart, "Knowing my great love for her, I would give everything I have. I would pray for her, fast for her, love her. I would do all within my power to influence her to return to the Lord. *I would never give up*. It wouldn't matter how long it took or what I had to invest, *I would never give up* until she was once again turned to the Lord." How strongly I felt the Spirit that morning! Yes, when one is filled with love, the Spirit comes in abundance.

Just after I returned from my mission, my bishop called me to be the assistant clerk in our ward. As I sat in various leadership meetings, occasionally those attending would discuss a Sister Smith who lived in our ward. I heard comments like, "Well, you know how Sister Smith is," or "Home teaching Sister Smith is no picnic; in fact, home teachers haven't been in her home for the past two years," or "Sister Smith is the worst housekeeper in the ward," or "Sister Smith does nothing but mope around her house and collect newspapers. If you went to her home you would see newspapers on her porch and stacked to the ceiling in her living room." I thought, "I hope I never get assigned as a home teacher to Sister Smith."

One day my younger brother and I were in a market purchasing some groceries for my mother. As we walked out, the thought came to me, "Why don't you go back behind this store and see Sister Smith?" I was a little surprised at the thought, and probably from curiosity more than anything else, I said to my brother, "Why don't we go back and see where Sister Smith lives?" I suppose the idea was, "We'll see if everything people have said about her house is true."

As we went around the back of the store and looked at her home from a distance, we could see that at least some of the stories were true. The house was dilapidated. The fence was broken down and unpainted, and her yard was full of junk. As we stood there, an impression came: "Go visit Sister Smith." I was taken aback and thought, "I'm not her home teacher." But the impression continued: "Go visit Sister Smith."

I said to my brother, "Let's go visit her." He was surprised, but nonetheless we headed for the door. I remember praying rather intently, "What shall I say? What will we do? Why are we going there?" As we entered her yard, we saw the newspapers. Sure enough, they were stacked all over the porch. I could see through the window that newspapers were stacked inside her house as well.

We knocked on the door. She opened it and rather gruffly said, "What is it? What do you want?" I struggled to know what to say, but finally I blurted out, "Well, we're members of your ward." The moment the word *ward* came out, she said, "You mean you're Mormons? I've told that bishop ten times not to send anybody to my home. I want nothing to do with the Mormon church, so leave." As I prayed in my heart what to say, the words came out, "Well, Sister Smith, this is my younger brother, and he and I just came by to tell you that we love you. Even if you don't particularly care about us, we do love you. We just wanted to ask if there was anything we could do to help you today."

She stood there staring at us and finally said, "What did you say?"

I repeated myself, trying to have her really feel of our love.

She said, "You've come to ask if you could help me?" Then tears came to her eyes. Then lots of tears. She invited us in. We spent nearly two hours listening as she told us about her problems.

She apologized for the condition of her house and yard. She told us about the leak in her roof. She said she had no one to help her—she didn't have any family. She told us about her problems at the death of her husband a few years earlier when she had felt offended by some Church members. She just poured out her tears. She got it all out. We rejoiced, perhaps more than she did, in finally seeing all the bitterness come forth.

You can imagine the joy my brother and I felt as we accompanied her to church the next Sunday, and she attended church many other Sundays until she passed away about six months later.

I've often thought, "What if we had not responded to the promptings? What if we had not been told what to say?" It surely would not have turned out the same way. It is most impressive to understand that when sincere love or gratitude is expressed, the Spirit of the Lord comes in abundance. Let us be filled with love in our families and thus be filled with the Spirit of the Lord.

## 6. SHARE SPIRITUAL EXPERIENCES

In your family, when you are prompted to do so, share a spiritual experience. Don't just have some repertoire of experiences you traditionally tell (although it's good to have a repertoire), but be praying that the Lord will draw from you the one that needs to be shared. If you do so, who knows the good it may bring? Sometimes we might not give our best effort in teaching because, after all, who is listening? "Just our family." But who is more important?

We really must do our best to have the Spirit of the Lord when we're teaching our families. Have you ever tried to share a spiritual experience when the timing was wrong? Or have you ever told an experience that perhaps you shouldn't have? How do you feel when you've just related an experience and it doesn't go over at all? Most people feel a spirit of rejection from those being taught. One of my greatest fears in teaching and in life is to feel a withdrawal of the Spirit, to feel that I'm left standing alone. I have felt that sometimes, and I don't like it. It is a rejection in a sense. It is an affront to the Lord. And you feel the affront as well. In sharing a spiritual experience, be sure to do so only when prompted. Alma gave some strict counsel about when it is appropriate to share spiritual things: "It is given unto many to know the mysteries of God; nevertheless they are laid under a strict command that they shall not impart only according to the portion of his word which he doth grant unto the children of men, according to the heed and diligence which they give unto him" (Alma 12:9). Some things can be delivered only by the Spirit. Some things are to be delivered only when those listening will receive them with "heed and diligence."

Instead of just teaching principles or even telling our children what to do, we can tell them about a spiritual experience and help them relate it to the challenge they are facing. This will have much more of an impact in changing their hearts. If we do this, we will influence them for righteousness' sake because the Spirit of the Lord is with us.

I've also found that many experiences with my family have been of great benefit to others, and I believe strongly in recording in some detail my key experiences week after week. I have learned, as have many others, that if I do not record them when they occur, the impact of the experiences or the feelings that attended them are soon lost. However, if I record them and remember them, I can use them to help others.

During a stake conference in the Midwest, I learned that the mission president and his wife were bringing an investigator to the meeting. She had taken the missionary lessons a number of times and had read much about the Church, but she just could not make the decision to be baptized. As a professional psychologist, she was having trouble with the intellectual decision about whether the Church was true. The president and his wife asked if I would talk with her.

Before the Sunday meeting, I was shaking hands with people in the congregation, and I talked with this woman for a few minutes. She seemed to me to be one of those people who have a testimony but just don't realize it. I asked her to listen carefully during the conference, suggesting that the

Lord would tell her in her heart as well as in her mind what she ought to do, and that she should then be courageous enough to follow those promptings.

During my talk, I discussed the need to trust one's feelings, and I told a story about a scientist I had met who had wanted to calibrate everything in a test tube, so to speak, before accepting it as true. However, he deeply loved his wife and children, and he finally realized that this truth of the heart was greater than anything he might learn through the scientific method.

Six weeks later I received a letter from her. She wrote: "My greatest stumbling block in getting closer to the Church is my fearfulness in trusting my feelings as a valid basis for a decision. I respect the commitment of baptism too much to join the Church lacking conviction and confirmation on which to build the foundation of a testimony and solid membership. I sincerely desire to believe. I have fasted and prayed and read the scriptures. I attend meetings, keep the commandments and Word of Wisdom, and pay tithing. I feel weary and frustrated, and I know the deficit is in me. Although this is not one of those decisions one can intellectualize entirely, or get swept away by nice feelings or programs or friendly people, it is hard for me to know how to discern the appropriate devotion and cause of action. This is the most important decision I will ever make, and I feel terribly accountable and rather inadequate. This circumstance makes me feel very humble and reliant upon God for help—which is probably good.

"Regardless of any decision I eventually make, I am grateful for what I've learned. Whether or not I join the LDS church I will always feel kindly toward it because I have been given much by it and because of it. Thank you."

As I read her letter, I thought, "I'll call her this week sometime, or maybe write her a letter." But as I was working at home that morning, the impression came a couple of times that I should call her, and that I should do it *now*. I called the mission president, got her phone number, and called her home only to reach her answering machine. I thought, "Well, she's probably at work, so I'll just leave my phone number." Why, then, had I received those urgent impressions?

To my surprise, just two minutes later, she returned my call. She said, "I just got home a minute or so after you left your message. "

I thanked her for her letter and said I had felt I should call and talk with her about her feelings.

She told me that it wasn't just by chance that I had called, and she was very touched by the fact that I would call. She said, "You wouldn't have known this, but I've been somewhat discouraged about all of this and in the past couple of weeks have been somewhat turned away, almost deciding I ought not go in the direction of becoming a member of the Church. At least I've been discouraged about it and have about determined to just forget it all. I was thinking those thoughts even this very morning. It's interesting that you would call me right now when I needed something."

Her greatest concern seemed to center in her inability to trust her *feelings* as a valid basis for a decision. It was evident as I interviewed her on the phone that she was morally clean, keeping the Word of Wisdom, and even paying tithing. She was obedient to the commandments. She just didn't know for sure that it was all true or at least did not know how to obtain a confirmation so she would *know* that she knew it was true.

I talked with her about the times she had felt the Spirit as a swelling in the breast (see Alma 32:28), as a burning in the bosom (see D&C 9:8), and as a feeling of peace (see D&C 6:22–23), and about the need to trust in the Spirit and thereby receive its fruits and the witness she lacked (see D&C 11:12–14).

I had previously discussed with my wife a couple of stories that I might share to help this woman understand how to trust her feelings in faith, and I decided to tell her about one of my sons.

This son had decided to go to college, but he didn't have a job to support himself while he was there. Nevertheless, he went in pure faith that he would obtain employment, trusting that the Lord would deliver something up. As the days passed, though, nothing came through. Finally, out of funds, he called to tell us he would have to come home. Our family fasted and prayed for him, and within twenty-four hours of the time he was going to leave, he had three job offers. He is now working two of the three jobs. I told this woman that such things happen through faith, after our faith has been tested and tried.

I challenged her not to do what anyone else told her to do, that we would never want her to feel pressured to be baptized, but that she now needed to go to the Lord and humbly pray again for direction as to what he would have her do. I promised her in the name of the Lord that if she would do that, she would receive the impression in her heart and mind of what she ought to do and that she ought to then be spiritually mature enough to act on those impressions given by the Spirit.

The next day in my office, I received a message from the mission president that the woman had asked for baptism the coming Saturday.

During our phone conversation, this good sister and I discussed many of the principles of how to gain a testimony. But I think it was the story of my son at college—a story I had written in my journal so I would not forget it—that really helped her understand what she needed to do.

Seek to have spiritual experiences. Then record them. And then pray during your time of need that the appropriate ones will come back to your mind to help people in need. Spiritual experiences have great impact upon the soul. Share them as prompted by the Spirit (see D&C 50:21–22; Luke 10:25–37; Acts 26:1–32).

## 7. USE PRIESTHOOD ORDINANCES

What a blessing it is to have the priesthood in the home, either in a worthy father or a worthy son. Those families who have neither can still turn to a relative, or to a friend who is a priesthood leader, home teacher, quorum leader, or neighbor. Using the priesthood and its ordinances in your home is another way to invite the Spirit of the Lord to help you in raising your family.

Without question, the Spirit can be felt in the ordinances, such as baptism, the sacrament, and the temple ordinances. The scriptures teach that "in the ordinances . . . the power of godliness is manifest" (D&C 84:20). Also, the Lord will greatly bless those who seek a patriarchal blessing. Parents should always encourage their children at the appropriate time to obtain such a blessing from an ordained patriarch of the Church. It will be of great guidance to them, and if they read it humbly, they will have the Spirit of the Lord come to them each time they ponder these personalized words of the Lord to them.

A priesthood blessing is an ordinance that can greatly help individuals and families. I don't know of anything that can bring the Spirit more quickly than when a child asks for a blessing. Sadly, however, most members of the Church probably do not take sufficient advantage of priesthood blessings. How long has it been since you sought one? We are not told how often to have one, but wouldn't it be appropriate to have a blessing during times of stress or trouble or decision throughout the year? Some members of the Church, including mothers and fathers, go for many years without having a blessing. Sometimes we wait until we're in a crisis before we ask for one. But sometimes there is a benefit in just asking for a blessing to see if the Lord has any additional direction for us.

Let us be quick to teach our families the necessity of having a blessing. Single-parent and part-member families may face special challenges in that respect. But, just the same, they ought to faithfully seek a blessing from worthy priesthood leaders. Grandparents can often be of great help in these things.

Sometimes some have asked, "Is it proper to give a blessing if someone hasn't asked for one?" They typically quote the passage that says: "Require not miracles, except I shall command you, except casting out devils, healing the sick, and against poisonous serpents, and against deadly poisons; and these things ye shall not do, except it be required of you by them who desire it, that the scriptures might be fulfilled; for ye shall do according to that which is written" (D&C 24:13–14).

Some people have misinterpreted those verses, I think, to mean that we shouldn't give a blessing unless asked to do so. Let me give you an example. A serious earthquake occurred in a Central American country where I was serving as the area president. Nearly ten thousand people were killed, including several members of the Church.

On the first evening after the earthquake, I went into a chapel where we were housing some of the injured. The electricity was out, and the church was dark. People were suffering, and they had no medical supplies. The first three people I came upon had serious injuries—one had a broken hip, another had a broken arm, and the third had serious internal injuries. I asked each one, "Have you had a priesthood blessing?" Each said no.

I was quite surprised at this. I took the bishop into the hall and asked, "Bishop, why haven't these people had blessings?"

He answered, "No one has asked for one, Elder Cook. I couldn't give a blessing unless I was asked, could I?" Well, that wasn't too wise, was it?

When people seem to need a blessing but have not asked for one, we might review with them the counsel found in James 5:14–16: "Is any sick among you? let him call for the elders of the church; and let them pray over him, anointing him with oil in the name of the Lord: and the prayer of faith shall save the sick, and the Lord shall raise him up; and if he have committed sins, they shall be forgiven him. Confess your faults one to another, and pray one for another, that ye may be healed. The effectual fervent prayer of a righteous man availeth much."

Then we might bear testimony to the healing power of the priesthood and say something like, "You know, Sister Brown, I wonder if you would like to have a blessing. You don't have to have one, of course. But if you would like one, I would be pleased to give it to you." When I have used such an approach, no one has ever said no.

We walk a fine line in such matters. The Lord wants people to ask for a blessing as a measure of their faith. But many people don't even know a blessing is available. Others are not sensitive enough to ask, or they may have forgotten about the possibility and need a gentle reminder. We can at least set the stage and then hope they will ask.

I believe parents should teach their children to ask for priesthood blessings fairly regularly when they have a need. We probably need a blessing many more times than we ask for one. Perhaps we don't want to bother anyone, or we aren't humble enough to ask. Maybe we have thought: "I can handle this. I don't need the Lord on this problem. I can take care of it."

Children learn to ask for blessings if they see their parents having blessings. They learn to ask for blessings if parents, through faith, teach them the importance of having a blessing. Then the Lord will help them more because of their faith. If your children can see the results of a priesthood blessing, you will not have to tell them to ask for one.

When we returned to the United States from living in Mexico, one of my daughters was having difficulty adjusting because she could not find a friend. She didn't feel close to anyone, and she didn't feel that anyone at school particularly liked her. Worst of all, her best friend had left on a mission with her family just one day before we arrived home. The two girls wrote to each other often, talking about how much they missed being together.

Even after many weeks, things got no better. We encouraged our daughter to make more friends and to become more involved in activities at school. We talked to her about the different girls in her seminary class and in our ward, but to no avail. After some time, we determined that what she really needed was a priesthood blessing. We suggested this to her, and in a few days she prepared herself for a blessing and asked for one.

In the blessing, she was told that she would find not only one friend but several. She seemed very encouraged by this, and I'm sure she believed what was said. However, the next few weeks went on in much the same way. No new friends appeared—not even one.

We told her not to lose hope, explaining that the Lord will sometimes try us to see if we will really believe. We reminded her of these words of Moroni: "I would show unto the world that faith is things which are hoped for and not seen; wherefore, dispute not because ye see not, for ye receive no witness until after the trial of your faith" (Ether 12:6). She persisted in faith. Within a few weeks, she began to "pal around" with one of the girls in our ward. Soon they became true friends. Then another friend came on the scene, and then another. Our daughter was happy again, and she learned much from having this new set of friends. In addition, three years later when her old friend returned, within a matter of minutes they were back into their old friendship.

I think my daughter learned a great lesson about the importance of seeking a priesthood blessing when prayer alone doesn't seem to be enough. It surely gave the family an opportunity, after the blessing and with her permission, to pray that she might find friends. Thus, the experience helped all of us increase our faith.

A priesthood blessing may also be given over your home. Especially during times of contention or difficulties, would it not be wise to bless the home and all who live there? The

Lord has told us how to do that (see D&C 75:18–22; Luke 10:5–9).

In addition, we are told by the presiding brethren that we can dedicate our homes. The Church's *General Handbook of Instructions* notes:

> Church members may have their homes dedicated, whether or not the homes are free of debt, as sacred edifices where the Holy Spirit can reside, and as sanctuaries where family members can worship, find safety from the world, grow spiritually, and prepare for eternal family relationships. Unlike Church buildings, homes are not dedicated and consecrated to the Lord (see the *Melchizedek Priesthood Leadership Handbook* for additional instruction on dedicating homes).

Living in a dedicated home can be a great blessing to the family. Such a priesthood blessing may assist you greatly as you move forward in creating a more celestial home.

The seven suggestions in this chapter will always help bring the Spirit of the Lord as you work with your family or with others. Are these not some of the spiritual gifts that Christ gave to prepare the way for the Holy Ghost to testify and change people's hearts? Give of yourself spiritually, and you will be able to discern the needs of family members and commit them, in the Spirit, to act. Then they will repent and come unto Christ.

You may have children who will not respond to the Master's voice at this time—I repeat, *at this time*. Jesus taught that he could bring people to himself only upon their repentance (see D&C 18:12). But with wayward children and others, we just go on loving them and trying again and again at other times when they may have a more repentant heart and will respond to the Spirit (see 3 Nephi 18:32).

Let us not be discouraged by any of these suggestions. Some might think, "I can't do all of those things. I'm really not able to do them." My answer would be, "Anyone can do these things. We just have to humble ourselves and be believing." Someone might ask, "How do you pray humbly? How do you humble yourself that much to cause those things to happen?"

An excellent but difficult question. Let's look in Alma 38:13 for just one example: "Do not pray as the Zoramites do, for ye have seen that they pray to be heard of men, and to be praised for their wisdom. Do not say: O God, I thank thee that we are better than our brethren; but rather say: O Lord, forgive my unworthiness, and remember my brethren in mercy—yea, acknowledge your unworthiness before God at all times."

That's a great key. Over the years my prayers have been filled increasingly with that thought—to ask the Lord for forgiveness, to try not to judge someone else or be worried about what they're doing wrong but to recognize my own weaknesses before him. I am convinced, as you are, that the closer you draw to the Lord the further away you realize you are.

Brigham Young, at one time, preached a fiery sermon on repentance. John Taylor and Wilford Woodruff went up to the prophet after the sermon to resign as apostles. They said, "We don't feel worthy to go on, President Young, as apostles of the Lord." And Brigham Young answered them, "No, my brethren, you'll find that the closer you draw to the Lord, the further away you'll recognize you really are, and that brings true humility." If you will acknowledge who the Lord is and who you are, that will bring the spirit of humility. I would venture to say there is not one of us who does not have much to ask for in the spirit of forgiveness daily. Remembering that will help us be more humble.

When problems or questions occur in our family, instead of reacting so quickly or giving a pat answer, as some of us do, let us try to humbly turn our hearts to the Lord and to find a way to turn our children's hearts to the Lord. If we will do that, we will have much more success in our families.

Let us not forget to be vigilant against Satan. He will do

all in his power to destroy our understanding of these principles. Let us not discipline when we are angry; true teaching can take place only in a setting where the Spirit of the Lord is present. Then the teaching will be permanently received in the heart of the one who is listening. The single greatest thing a teacher does is provide the environment in which people can have a spiritual experience. How does a teacher do that? These seven spiritual keys will help you provide such an experience. I pray we may all learn how to do it better.

As parents learn to teach with the Spirit, children will learn to hear the voice of the Lord for themselves. They will learn the power of the Spirit through the example of their parents. They will know how to obtain answers to prayer. I bear testimony that if the Lord is humbly invited into a situation, he will be there immediately through the power of the Holy Ghost. Isn't that a great indication of his love?

If parents and children are humble in their hearts, the Spirit of the Lord will come to them immediately. They will feel direction come to them, individually and uniquely. Each will know that the Lord has spoken. That's a great truth that ought not to be overlooked or taken for granted.

## CONCLUSION

May the Lord bless you, above all else, to be a great teacher in your family, in the Church, or wherever you go. I think one of the greatest tributes that could be paid to teachers is, "With all of their teaching, they magnified the Lord in the eyes of the people." Moses couldn't go into the promised land because he wouldn't magnify the Lord in the eyes of the people (see Numbers 20:12). If you will turn your family and others to God, if you will help them to humble themselves and go to the Lord for their strength and for their answers, I bear witness that he will magnify you as a teacher. You will have the Spirit of the Lord with you, and he will use you as an instrument to change the hearts of your children as well as the hearts of others to seek after

God, to seek after the blessings he has promised to all who follow him.

I bear testimony that these things are true. They might have been said in weakness or not been communicated clearly, but if you've listened by the Spirit, the Lord has been able to speak some things to your heart that may set you on a quest of learning better how to receive the Spirit and thereby bless the lives of all you might be able to teach. May the Lord bless you to do that. Get the Lord involved and lives will be changed.

I bear testimony that God lives. I express my love to him who faileth not his children, nor will he fail to help you with his children who are yours as well. He stands ever ready to respond through his Son, Jesus Christ, for any blessing they desire of him. I bear witness of Jesus Christ, as a special disciple of his, even one of the Seventy, that all he has taught us is true, that he is the way, that he is the model. If you have any question about teaching by the Spirit, just ask, "What would he do?" If you'll pursue that thought, you'll begin to teach more as he did and ultimately become as he is.

May the Lord bless you and your family. I leave a blessing upon you, in faith, that if you will exercise your righteous desires, prayerfully think about them, ponder them, and work on them, the Lord will lead you step by step along the way until you obtain those things the Lord desires you and your family to have.

# CHAPTER THREE

# TEACHING YOUR FAMILY TO PRAY

While our family was living in Montevideo, Uruguay, we were out for a drive one day when we passed a dog pound. Our children had been after us for some time to buy a dog, as in Montevideo dogs could run free—they didn't have to be chained up or fenced in. We debated the issue for some time and finally went inside, where we were surrounded by scores of dogs of all kinds. After looking around, we finally found her—a mongrel pup with curly golden hair. She seemed to have been made just for our family. We bought her and headed home amid great noise and excitement.

Our oldest son, then eight years of age, soon became the one who took care of her. She responded to all of the family but most of all to him. He fed her, took her on long walks, listened to her howl at night, and did all the rest that comes with the proud ownership of a puppy. He named her Dixie. Dogs seem to exist to wag their tails and make people happy, but Dixie did much more than that. She soon became an important part of the family.

One afternoon when I came home from work, I was met by our oldest boy, who was crying. Dixie had been lost most of the day and could not be found. The search had gone on for two or three hours. My wife had driven several of the children, who had been praying most of that time, to look throughout the neighborhood and in the surrounding blocks. By the time I arrived home, they had lost nearly all hope, as thievery ran high in that area, and the chances were good that someone had stolen our pretty little pup.

However, the faith of our oldest boy was not diminished. He tearfully told me that he had prayed and prayed, but that the Lord had not yet helped him find Dixie. Yet in confidence and faith he said, "Dad, I *know* if you will pray with the rest of the family, all together in family prayer, Heavenly Father will show us where Dixie is."

As we headed for the living room to have a prayer, my own faith needed strengthening. How I prayed that the Lord would answer this boy and strengthen his faith in prayer! Because the situation was serious, and because it offered an opportunity to teach our children about the power of prayer, each family member (all six of us), from the oldest to the youngest, prayed aloud that the Lord would show us where Dixie was. The oldest boy, guided by the Spirit, prayed that wherever Dixie might be, she would be protected, and that if someone had taken her and would not give her back, they would love her and take good care of her.

After the prayer, we talked about the need to do all in our power to find Dixie if we expected the Lord to help us. The whole family got into the car, and we began backing out of the driveway to begin another search. As the car reached the street, we saw a neighbor girl running toward us. To our great joy, she was yelling, "I have Dixie!" The dog had been trapped in the neighbors' garage all that time. As many little arms reached for her, my wife and I had much gratitude in our hearts that the Lord had honored our prayers, *even in the moment* when our prayers were being offered.

As things quieted down and we brought Dixie into the house, one of the younger boys said how grateful he was and that we ought to thank Heavenly Father. Thus again, on bended knee, the entire family offered individual thanks to the Lord for having answered our prayers.

As pleased as I was about finding the lost dog, I was even more pleased that when the dog was lost, our son had the natural inclination to pray, and he knew that if he could get the whole family to pray for something, it would happen.

Many families do not think it necessary to pray over such small temporal problems as a lost dog. Perhaps they think prayer should be used only for serious problems or for purely spiritual matters. But I think small incidents like the one our family experienced bring great faith to children (and to parents). Then, when larger problems come, they will better know how to obtain answers through prayer.

## TEACHING CHILDREN TO PRAY

No other teaching seems to affect young people (and older people too, for that matter) more than individual and family prayer. That should not surprise us, for the scriptures are filled with the injunction to pray. The Lord's direction to parents is, "They shall . . . teach their children to pray, and to walk uprightly before the Lord" (D&C 68:28).

In the Book of Mormon, the Lord instructed, "Pray in your families unto the Father, always in my name, that your wives and your children may be blessed" (3 Nephi 18:21). What if we do not pray in our families? Then perhaps our families will not be blessed, at least not to the same degree they might be.

Through the Prophet Joseph Smith, the Lord gave this counsel to one of his servants: "Newel K. Whitney . . . , a bishop of my church, hath need to be chastened, and set in order his family, and see that they are more diligent and concerned at home, and pray always, or they shall be removed out of their place" (D&C 93:50). Evidently Bishop Whitney, like many of us, did not have his home in good enough order with respect to praying to the Lord.

One of the greatest gifts we can give our children is to teach them to rely more fully on the Lord through prayer. What a blessing it would be for them to know that the Lord lives and will answer their prayers. What a blessing it would be for them to know how to pray to him, and what some of the laws and conditions are to obtain answers to prayer. Such blessings may be the greatest gifts we could give them.

The best way for children to learn how to pray and to know the power of prayer is to see it in action in their own family. If they see parents who humbly kneel and offer prayer, they will do likewise. If they see parents who, when first confronted with a problem, turn immediately to the Lord, so will the children. Our children ought to see us daily give thanks to God in prayer. Again, if children see parents who are truly grateful, so will the children be.

A father ought to take the lead as patriarch in his home in giving an example of prayer and calling upon other members of the family to pray. Perhaps what they say in prayer isn't so important as what they feel. Children need to hear us pray for them *by name*, when they have a problem with a friend or in school or in work. We should pray over the years that they will be blessed when they go on missions, and then pray for them fervently while they're on their missions. With such an attitude, parents can pray all of their children into the mission field.

I believe we should teach our children to pray over "little things" so that when they have to pray for more important matters that will require a lot of faith and repentance and sacrifice on their part, they will know how to go about it. If they obtain the attitude, the habit, and the skill of praying over all things, then when a crucial answer is needed, they will be prepared to obtain it.

## ANSWERS TO TEMPORAL PROBLEMS

Another experience our family had with prayer helped us realize that the Lord will indeed help us with all our problems, be they temporal or spiritual.

A couple of years ago, one of my sons and his two friends, one in the front seat and one in the back, were driving down the hill in Bountiful, Utah, toward the freeway. Suddenly a car two cars in front of them made an unusual turn, and the man in the car in front of my son slammed on his brakes and came safely to a stop. My boy slammed on his brakes and stopped safely as well. However, a young man behind them was looking down and did not see that the cars in front of him had stopped. He smashed into the back of our 1984 Honda, crushing the back bumper and trunk. The back window exploded into a thousand pieces, filling the back seat with glass and cutting my son's friend in the back and neck. The car in back of ours also pushed the Honda into the car in front, crushing the headlights and the left side of the front of the Honda.

Soon the police arrived. Our son called me, and I drove down to the scene of the accident. There was quite a stir on that busy corner. After taking statements from all concerned, the police cited the other driver and put a damage sticker on our car to permit us to drive it, which we were fortunately able to do. Then everyone departed, leaving the matter in the hands of the insurance companies.

Our car sat in our garage for nearly a week. No appraisers came by as promised. After numerous calls, an appraiser came and spent nearly two hours examining the car from top to bottom. A few days later, we learned that he had declared the car to be totaled. We could hardly believe it! We had thought the dents could be pounded out and painted for under a thousand dollars. The insurance company said they would give us around $3,500 to buy a new car and considerably less if we wanted to repair the old one.

I spent most of the next day checking car lots to see if the amount the company had offered was fair, as it seemed low to us. I found three car dealers who were willing to confirm that the true value of our car was around $4,500. I asked the insurance company to contact these dealers, and I told them we wouldn't accept their offer.

Over the weeks, the idea that we had a wrecked car in the garage and that we were going to have to spend at least another $1,000 to buy another one left us in great anxiety. On our budget, it was simply out of the question.

During that time I also took the car to four or five repair shops to see what it would cost to repair it. Two places said the car was totaled, and they wanted nothing to do with it. Two other places thought they could fix it, but the price was so high that it wouldn't be worth it. One practical man said, "Your car has 92,000 miles on it. It would be better to put your money into another car. This one could go out on you next week, and then all your money would be lost."

My wife and I stewed over the matter day after day. To make things worse, our lawn mower broke down during this time, and we had to buy another one, which was hard on our budget. Both of our vacuum cleaners went out the same week, as did our weed eater and my electric razor. Things were getting downright depressing. Our temporal problems seemed to have a hold on us—something we had seldom allowed to happen.

A couple of days before my wife was to go to girls' camp for a week, she and I were sitting on the couch trying to decide what to do. I didn't want her to leave before we had made up our minds because I knew the insurance company would be calling for a decision. We had penciled out our alternatives—the pluses and minuses of each—but we were still in turmoil. Each alternative seemed a poor one.

As we discussed our problem, it was as if a light turned on. We asked ourselves, "Have we really asked the Lord?" The answer was, "Yes, we have been praying about the problem, but not very specifically, and not with real intent. We have been relying too much on our own strength." We bowed our heads together and prayed fervently that the Lord would inspire us in that very moment, that he would tell us what to do.

At the conclusion of our prayer, the name of a man in our ward popped into my mind. I remembered that on the day of the crash, my son had told me about this fellow, who used to work in a body shop. I called him on the phone. His wife said he no longer did that kind of work but that their son (who also lived in our ward) was as skilled as the father.

I called him, and ten minutes later we were at his house, showing him the Honda and asking him what could be done. Somewhat to our astonishment, he told us that this was not a totaled car, and that with some work and very little money, the Honda could be put back into operation and even look just fine.

When my son got home from work, we went back to our neighbor's home. The young man and his father instructed us in how to bend the dented places back into shape. My son listened with great interest, and that very night he and his friend spent several hours pounding out the back of the trunk. Several days later, after many hours of pounding and bending and counsel from our neighbor, we were able to get the car back into shape.

I also went shopping a number of times for parts at wrecking yards. The Honda dealer wanted $300 for a new back window, but I bought a salvaged one for $53. The dealer wanted $189 for the headlight assembly; I got it for $35. It did take time to look for the parts; in fact, I had to call as many as forty-three places to find some of the parts we needed. But it was worth it; at the completion of the project, we had spent only about $300.

The result of all this was that we got to keep our Honda. We didn't have to spend a lot of money to fix it, and we didn't have to put a lot of money into a newer car. We did receive the money from the insurance company, which we held in the bank until we had to buy another car.

As my son and I looked over the newly cleaned and repaired car, we could hardly believe it was to have been sent to a wrecking yard. It looked as good as it had before the crash and was probably worth almost as much. We truly felt that the Lord had blessed and inspired us, and that we had learned some things of great value. We were so pleased with our work that we took a drive around the block, marveling at our good fortune and feeling grateful for all that had happened.

I bear testimony that in many of our problems, we do not ask specifically enough or with real intent. How badly the Lord wants to bless us, and yet many of us will not ask. Thus he cannot bless us nearly as well as he would like. How beautiful are the words of the Lord as he laments this fact: "What doth it profit a man if a gift is bestowed upon him, and he receive not the gift? Behold, he rejoices not in that which is given unto him, neither rejoices in him who is the giver of the gift" (D&C 88:33). But if we will recognize the hand of the Lord in our lives, asking for and receiving every good gift from him, then the Lord will respond.

I again bear testimony that the Lord does answer the prayers of his children that are offered in faith. He will answer them on any issue that is of concern to the one praying, for he has great love for each of his children. May each of us pray more specifically and with real intent, that the heavens may more effectively respond to us.

The Lord has commanded us to pray over all things, no matter how trivial they may seem:

> May God grant unto you, my brethren, that ye may begin to exercise your faith unto repentance, that ye begin to call upon his holy name, that he would have mercy upon you; yea, cry unto him for mercy; for he is mighty to save. Yea, humble yourselves, and continue in prayer unto him.
>
> Cry unto him when ye are in your fields, yea, over all your flocks.
>
> Cry unto him in your houses, yea, over all your household, both morning, mid-day, and evening.
>
> Yea, cry unto him against the power of your enemies.
>
> Yea, cry unto him against the devil, who is an enemy to all righteousness.
>
> Cry unto him over the crops of your fields, that ye may prosper in them.
>
> Cry over the flocks of your fields, that they may increase.
>
> But this is not all; ye must pour out your souls in your closets, and your secret places, and in your wilderness.
>
> Yea, and when you do not cry unto the Lord, let your hearts be full, drawn out in prayer unto him continually for your welfare, and also for the welfare of those who are around you (Alma 34:17–27).

## THE POWER OF FAMILY PRAYER

I have asked various families and individuals around the Church why they do not pray about the kind of things described in this chapter. Some have expressed surprise over the very idea. Some have simply not thought of praying about such things. Others have simply not made much of an effort. But children need to see prayer in action. As they see what can happen through family prayer, they will develop the faith and the knowledge to pray individually for the things they need.

Perhaps our most demanding challenge is to faithfully hold family prayer both morning and evening. Many Latter-day Saints have not yet established that tradition. When I have asked people why they do not hold regular family prayer, I have heard reasons like the following:

- We don't have time in the mornings.
- We just haven't gotten into the habit.
- Our children get up at different times, so we can't be together in the mornings.
- Our children are all going different ways, so we can't be together at night.
- Our own families didn't pray, so we haven't been able to either.
- Our children don't want to have family prayer. They resist, and sometimes we have real contention at prayer time.
- I hate to admit it, but I don't believe that family prayer can make much of a difference.

I believe all of these answers are just excuses, or, to put it more boldly, they are lies. It is the devil himself who tries to get us not to pray. Nephi taught that principle clearly:

> My beloved brethren, I perceive that ye ponder still in your hearts; and it grieveth me that I must speak concerning this thing. For if ye would hearken unto the Spirit which teacheth a man to pray ye would know that ye must pray; for the evil

spirit teacheth not a man to pray, but teacheth
him that he must not pray.

But behold, I say unto you that ye must pray
always, and not faint; that ye must not perform
any thing unto the Lord save in the first place ye
shall pray unto the Father in the name of Christ,
that he will consecrate thy performance unto thee,
that thy performance may be for the welfare of
thy soul (2 Nephi 32:8–9).

Clearly, we are to pray over all things; then they will be
consecrated for our good. The opposite is also true. If we do
not pray over the things we are doing, they will not be consecrated for our good or for the welfare of our souls. It is
also clear who it is that teaches us not to pray. I believe that
some of Satan's best-trained emissaries offer such simple
lies as these: "You're too tired." "You can do it tomorrow."
"Prayer doesn't work. Don't you remember the time you
prayed and nothing happened?"

In my judgment, all the excuses can be easily solved if
we will just believe that prayer will work, decide we ought
to be praying, and decide how and when we will do it. *If
we're too busy to pray, we're just too busy.*

Holding family prayer in the morning may require two
separate prayers, one with younger children and one with
older ones. But the one unacceptable alternative is not to
pray. If we are not in the habit, it is time to get into the
habit. If we don't believe that prayer will work, it is time to
get more involved, to discover the power of the great truths
the Lord has taught.

## WHY SHOULD WE PRAY?

Perhaps the most important reason we should pray is
because the Lord has told us to. Prayer is a way to communicate with our Heavenly Father. When he sent us to earth,
he gave us the opportunity to live by faith, and one of our
principal ways to receive instruction, counsel, and direction is through prayer.

## WHEN SHOULD WE PRAY?

Families ought to pray, without question, in the morning and in the evening, every day without fail. Family prayers should also be held on special occasions. Sometimes when a family is simply feeling joy and happiness, they might kneel and have a family prayer. When a child is having a difficult time, what a great opportunity to say, "Let's have a word of prayer together." When family members are facing a crisis, a special family prayer could do much to solve the problem while teaching children to pray. When there is contention at home, if one or more of the family members were to say, "Let's have a special prayer," the spirit of contention would immediately leave, and the Spirit of the Lord would enter.

## WHAT SHOULD WE PRAY ABOUT?

The Lord has commanded us to pray over all things. Some have the idea that they should pray only over critical matters or over spiritual problems. But the Lord has told us to pray for whatever we stand in need of, and we should be sure to thank the Lord in all things. We should pray for our families, for our neighbors, for personal things, for help in overcoming weaknesses, for help at school, and on and on.

## WHERE SHOULD WE PRAY?

Some families struggle with something as small as where to pray. Maybe they have just not decided where would be the best. In truth, they could pray anywhere—in their hearts, on their knees, alone, or together. Whenever possible, family members should pray both individually and as a family. Some families kneel around the bed in a quiet bedroom. Others kneel around the table before breakfast or supper. Others find it easier to pray in the living room after reading the scriptures together.

## WHO SHOULD PRAY?

A righteous father will set the example in prayer, as will

a righteous mother, but each of the children ought to be given ample opportunity to pray. Most families have found it helpful for each person to take a turn. Even the littlest ones can be helped to repeat after their parents or an older child so they, too, will learn to pray.

Taking turns should not always be required. At times someone who is having problems may need to pray even though it's not that person's turn. The important thing is that all should have the opportunity to pray.

Some parents have found it helpful to remind the family of someone for whom they might pray, or to mention some other special need of which they are aware.

In the long run, how or when or where we have family prayer is not nearly as important as the fact that we have it. Praying together regularly will bring great blessings to the whole family.

## A PRAYER FOR PEACE

When one of our sons was about ten years old, he was having some challenges trying to get to sleep. Often he would get so keyed up he couldn't sleep at all. One night when he was very excited about the first day of school, he had been in his room for about an hour and a half and was still not asleep by the time I was ready to go to bed. I heard him crying in his room and went in to talk with him.

He told me he was having problems and just couldn't sleep. He was very upset and tense. I asked him if he had prayed about it, assuring him that Heavenly Father would help him go to sleep. He said, "I have already prayed about four times."

I then told him the Lord couldn't help him unless he did his part, and I discussed with him what his part might be:

• To calm down and not be so emotional.
• To not be so tense about thinking that he had to go to sleep.
• To just concentrate on the fact that his body was lying

in bed resting. That wasn't quite as good as sleeping, but it was good enough. If he would quit trying so hard, he could go to sleep.

He seemed to receive that counsel well and calmed down considerably. I knelt with him as he prayed, exercising my faith with him that he would be able to go to sleep quickly.

He told us the next morning during scripture reading how his prayer had been answered and that the Lord had truly helped him fall right asleep. Within five minutes of our prayer, he was asleep, and he slept through the whole night.

Clearly if someone will exercise faith, especially a little child or we as adults trying to be as little children, the heavens will respond. The Lord is very kind and anxious to bless his people if, in faith, they will ask.

I was thankful the Lord would respond to our prayer in such an immediate way. Some might feel this was a small thing, but to my son it was not. The thing that was most significant to me was that my son knew that the Lord had directly answered his prayer.

It is amazing how the Lord can give peace and comfort. When the Lord answers prayer, he usually does it through a feeling of peace in our minds and hearts. He told Oliver Cowdery: "If you desire a . . . witness, cast your mind upon the night that you cried unto me in your heart, that you might know concerning the truth of these things. Did I not speak peace to your mind concerning the matter? What greater witness can you have than from God?" (D&C 6:22–23).

Having peace is as great a witness that the Lord has answered our prayers as any other thing we might receive. I truly saw that in the case of my son that evening.

## PRAYERS TO FIND A HOME

Let me recount another experience in which the whole

family was involved and that greatly strengthened our faith that the Lord hears and answers prayers.

When we returned home from living in South America, our family had grown from six persons to eight, and we decided to sell our small home. First we tried selling it on our own and then with two different real estate companies.

These were difficult times economically. Mortgage rates were up around 20 percent, and almost no homes were selling. To sell our home and buy another one seemed just this side of impossible. Some people came to see it, but for a year and a half no one made a concrete offer of any kind.

Neither realtor brought anyone to see the house, even though we cleaned it from top to bottom to make it more appealing. We recarpeted, painted, and so on. We prayed off and on about the sale of the home and about finding another one. Nothing seemed to fall into place.

During this time we found a house to buy in our own ward, and then a house in another one. We actually made an offer on both houses contingent on the sale of our own. However, neither realtor would take our home on a trade, and because it didn't sell, the deals on the other two houses fell through. We felt as if all the doors had closed.

About six months later we began feeling strong impressions that we should have another child. Yet we said to ourselves, "How can that be when there's really no place to put a baby except in our chest of drawers?" Although we felt awfully crowded in our home, we decided in faith to have another child.

We wanted a larger house not just because of our growing family. We also wanted a place where we could grow crops and fruit trees and have some running space for teenage children, a place where they could bring their friends. We seriously began to consider moving to another town.

A few months later, my wife and I were driving through another area of the city, and I told her of a strong impression I had had the day before that we should stop worrying about moving to another town, buying a new home, or building a new home. I told her about a dream I had had in which we were living in a large older home with a garden and mature fruit trees, and I felt strongly that it would be given to us in time. These impressions seemed to quiet my wife's heart.

Six months later we again listed our home with the realtors, and this time we began to pray intently, knowing we were just six weeks away from the delivery of our new baby. We and our children prayed morning, noon, and night in our family prayers and in our personal prayers that the Lord would show us a house that we should buy, and that he would bring someone to buy our home. The difficulty with selling our home centered in the fact that we had paid it off before going to South America, and thus there was no mortgage to be assumed. Also, we wanted to be cashed out of the home, and in those days, when almost no one could get a loan, that seemed nearly impossible. Anyone who had that kind of cash would put it into a lot nicer home than ours. Nevertheless, we went on praying intently for two or three weeks.

About this time a home in a beautiful area of our city came to our attention. It had been for sale privately for a couple of years, and it had a big yard and fruit trees. We went over and looked at it two or three times within a few days. After praying about it, we felt strongly that it was the house we should buy, although we felt uneasy about doing so without having sold our old one. But after more prayer, we determined to buy it in faith.

We began bargaining with the owners. Originally they agreed to take our home in on the deal, then later agreed to take just a lot that we owned. Now we were really committed, and our whole family began to pray even more fervently that before the baby came, the Lord would bring someone to buy our old home.

The Lord seems to like close calls. To our delight, just before our new son was born, some Church members moving from California came to see our house. The wife, especially, was impressed with it. They made an offer on the home and paid us *in cash*, which was almost unbelievable.

We felt that the Lord had directly intervened because of the faith of our children, and in fact the whole family, in helping us find a home with fruit trees, a level lot (which in our city on a hill is hard to come by), ample bedrooms, and all the space we wanted inside and out. It would provide work for the children and enough land that we could be self-sustaining, with plenty of room for the new baby. What more could we have asked?

Without question, the Lord will answer a family's sincere prayers, regardless of their situation. We should never use the excuse that we don't have a normal family or a completely active family. I have a feeling that many of us go on trying to resolve our own problems—spiritual, temporal, or emotional—without turning to the Lord as we should. We can have nearly any blessing we would like from the Lord, but we must ask, and we must do it in faith.

A family united in prayer can have real spiritual power. I believe that if a family is praying for what is honorable and right, they have every right to believe that the Lord will respond, blessing them with what they desire or even with something better, giving them some indication why they cannot have what they want, or indicating that they should quit praying for something they will not receive. It was truly satisfying to our family to have our prayers answered as they were.

## PRINCIPLES OF PRAYER

The scriptures provide a number of principles that, if obeyed, will help us receive answers to our prayers. They include:

1. Humble yourself (see D&C 112:10).
2. Kneel as you pray (see D&C 5:24).
3. Pray fervently.

4. Pray in faith, believing that you shall receive (see D&C 18:18; 29:6; Alma 32:28).
5. Pray sincerely and be of a sincere heart (see D&C 5:24).
6. Find a still place to pray (see D&C 6:22–23).
7. Discipline your mind to concentrate on prayer (see Jacob 3:1).
8. Ponder, study your feelings and ideas out in your own mind (see D&C 9:7–9).
9. Pray for the Holy Ghost beforehand to know what to pray for (see D&C 46:30).
10. Use the power of fasting (see D&C 88:76).
11. Obtain the Spirit by the prayer of faith (see D&C 42:14).
12. Confess your sins; acknowledge the things you have done wrong (see D&C 5:28).
13. Obey the commandments—be worthy (Mosiah 2:41).
14. Rid yourself of disputes, contentions, covetousness, and impure desires (see 4 Nephi 1:1–2; D&C 88:123).
15. Prepare yourself to receive tests (see D&C 58:3; 101:16).
16. Recognize the hand of the Lord in all things (see D&C 59:21).
17. Be grateful (see D&C 46:32).
18. Let the Lord enlighten your mind (see D&C 11:12–13; 6:15–16).
19. Pray for the will of God. Pray to be subject to his will, to know his will beforehand (see Romans 8:26–28; Matthew 6:8).
20. Pray for others, perhaps even more than just praying for yourself (see D&C 112:11–12).
21. Increase your desire to talk with the Lord (see 3 Nephi 19:24; D&C 11:17).
22. Don't speak words so much—rather communicate.
23. Use pauses, wait, listen.
24. Don't multiply words (see 3 Nephi 19:24).
25. Pray without ceasing (see D&C 10:5).

26. Use the familiar form of language to the Lord (thee, thou, thy, thine, and so on; see Matthew 6:9).
27. Practice by praying (see 2 Nephi 32:8–9).
28. Be specific. Ask specifically for what you need (see D&C 103:31).
29. Recognize you are a child of God, a servant of the Lord. Pray, "Speak, Lord, thy servant heareth" (see 1 Samuel 3:10).
30. Pray while helping individuals, "Deliver me his heart." "How may I help this person now?" "How might I lighten this person's burden?"
31. Listen intensely during and after prayer.
32. Pray over all things, that the Lord may consecrate them for your good (see 2 Nephi 32:8–9; D&C 46:7).

We can learn many other principles from the scriptures and from our own experiences with prayer.

### PRAYER FOR A MISSIONARY

As a young missionary in Uruguay, I learned through experience the power that the prayers of others can have, even over great distances. On my mission, I struggled with many digestive problems. They were so bad, in fact, that the mission president considered sending me home. To compound these problems, one day while out walking I experienced a severe pain in my left foot. I couldn't even walk to the discussion my companion and I had planned. We went to the doctor, who told me, "It's just arthritis caused by the damp weather. If you'll stay off your foot for two or three days, the pain will pass."

I did so, and I also had a priesthood blessing, but my foot felt no better. I was a district leader, and my district had just begun to baptize in a city where there had been no baptisms for some time. I couldn't understand how the Lord could allow me to remain down for those days when my district was just beginning to succeed.

A week went by, then two weeks, then three and finally

a month in bed. I was still incapacitated, with no change in the pain in my foot. Finally, I was taken to the mission home in the capital city, where more suitable medical facilities were available.

An X-ray showed that one of the bones in my foot had been fractured and then grown back together incorrectly. The doctors talked about breaking the bone again or giving me electrical treatments that were supposed to fuse the bone correctly, but either treatment would take another month. I started going for electrical treatments twice a day, but they didn't seem to make any difference. This problem on top of my other health problems had me somewhat discouraged.

One morning after nearly three months of struggling with this affliction, I stepped out of bed to find absolutely no pain in my foot. I stepped on the foot gently, then stamped on it, then ran with my companion for a mile that morning, totally healed. With great joy I returned immediately to the field to work.

Two more weeks went by. A letter arrived from my parents that said, "Dear son," followed by a paragraph or two of chastisement for not having told them about my ailments. They said they had learned of my problems from another missionary, a friend of mine, who had written home. In great love they wrote, "We have begun a fast and constant prayer for you as a family. We have also placed your name on the temple prayer list and hope that it might be of help to you."

As I tearfully read the letter and examined my journal, I found that the day I had been healed was the very day the letter had been written—the very day my family had placed my name in the temple and begun praying and exercising faith for their distant son and brother.

To me, this showed clearly that the faith of Saints even at a great distance can have a real impact on someone who needs help. The doctors could do nothing, but the Lord intervened. In an instant, largely because of the faith of others, my foot was healed. For the Lord, nothing is impossible. In fact, the more impossible something is, the more he seems to get involved if we exercise faith in that near-impossible thing.

## LISTENING FOR THE
## STILL, SMALL VOICE

When we are attempting to obtain answers to our prayers and to be directed by the Lord, we must surely learn to follow the promptings of the Spirit. Those promptings will come to help us through the problem we are experiencing. They help us know what to pray for. In fact, the scriptures tell us we should pray to have the Holy Ghost in order to know what to pray for: "The Spirit also helpeth our infirmities: for we know not what we should pray for as we ought: but the Spirit itself maketh intercession for us with groanings which cannot be uttered. And he that searcheth the hearts knoweth what is the mind of the Spirit, because he maketh intercession for the saints according to the will of God" (Romans 8:26–27). Also, notice that the Spirit itself will intercede for us in our prayers.

The promptings of the Spirit will also tell us how much more faith we may need to exercise. We may have promptings come to us about what we need to repent of, and so on. In summary, the Lord will guide us through our experiences if we will seek his direction.

Certainly, if we pray constantly, we will hear the Spirit's voice much more easily. We must concentrate in order to hear the voice. It is felt more than it is heard. Because of that, if we are too busy or preoccupied or hardened in our feelings, we may not feel the words. As Nephi said to Laman and Lemuel: "Ye are swift to do iniquity but slow to remember the Lord your God. Ye have seen an angel, and he spake unto you; yea, ye have heard his voice from time to time; and he hath spoken unto you in a still small voice, but ye were past feeling, that ye could not feel his words; wherefore, he has spoken unto you like unto the voice of thunder, which did cause the earth to shake as if it were to divide asunder" (1 Nephi 17:45).

The voice of the Spirit truly is a still, small voice. The Book of Mormon describes the voice of the Lord in this way: "It was not a voice of thunder, neither was it a voice of a great tumultuous noise, but behold, it was a still voice of perfect mildness, as if it had been a whisper, and it did pierce even to the very soul" (Helaman 5:30).

It surely seems clear to me that the Spirit speaks in a still, small voice, and we have to really listen and expect to be able to hear it or we will not be able to. If we would like to increase our facility to hear the voice, we may best accomplish that by learning how to pray without ceasing. The more we learn to pray throughout the day, in my experience, the more the promptings will come to inspire us about what to do.

I have surely seen that gift manifest many times in my wife, who has had feelings or impressions about things that were needed for our children. When we have followed those promptings, they have led us to additional experiences in faith, sometimes even saving a child from a life-threatening situation. Other times they have been much simpler experiences where the children could have weathered something through on their own, but because we listened to the Spirit, things turned out better than they would have otherwise.

We once learned a great lesson on a trip to Arizona from Utah. After family prayer, we left early one morning in a van and drove for about an hour into Southern Utah. Suddenly we realized we had left behind the bag containing all of our clothes. The only alternative, we felt, was to drive back and get it, which we did. Then we drove south again, losing more than two hours. None of us was upset, although we were a little disappointed as we had lost some of the swimming time we were going to enjoy at Lake Powell. We felt pressed somewhat, since my wife and I were to board a plane the next morning in Phoenix for an international flight. We had to make it on time.

My wife was driving and apparently did not realize that the car was in second gear. When it was my turn to drive, after a few minutes I noticed that the car had overheated. We immediately pulled over, and fortunately (I think it was more than fortunately), we were driving alongside a river. We could have been in a lot of other places when the car boiled over, but we were right there. We tried to pour water into the plastic container that feeds into the radiator, but the radiator didn't take the water. I felt there was no choice but to take the radiator cap off. (I learned later that the radiator won't take the water until it cools down.)

To make things a little more tense, while I was trying to get the radiator cap off, one of my daughters turned on the air conditioning, which unsettled me. Then a son accidentally honked the horn while I was under the hood, scaring me, and I bumped my head. I took a walk so I wouldn't get too upset with him. Then one of my sons dropped a rock on his brother's head and made him cry. Things were going from bad to worse.

I finally got the radiator cap off, losing most of the coolant in the process. Using water from the river, I got the radiator filled and cooled down. Then we tried to start the car, but it was totally dead. There was not even a sound from the starter.

After we calmed down, we had a word of prayer that the Lord would save us and that the car would function. We tried to start it again, but it was still dead.

Just then a man came by in a truck. He "just happened to be in the area" checking the river. He had some jumper cables, but we tried the lights and they were working, so I didn't think the problem could be the battery.

He finally determined he would tow us into the nearest city, about thirty minutes away. He hooked a chain onto our car and began towing us backward up the hill. It was hard going, but he kept pulling. Suddenly he said, "You know, I've heard you're not supposed to tow these automatics." I remembered then that you have to lift the rear wheels off the ground if you're going to tow it.

I said, "Well, my oldest daughter and I will go in with

you to the town and come back with the tow truck." Even if we could find a tow truck, the man didn't think we could get a mechanic to look at our car on a Saturday afternoon.

We were just sick about this whole experience and felt that our family trip would be ruined. We imagined losing the whole day or maybe two in this little Southern Utah town. I thought about what we would do if we had to get a hotel and stay that night and miss our plane the next morning.

Just as we were going to drive into town, the man asked, in a moment of inspiration, "Shouldn't we try the jumper cables anyway as long as we're here and we've got them?" (I don't think the Lord gave *me* that thought because I was still upset about the whole experience. It's difficult to receive inspiration when you're mad.)

I said, "Well, yes, let's do it as long as we're here." We hooked up the cables, and, to our amazement, the van started right up. We thanked the man with the truck for his kind help, and he drove away.

One of our sons immediately said, "We ought to have a prayer of thanks," which we did. Then, instead of spending the whole day and the next day there, we were on our way. The van gradually heated up again during the next hour until the last hill before the next city. It boiled over the last few minutes, but we pushed on anyway. Again, "fortunately" we found an honest mechanic who said, "We'll put the coolant in." Then he noticed that the belt to the alternator was broken, which was why the battery had not been charging. He charged the battery, put on a new belt, and replaced the coolant. It took about forty-five minutes, and we were once again on our way.

We surely felt blessed that the problem was fixed. We drove right on to Phoenix late that night, and we were very thankful that the next morning we made our international flight.

Question: When our car boiled over, why did we just happen to be next to a river? Did the man with the truck just happen to be there? Did he just happen to have jumper cables? Did the mechanic just happen to be honest and to have the right belt for our van? Most important, why did the first man say, "Shouldn't we use the jumper cables before we go into the city?" Had the question not been asked, we would have wasted a whole day or more. It surely shows that the Lord leads people in a variety of ways to solve a problem. He is very kind to us, even at times when we may not deserve it.

The Lord watched over us and blessed us in that experience. The Lord truly does answer prayers, but his answer can be at a first level of blessings, a second level of blessings, or a third level of blessings, depending on how we listen and how we exercise our faith. Things would have been very different if the Lord had not answered the prayers of the family and if the man with the truck hadn't asked the question. We could have stayed all night in that town. We would still have prayed with thanksgiving that night that we didn't have to spend the night out in the wilderness. We could have gone on to that secondary level, never knowing that the problem could have been solved right there the way it was if we had exercised a little more faith. It was an interesting experience.

Hearing the impression to use the jumper cables saved the trip overseas, saved us from going back to the city, and saved an awful lot of money—all from hearing the still, small voice in just a few seconds.

This experience certainly caused our family to be very thankful, and it impressed upon us again the importance of really listening and *expecting* the Lord to be of help to us. I believe that truly is what faith is, for the Lord said, "Whatsoever ye shall ask the Father in my name, which is right, believing that ye shall receive, behold it shall be given unto you" (3 Nephi 18:20).

## PRAYING FOR THE PROPHET

Let me conclude this chapter with one last experience in which we learned a great lesson about getting our children to pray for the prophets by name. It was a rather humorous experience, but President Spencer W. Kimball, in the process, taught us a great lesson about family prayer and specifically about praying for the Brethren.

It was Christmastime in 1973. The traditional excitement was in the air, and particularly in Salt Lake City with the Tabernacle Choir Christmas program and other activities that tend to increase that spirit.

Our family was especially pleased to be invited to a Church employees Christmas reception in the general board room of the Quorum of the Twelve. My wife and I and our oldest boy had entered the room, trying not to be too nervous as we watched the General Authorities assembling to shake hands and give each other Christmas greetings. After we had shaken hands with a few of them, we each took a glass of punch and some cookies and went into one of the far corners to get out of the way and allow other employees the opportunity to talk to some of the Brethren.

We were just beginning to feel secure in our little world of three when suddenly a door in the corner where we were standing opened and in walked Spencer W. Kimball, then president of the Quorum of the Twelve. He greeted us, shook our hands, and then took our son's face in his hands to ask him if he was going on a mission. Our son said he was. President Kimball then told him that he would be a great missionary, which we considered a prophetic statement to be fulfilled through the faith of our son and ourselves.

During the conversation, we told President Kimball of a rather humorous experience that had occurred in our family the preceding week. Our children had been in the habit of praying for the presiding Brethren by name. Our second son was praying and said, "Bless Pwesident Wee, Pwesident Tanno, and Pwesident Womney." He then began to go on in his prayer, having forgotten to bless President Kimball.

His older brother whispered, "You forgot President

Kimball," whereupon the second boy answered, "He didn't need it tonight."

President Kimball chuckled at the story but then in dead seriousness pointed his finger at me and then at my son, saying, "You tell your second son that he should never forget me again. We need the prayers of all the children of the Church to sustain us. I could never do what I have to do if it were not for their prayers." He then told me again, "You be sure your children pray for me every night."

We were tremendously pleased with those few moments with President Kimball and even more so for the lesson he taught us about the power of children's prayers. As he literally spoke the words of the Lord to us that night, little did we know that within a matter of days President Harold B. Lee would pass through the veil to the spirit world and President Kimball would be president of the Church, making his words to us even more prophetic.

We did try after that to make sure our children always prayed for the Brethren and to recognize that what President Kimball had told us was true—the prophets, apostles, stake presidents, bishops, and heads of families truly do need the prayers of children. One child's prayer is sufficient to obtain an answer from heaven. Let us therefore pray faithfully for all the Brethren. Let us pray for the First Presidency, for the Quorum of the Twelve, and for the other General Authorities. Let us pray for our stake presidents and for our bishops. I am confident that if we do that, it will greatly bless those priesthood leaders and greatly bless family members as they pray for the Lord's anointed.

## CONCLUSION

Prayer is truly one of the fundamental building blocks of raising up a family to the Lord. If families pray together, the children will learn to pray on their own, and they will then be far more likely to go on missions, obtain the priesthood, and be endowed and sealed in the temple.

Not much has been said in this chapter about individual

prayer. Because of their personal nature, it would not be appropriate to share experiences with personal prayer in a book like this. It's difficult even to share many of these things about the family. But all that has been said here about family prayer also applies to individual prayer, which sets the example for family prayer.

Also, fasting was not illustrated as amply as ought to be the case. When there is time, families certainly ought to fast to add to their spiritual preparedness. There is great strength and power in fasting and prayer.

We must teach our children to fast. As they try to solve problems in life, they should see the example of their parents who fast more frequently than just the minimum of once a month asked by the Church. Members of the Church are free to fast as often as they feel a need to do so. We have always felt it important to teach our children early that principle so they could better learn to resolve their problems under the direction of the Lord. We have taught our children some months before they reach age eight to begin fasting one meal, and then at baptism they begin fasting the full twenty-four hours without food or water. It has been a challenge for a few of them at the beginning, but they have quickly learned the principle and can then use it often throughout their life.

Let me remind you again that Satan will do all in his power to keep you and your family from praying. He will try to bring about contention in the family. He will try to make you forget to pray. He knows well that if he can somehow weaken or destroy the spiritual link between you and your Heavenly Father, he will have obtained a major objective.

Lastly, lest anyone misunderstand, our family has had many problems and challenges. Things have not always gone forward smoothly. However I bear testimony that when problems have arisen, prayer has been of great help in solving them. Regular prayer, on the part of children and parents, will bring about inspired solutions to the problems faced in a family.

May the Lord bless all of us to learn better how to use prayer to change our hearts and humble the hearts of our children. The key seems to be to turn the children to the Lord. You will thereby save them and yourself.

# CHAPTER FOUR

# TEACHING YOUR FAMILY THROUGH SCRIPTURE READING

I will never forget one time when I had been reading stories from the Book of Mormon to our five-year-old son. I told him the story about Nephi going back to Jerusalem to get the plates, trying to teach him the importance of having his heroes be the Lord's servants in the scriptures, men like Nephi.

After having read the story, I thought I should check his understanding. I asked him, "Son, why do you suppose Nephi had to go back to Jerusalem to get the plates?"

He thought a moment and said, "Well, Dad, I guess they didn't have anything else to eat on."

I was flabbergasted. Here I was talking of brass plates, and the only plates this five-year-old had ever heard of were the ones on the table. This father learned a good lesson that day about checking people's understanding and being careful not to teach over their heads.

Some time later when one of my other children heard of the incident, he said, "Dad, I guess you know why the Lamanites always had bruised knees, don't you?"

"Why?" I asked.

His answer: "Because of all the knee-fights!"

Some families seem to think reading the scriptures together must be dry and boring. Nothing could be further from the truth. Reading the scriptures together can be enjoyable and enlightening in many ways.

## BENEFITS OF FAMILY SCRIPTURE READING

Just a few of the great benefits that can come from family scripture reading are:

1. Finding Jesus Christ and learning of his atonement.

2. Learning how to obtain answers to prayers.
3. Learning how to humble oneself.
4. Learning how to exercise faith.
5. Learning how to repent.
6. Help in setting family values.
7. Learning to resolve life's problems.
8. Keeping the whole family focused on the Lord.

On and on goes the list. We can learn many valuable things through reading the scriptures together. They truly are instructions from heaven to us on the earth. If we will receive them in the right spirit, we will be taught by the Lord how to return to our heavenly home.

## THE VALUE OF THE LORD'S WORDS

How does the Lord feel about the value of his own words? What follows is his answer from the scriptures. These passages explain the purpose and the value of his holy word:

> The words of Christ will tell you all things what ye should do (2 Nephi 32:3).

> From a child thou hast known the holy scriptures, which are able to make thee wise unto salvation through faith which is in Christ Jesus. All scripture is given by inspiration of God, and is profitable for doctrine, for reproof, for correction, for instruction in righteousness: That the man of God may be perfect, throughly furnished unto all good works (2 Timothy 3:15–17).

> [The scriptures] shall be with him, and he shall read therein all the days of his life: that he may learn to fear the Lord His God, to keep all the words of this law and these statutes, to do them (Deuteronomy 17:19).

> The scriptures are given for your instruction, they contain the fullness of the Gospel; and the scriptures shall be given, even as they are in mine

own bosom, to the salvation of mine own elect (D&C 35:20).

They shall pray always that I may unfold the [scriptures] to their understanding (D&C 32:4).

When ye shall receive these things, I would exhort you that ye would ask God, the Eternal Father, in the name of Christ, if these things are not true; and if ye shall ask with a sincere heart, with real intent, having faith in Christ, he will manifest the truth of it unto you, by the power of the Holy Ghost. And by the power of the Holy Ghost ye may know the truth of all things (Moroni 10:4–5).

It is my voice which speaketh [the scriptures] unto you; for they are given by my Spirit unto you, and by my power you can read them one to another; and save it were by my power you could not have them; Wherefore, you can testify that you have heard my voice, and know my words (D&C 18:35–36).

They said one to another, Did not our heart burn within us, while he talked with us by the way, and while he opened to us the scriptures? (Luke 24:32).

Faith cometh by hearing, and hearing by the word of God (Romans 10:17).

Whosoever will may lay hold upon the word of God, which is quick and powerful, which shall divide asunder all the cunning and the snares and the wiles of the devil, and lead the man of Christ in a strait and narrow course across that everlasting gulf of misery which is prepared to engulf the wicked (Helaman 3:29).

As many of them as . . . are led to believe the holy scriptures, . . . [are led] to faith on the Lord, and unto repentance, which faith and repentance bringeth a change of heart unto them—Therefore, as many as have come to this, ye know of yourselves are firm and steadfast in the faith, and in the thing wherewith they have been made free (Helaman 15:7–8).

## A MODERN-DAY PROPHET ON THE VALUE OF THE LORD'S WORDS

A modern-day prophet, President Ezra Taft Benson, has often explained the value of the scriptures. Read these statements from him carefully, as they will give you a new and deeper appreciation for the value of word of the Lord:

[We Latter-day Saints have] not been using the Book of Mormon as we should. Our homes are not as strong unless we are using it to bring our children to Christ. Our families may be corrupted by worldly trends and teachings unless we know how to use the book to expose and combat falsehoods ("The Book of Mormon Is the Word of God," *Ensign*, May 1975, p. 65).

Let us use that standard [the Book of Mormon] to judge what we read, the music we hear, the entertainment we watch, the thoughts we think ("A Sacred Responsibility," *Ensign*, May 1986, p. 78).

Children, support your parents in their efforts to have daily family scripture study. Pray for them as they pray for you. The adversary does not want scripture study to take place in our homes, and so he will create problems if he can. But we must persist (p. 78).

I bless you with increased discernment to judge between Christ and anti-Christ. I bless you with increased power to do good and to resist evil. I bless you with increased understanding of the Book of Mormon. I promise you that from this moment forward, if we will daily sup from its pages and abide by its precepts, God will pour out upon each child of Zion and the Church a blessing hitherto unknown—and we will plead to the Lord that He will begin to lift the condemnation—the scourge and judgment. Of this I bear solemn witness (p. 78).

Let us not treat lightly the great things we have received from the hand of the Lord. His word is one of the most valuable gifts He has given us. Recommit yourselves to a study of the scriptures. Immerse yourselves in them daily. . . . Read them in your families and teach your children to love and treasure them. Then prayerfully and in counsel with others, seek every way possible to encourage the members of the Church to follow your example ("The Power of the Word," *Ensign*, May 1986, p. 82).

There are three great reasons why Latter-day Saints should make the study of the Book of Mormon a life-time pursuit.
  a. It is the keystone of our religion
    • It is the keystone in our witness of Christ.
    • It is the keystone of our doctrine.
    • It is the keystone of our testimony.
  b. The Book of Mormon is written for our day. It gives the pattern for preparing for the Second Coming. The major portion of the book centers on the few decades just prior to Christ coming to America. It tells why some were destroyed and others were standing at the temple when Christ came.
  c. It will help us to draw nearer to God (See "The Book of Mormon—Keystone of Our Religion," *Ensign*, November 1986, pp. 5–7).

If [the Book of Mormon writers] saw our day, and chose those things which would be of greatest worth to us, is not that how we should study the Book of Mormon? We should constantly ask ourselves, "Why did the Lord inspire Mormon (or Moroni or Alma) to include that in his record? What lesson can I learn from that to help me live in this day and age?" (p. 6).

In the Book of Mormon we find a pattern for preparing for the Second Coming (p. 6).

It is not just that the Book of Mormon teaches us truth, though it indeed does that. It is not just that the Book of Mormon bears testimony of Christ, though it indeed does that, too. But there is something more. There is a power in the book which will begin to flow into your lives the moment you begin a serious study of the book. You will find greater power to resist temptation. You will find the power to avoid deception (p. 7).

These two great books of latter-day scripture [the Book of Mormon and the Doctrine and Covenants] are bound together as revelations from Israel's God for the purpose of gathering and preparing His people for the second coming of the Lord ("The Gift of Modern Revelation," *Ensign,* November 1986, p. 79).

The Book of Mormon title page declares its purpose is threefold: to show what great things the Lord has done, to teach of the covenants of the Lord, and to convince both Jew and Gentile that Jesus is the Christ.

The Doctrine and Covenants is the only book in the world that has a preface written by the Lord Himself (p. 79).

We must honor [the Book of Mormon] by reading it, by studying it, by taking its precepts into our lives and transforming them into lives required of the true followers of Christ (p. 80).

No member of this Church can stand approved in the presence of God who has not seriously and carefully read the Book of Mormon (p. 80).

The Book of Mormon is the instrument that God has designed to "sweep the earth as with a flood, to gather out [His] elect" (Moses 7:62). This sacred volume of scripture needs to become more central in our preaching, our teaching, and our missionary work ("Flooding the Earth with the Book of Mormon," *Ensign*, November 1988, p. 4).

One of the most important things learned in reading the scriptures is how to hear the voice of the Lord *to us*. Instruction comes not only from reading the words; when we prayerfully ponder them, the Lord can speak "between the lines" to us. In other words, he can speak to us about our current problems while we are reading the content of the scriptures. In fact, the very act of reading them (it almost doesn't matter where) seems to open the door to direction from the Lord if we approach our reading humbly. The scriptures are one of the greatest tools we have for communicating with the Lord. Elder Bruce R. McConkie once told me he had received more revelation while reading the scriptures than in any other way. I bear testimony that the same is true for me.

What parents would not want their children to learn and apply the principles discussed above? I'm sure we all desire that for our family members. And of course, the best possible way to teach those skills to our families is through example. We need to work and learn how to read the scriptures ourselves; then we will be in a better position to teach our families. However, if we are not sure about how to do it, one of the best ways to learn is just to *do* it.

The best way to make sure children learn those skills is for faithful parents to model them in family scripture reading. If children day after day learn from personal experience to read the passages, to understand them, to cross-reference them, to learn from the Lord, to believe in the standards taught, and to apply them in daily life, then when they are on their own they will almost automatically know how to do those things. The Lord said in D&C 98:16: "Seek diligently to turn the hearts of the children to their fathers, and the hearts of the fathers to the children." If parents want to have the hearts of their children turned to them, and to have their own hearts turned to their children, I know of no better way to accomplish that than through family scripture reading. In that process, both generations—parents and children—assimilate values from heaven, and thereby their hearts are drawn together. The promises to parents and children before they came to this world begin to bear fruit in this life.

Testimonies knit together in love, with the Spirit confirming to parents and children the pure message of heaven, will truly turn the hearts of parents to their children and the hearts of children to their parents. When parents study together with their children, their gospel understanding, love, and unity will grow geometrically.

Plainly the Lord feels strongly about our studying his words. Doing so may be one of our most important tasks in learning of the Lord and how to return to him.

## EXCUSES FOR NOT READING
## THE SCRIPTURES

Despite inspired counsel to the contrary, many families in the Church still do not read the scriptures together regularly each day. As I have traveled around the Church, I have estimated that perhaps 10 to 15 percent of the members read the scriptures together as families. Why is that so? As I've talked with a number of families, I've heard things like:

- We're just too busy as a family.
- We're all going different ways and can't ever seem to get together.
- We've tried it many times and have gone for a few weeks and then given up.
- We're just not sure where to start or how to go about it.
- I'm not confident enough to read the scriptures knowing that I'll have to explain them to my children. I might be embarrassed.
- We've just never made the effort to get our children their own books of scripture.

- I guess we just never really decided that we would do it.
- When we've tried to read the scriptures together, it's just caused contention.
- Our children have just rebelled against it. They don't like to read the scriptures.
- Our children complain that they can't understand what the scriptures are all about.

Speaking to the youth and children of the Church, President Ezra Taft Benson gave great counsel concerning family scripture study: "Children, support your parents in their efforts to have *daily* family scripture study. Pray for them as they pray for you. The adversary does not want scripture study to take place in our homes, and so he will create problems if he can. But we must persist."

The list of excuses seems to go on and on. I think we would have a difficult time giving any of those excuses to the Lord. Do we really think he'd say, "Well, I suppose I understand. It's okay, then, that you didn't read the scriptures."

Some people seem to have a problem with pride or lack of humility. Sometimes they are afraid to admit they don't understand the scriptures and begin working forward from there. They don't want others to know they don't know. But then their growth is stymied. People must truly humble themselves before they read the words of the Lord or they will not understand them, enjoy them, or grow from the experience.

I believe that one of the main reasons families have not regularly read the scriptures together is that they have just not decided in their hearts that it was important enough to do. They have not made the decision that they would find out how to do it at all costs. If they understood the importance of this family activity, they would surely do all in their power—both husband and wife or single parent—to make sure that this family practice became a foundation stone of their family traditions. It might very well do as much as any other thing to help exalt their family.

## LEARNING FROM ONE ANOTHER
## IN SCRIPTURE READING

I will never forget one time when we were reading in the Book of Mormon about the importance of having a testimony. We stopped and asked the question, "Are there different kinds of testimonies?" We discussed that thought for a little while.

Then I asked the family to take turns telling how they knew the gospel was true. I asked, "How do you know that for sure?" We closed our eyes and prayerfully pondered the answer to that question. The answers from the family surprised me because of their great variety.

One daughter, age twelve, said: "I know the gospel is true because I have seen the Lord answer prayers. He has answered our family's prayers. He has answered my prayers. The Lord truly does answer us when we ask, and he will help us with our problems. My testimony is based heavily on that knowledge."

A seventeen-year-old boy said: "I believe my greatest testimony is that the Lord will heal people through priesthood blessings and that faith really works." He then related an example or two that had strengthened his testimony in those things. He concluded, "I could never be convinced now that the Church is not true. I have seen the power of the priesthood in operation. I know that faith is a real power and that it works."

Another boy, a recently returned missionary said: "I know the Church is true because of the Book of Mormon. I have come to know, as Joseph Smith said, that 'The Book of Mormon [is] the most correct of any book on earth and the keystone of our religion and that a man will get closer to God by abiding by its precepts than by any other book.' He then bore testimony of how he had obtained his testimony through a personal revelation while reading of the Savior's visit to the Nephites.

A fifteen-year-old daughter said: "I know the Church is true because of Jesus Christ. Above all else, I know that he is the Savior of the world. I know that he loves me. I know that he has power to help me if I pray to the Father in his name. I have received a personal witness about Jesus Christ and thereby I know that his gospel is true, as is the Church."

My good wife then added: "I suppose all I have heard this morning teaches me that the Church is true. I would add one other thing: giving service to other people. To the degree I have lived the gospel through service, I have had witness after witness come to me that these things are true. My first testimony came through leading the music in Sunday School as a teenaged girl. As I memorized the words of the hymns and sang them with all the people, I felt the Spirit of the Lord come into my heart."

As she spoke, I could not help but think of Jesus' teaching: "My doctrine is not mine, but his that sent me. If any man will do his will, he shall know of the doctrine, whether it be of God, or whether I speak of myself" (John 7:16–17).

I learned a great lesson that morning as I listened to my family members share how they knew that the gospel was true. It showed me that testimonies can come in a variety of ways, that the Spirit will work upon people in different ways, but the result is the same: They come to know the gospel is true. It made me think of the passage in John 3:8: "The wind bloweth where it listeth, and thou hearest the sound thereof, but canst not tell whence it cometh, and whither it goeth: so is every one that is born of the Spirit."

What a choice experience would have been lost to the Cook family if we had not been reading in the scriptures that morning about the importance of testimonies!

## WHY WE SHOULD READ THE
## SCRIPTURES AS A FAMILY

The Lord gives many reasons for reading the scriptures,

and I believe those reasons are true for both individuals and families. Some of the blessings I have seen come from family scripture reading include the following:

• Reading the scriptures together creates a family worship time, a way to effectively worship God together.

• Scripture reading will give children a "new heart"—one of the most important blessings of all.

• Scripture reading builds faith in and among family members.

• Scripture reading makes it possible for the Lord's servants in the scriptures to become young people's heroes.

• Scripture reading allows families to be together. In today's busy world, that alone is a wonderful blessing.

• Scripture reading engenders humility and love in the family.

• Scripture reading helps the family get up in the morning and start the day, or, if they're reading at night, to conclude the day on a spiritual note.

• Scripture reading brings about a daily focus on God, on others, and on self, thus bringing about repentance and a desire to change.

• Scripture reading allows time for loving, sharing, understanding, and listening.

• Scripture reading gives children an opportunity to raise some of the concerns they face in school or with their peers and then to have those items discussed by the family and related to the words of the Lord.

• Scripture reading promotes the sharing of values between generations.

• Scripture reading provides the opportunity for testimonies to be gained and borne.

On and on go the benefits. Why then, do so many families have difficulty trying to read the scriptures? Surely Satan is working hard to prevent it.

President Benson made a powerful statement about the impact scripture reading can have in our lives:

> I bless you with increased desire to flood the earth with the Book of Mormon, to gather out from the world the elect of God who are yearning for the truth but know not where to find it (*Ensign*, May 1987, p. 85).

Elder Marion G. Romney said:

> I feel certain that if, in our homes, parents will read from the Book of Mormon prayerfully and regularly, both by themselves and with their children, the spirit of that great book will come to permeate our homes and all who dwell therein. The spirit of reverence will increase, mutual respect and consideration for each other will grow, the spirit of contention will depart, parents will counsel their children in greater love and wisdom, children will be more responsive and submissive to that counsel, righteousness will increase, faith, hope, and charity, the pure love of Christ will abound in our homes and lives bringing in their wake peace, joy, and happiness (*Conference Report*, April 1960, pp. 112–13).

We should not be surprised that the Lord's servants would so testify about the power of the scriptures. In his great intercessory prayer the Lord said: "Sanctify them [his disciples] through thy truth: thy word is truth" (John 17:17).

I bear testimony that family scripture reading is of great importance.

Our family had difficulty for many years in holding scripture reading. We would be faithful for a few days or a few weeks but then slip back into our old routine. We would then try to start all over again. We never could quite decide that we were going to hold it and have enough fortitude to do so. Finally, my wife and I fasted and prayed about it, and we determined, resolved, and decided that we would start scripture reading as a Cook family tradition—that we would do whatever it took, that we would pay whatever price it cost.

We called a family council meeting and discussed it with

our children. We bore testimony of its importance. Their hearts were touched sufficiently that we all agreed we really ought to do it. We discussed how we could put it into practice and laid out a plan to begin in the mornings.

It wasn't easy. We went through difficult times with some children not wanting to get up or coming late. At times we wondered if we would be able to continue, but we did, and our family began to see the results. After those initial months of difficulty, we finally established it as a Cook family tradition.

As I write this book, it has been seventeen years since that decision was made. I bear testimony that I know of no other thing that has had a greater impact on our family than being up nearly every morning praying together, reading the scriptures, loving one another, and trying to assimilate the doctrines of Jesus Christ. It has truly been of great benefit in helping us raise up a family to the Lord.

## WHEN TO READ SCRIPTURES
## AS A FAMILY

When should we read the scriptures together? Some families have found it best to do it early in the morning. That way, they can start their children off on a spiritual note and prepare them for the challenges they will face that day. If it is done early enough, generally everyone can be together. Other families have found it best to read in the evenings around the supper table or later before bedtime. I suppose it doesn't matter much when scripture reading is held as long as it is held, with a regular place and time set so it can occur each day.

Some families have to arrange their scripture reading around early morning seminary. Seminary, as important as it is, should never take the place of family scripture reading. Some families have had the idea that their children were learning the scriptures sufficiently at church and in seminary. That is not the case. Family scripture reading takes first priority. Some families have found it necessary to hold two brief scripture readings (and two family prayers) to accommodate all their children.

Our family has found it best to hold scripture reading in the morning, typically between 6:00 and 6:30, depending on when the children have to be at school. Our scripture reading has normally taken about twenty or thirty minutes. Getting up that early has always been a great blessing to our children. In fact, one of my sons said when he went on his mission that he obeyed the rules but still got to "sleep in" half an hour later than usual.

Some families have difficulties with children who do not want to get up early. When our children were young, we tried singing to them, tickling them, rewarding them, and punishing them. We even tried dragging them out of bed. Sometimes when a child missed scripture reading, I would have the rest of the family talk during breakfast about what a wonderful time we had had, trying to make the person feel a bit remorseful that he or she had been left out. Although we did this in a humorous way, it didn't work either, as the children saw it as a subtle form of manipulation, which I suppose it was.

One time one of our little daughters invented a punishment that if we couldn't get up for scripture reading early in the morning, it meant that we were too tired, so we had to go to bed an hour early. That seemed to work for a few weeks to get everyone up, but sooner or later Dad or Mom became "the sheriff" or "the enforcer" to try to get them to go to bed early, which was always difficult and caused hurt feelings.

We soon learned that such tactics ultimately create resentment, ruining the spirit of scripture reading for everyone.

When children are small, they may need to be awakened, but we realized that if we were going to have the right spirit in scripture reading, it had to be because each person wanted to be there. It couldn't be just because Dad and Mom wanted them there. Thus, we finally got each child an alarm clock and gave them the responsibility to get themselves up and come to scripture reading. Some of them tried us, thinking we would wake them anyway, but we didn't, and they slept through scripture reading. This went on for a number of days until they learned we really meant it. If they did not get up on their own, we would go forward without them. Then they began to set their alarms and get themselves up.

That has been a great side benefit of scripture reading. Our children have learned to get themselves up early in the morning. Some young people don't learn that until they enter the mission field. Waking children up every morning only makes them dependent upon their parents. But they need to learn independence and self-reliance and to be disciplined enough to get themselves up.

The key to getting children to come to scripture reading is to make the experience good enough, sufficiently full of the Spirit, and enjoyable enough that they will want to be there and will feel bad if they miss. When we first started reading the scriptures together, if someone missed we would announce it to the whole family or kid the person about it. But later, when we were a little wiser, we would privately ask if the person was sick or had other problems. Usually the child had simply slept through the alarm or forgotten to set it. If the problem continued, my wife or I would usually talk with the child in private, encouraging him or her, praying with him or her, and generally doing what we could to touch the child's heart. Our children soon developed the true intention to be with the family every morning.

In the past few years, because the tradition has been firmly set, scripture reading has become truly enjoyable, and everyone wants to be there. We have learned much as a family as a result.

## WHERE TO HOLD SCRIPTURE READING

Each family will need to decide where to hold scripture reading. Some have tried holding it around the parents' bed.

However, the temptation to fall asleep is too great if this is done early in the morning. Some have done it around the breakfast or supper table, although this makes it a little more difficult to manage your scriptures and to mark them. Some have tried reading while seated on the floor or around an empty table. Some have sat in the family room on the couch. I suppose it really doesn't matter where it is held if the environment is comfortable, inviting, and conducive to learning.

In our scripture reading we've tried to teach the children to have a red pencil, to mark important passages, to cross-reference things, and so forth. Thus, we've tried sitting around the kitchen table in the mornings, but for us that's a little bit formal. The children have enjoyed more sitting on the couch in their bathrobes or snuggled up under a blanket.

## HOW TO HOLD SCRIPTURE READING

One of things a family has to decide is what to read. We have found, especially when the family was younger, that the Book of Mormon is by far the easiest book of scripture to understand. The Old Testament seems to be the hardest. For a number of years we just read the Book of Mormon three or four times until our family was a little older. Then we began to read in the New Testament and the Pearl of Great Price. We also read some of the stories in the Old Testament.

Families will have to decide whether to study the Book of Mormon from beginning to end or to study it by subject. We have found that both are important ways of learning. We tend to read from beginning to end, but we stop anyplace we are interested in a particular concept. Then we may study that subject for a number of mornings, using the Topical Guide and Bible Dictionary, until we understand it.

Whether it takes us one morning or five or six mornings, we do what we need to do to understand what we are reading, without feeling the need to rush on to continue a certain reading pace. One man said it well: "You ought not read for mileage." Thus, we read by subject as well as by sequence.

We have found it important that each family member have a set of scriptures. Our little ones, especially, have taken great pleasure in having their own books with their own names on them, their own marking pencils, and so on. This seems to add to the importance of the scriptures and of scripture reading. Then the little ones are much more prone to say, "Wait, it's my turn to read" or "Can I read another verse?"

In our scripture reading, we always start with a word of prayer. We try to remember to ask the Lord to bless us that our understanding might be quickened as we read the scriptures. We have learned, as I'm sure you have, that we cannot read the scriptures as we do other books. They must be prayed over, and we must humble ourselves if we really want to understand what the Lord is telling us. That thought was surely taught clearly in D&C 32:4, which says: "They shall give heed to that which is written [the scriptures], and pretend to no other revelation; and they shall pray always that I may unfold the same [the meaning of the scriptures] to their understanding" (D&C 32:4).

We have learned over the years that having a prayer is not just something traditional that we *ought* to do. In truth, to the degree we humble ourselves in prayer and ask for understanding, the Lord enriches our reading of the scriptures.

I have found that I need to be up earlier than my family to have my own personal scripture reading. If I've had a spiritual experience with the scriptures before my family joins me, it is much easier to lead scripture reading with the Spirit so that each person can have a spiritual experience.

After we have prayed, we usually call on one person to begin reading, and the person will read one or two verses after the place we last stopped. That person then calls on one of the others, without notice, to explain what was just read.

That keeps all of us awake and alert, and it has been very effective in helping us listen a little better.

After the person has explained the content of the verses, the reader tries to ask at least one question about the text that the whole family can answer. The reason for having children ask a question is to teach them how to read the scriptures, asking questions as they go. I am convinced that the scriptures are largely a book of answers. The problem is that we do not know the original questions. If we will get into the habit of asking questions verse after verse, we will understand much more. I've found that even little children are able to ask good questions. In fact, sometimes they ask questions that really surprise me. Parents should help children and each other to focus their questions on what their family needs to learn that day. We should always be thinking, "What does this mean to me personally?"

In the beginning children tend to ask knowledge questions like "What was Nephi's brother's name?" Later they begin to ask "feeling" questions like "How was it that Nephi had faith to be able to do that" or "Why did Alma believe the words of Abinadi? How could he have had so much faith when all he heard was Abinadi's preaching?" Still later they begin to ask more important questions like "How could we obtain faith like Samuel the Lamanite had?" Asking questions is very important.

The parents may also ask a question or two to direct the children's thinking to the more important parts of what was just read. We have felt no desire to hurry through any particular verse. Many times we have stopped on a verse and related an example from our own lives that illustrates the verse, or we have borne testimony about the verse. Many times we ask questions like, "Who can explain this verse in such a way that it will apply to what we are doing today?" or "How does this verse affect you personally?"

Many times we look up references in the Topical Guide, refer to the footnotes, or use the Bible Dictionary to gain further understanding. If we know a particular verse is important, we usually help the children cross-reference it to some other verse that may help them later when they are studying on their own. With my older children, many of the cross-references they wrote when younger have become more valuable to them over the years. Many times they've wondered how those references got into their books, having forgotten it had occurred during family scripture reading.

When we're concluding our scripture reading, sometimes we ask what the most important thing was that anyone learned that morning. An even better question is, "What is the most important thing any of you have *felt* this morning?" We then give the children a chance to respond, if they desire. Usually one or two do. Sometimes we try to take the most important idea and apply it that day, such as praying more frequently, humbling ourselves more, reaching out to other people more, and so on.

After our scripture reading, we sing a verse of a hymn (many times a Primary hymn), or someone is called on to share a scripture they have memorized. These things have had great impact on the family over the years. Singing, especially, helps quiet the little ones and puts them in a spirit to pray. Every week or two, family members, voluntarily and on their own, learn a new scripture to share with the family. This sets a great environment and allows parents to teach concepts that may not have been covered in scripture reading. Our children four years of age and up have begun learning the Articles of Faith this way.

After the song or scripture, family prayer is offered by the one called upon. Then, after the prayer, my wife and I throw our arms around each of our children, saying, "I love you. Have a good day." This is truly a great way to begin a morning. Many times our discussion of the scriptures carries over to the breakfast table and helps each of us again focus on the Lord as we begin our day.

We have never felt committed to read according to schedule, such as reading one chapter each morning. We have always read just a few verses, seeking for understanding, feeling, and application. I have always felt it was much more important for my children to love Alma, for example, than to know the names of his sons.

President Marion G. Romney illustrated this idea most clearly. Whenever he was not on a Church assignment, he would sleep out on the lawn in a tent with his son, George, on hot summer nights. Part of that experience usually included reading and discussing a chapter in the Book of Mormon. Once when George was sick and confined to the upper bunk of his room, President Romney quietly went in, lay down in the lower bunk, and offered to continue the practice that had come to mean much to both of them. George began reading aloud. While he was reading, he hesitated a bit. Then he asked, "Daddy, do you ever cry when you read these things?"

President Romney was touched, answering that indeed tears did come to his eyes when the Spirit bore witness of the truthfulness of what he was reading. George said, "Tears came to my eyes tonight, too" (See F. Burton Howard, *Marion G. Romney: His Life and Faith* [Salt Lake City: Bookcraft, 1988], p. 154).

Brother Romney understood the real importance of reading the scriptures together.

## OTHER ACTIVITIES FOR SCRIPTURE READING

Sometimes variety is needed during scripture reading, particularly if the family is a little sleepy or slow to respond. In such cases, you might call on one of your children to give a short talk on a certain topic. Give the child a minute or two to look up some scriptures, and that will be the scripture reading. Sometimes you might do some scripture chasing to teach the location of scriptures instead of reading. We have sometimes worked on learning the locations of books within the volumes of scriptures. All these things help add some variety.

All of our eight children have learned to read through

following along in the Book of Mormon during family scripture reading. The memory of doing so will stay with them throughout their lives, influencing them for good.

At times we have found it important not to read the scriptures every single morning. Sometimes we read Monday through Friday. Then, on Saturday, the children sleep in, and we ask one of them to share a spiritual thought or scripture at breakfast. After family prayer on Sundays, we normally hold our devotional, and that becomes our scripture reading.

Sometimes, instead of reading the scriptures, Dad or Mom may share an experience. Perhaps one of the children has had a special experience the night before, and we have him or her tell about it.

After general conference, for a week or two, we will read the conference talks from the *Ensign*. Sometimes we will assign specific talks to the children to report on in scripture reading. This gives us a chance to have a child learn more about a particular topic for which he or she has a need.

Reading the conference talks has been very effective in teaching the importance of relying upon the words of the living prophets. We usually do not read all the talks to the family but only those that best apply to our children. This has helped strengthen our family according to our needs as well as teaching the whole family more about the doctrine of the kingdom.

Another benefit that has come from reading the words of the living prophets has been to give our children some modern-day heroes. Telling the children stories about some of our modern prophets helps the children want to be like them. This practice counteracts the natural tendency of some young people to set up worldly heroes whom they may desire to follow.

Some mornings we have even used the time to plan a vacation or to schedule a particularly difficult day or week. When the children were younger, we marched around the house to some good music. We also occasionally share

important news events. Sometimes we listen to beautiful music or even do fifteen minutes of exercise. We might read an article in the *New Era* or the *Friend*; the Church magazines provide many opportunities to teach gospel principles while providing lighter reading for children. Our children have always delighted in receiving the magazines, especially the *Friend*. Parents can relate some of these articles back to the scriptures.

The most important thing about scripture reading is that it brings the family together for learning, loving, and sharing. If we can center on the Lord, we can make all our days more effective. I have always assumed it was my responsibility as a father to leave my family happy as I leave for work in the morning, thus making it easier for my wife to handle the children through the day.

## THINGS LEARNED THROUGH
## FAMILY SCRIPTURE STUDY

I have surely come to believe what was said by Mosiah: "It were not possible that our father, Lehi, could have remembered all these things, to have taught them to his children, except it were for the help of these plates; for he

having been taught in the language of the Egyptians therefore he could read these engravings, and teach them to his
children, that thereby they could teach them to their children, and so fulfilling the commandments of God, even
down to this present time" (Mosiah 1:4).

Doesn't a parent feel that way? Except for the plates,
except for the scriptures themselves, we would never be
able to remember all the things we should teach our children. However, when we read through the scriptures
systematically, all of the doctrines are treated in a balanced
approach, those with greater importance receiving the most
attention, the Lord himself having prioritized the content.
How thankful I am for these scriptures. Mosiah surely spoke
the truth.

The holy scriptures represent humanity's spiritual memory. When our connection with the scriptures is severed,
we are tragically denied an awareness of the spiritual history
that has come to us from the very beginning, even from the
premortal life. The scriptures truly preserve the great doctrines of the kingdom.

## HOW PRAYERS ARE ANSWERED

I will never forget one experience when we were reading
through the wars in Alma. One of my children said, "We've
read so many chapters. We're not getting much out of the
wars. I wonder why they're in here." We talked a little that
morning about the importance of the Lord having those
chapters in there and that there might come a day when we
would really need to know some of the specifics about war.
We also said there were many jewels buried in those chapters. That very morning we began reading in Alma, chapter
58. For the first time we took notice of these powerful
verses:

> We did *pour out our souls* in prayer to God, that
> he would *strengthen us* and *deliver us* out of the
> hands of our enemies, yea, and also give us
> strength that we might retain our cities, and our

lands, and our possessions, for the support of our people.

Yea, and it came to pass that the Lord our God did *visit us* with *assurances* that he would deliver us; yea, insomuch that he did speak *peace* to our souls, and did grant unto us *great faith*, and did cause us that we should *hope* for our deliverance in him.

And we did *take courage* with our small force which we had received, and were *fixed with a determination to conquer* our enemies, and to maintain our lands, and our possessions, and our wives, and our children, and the cause of our liberty. (Alma 58:10–12; italics added.)

Just as Satan tries to influence us for evil, the Spirit of the Lord influences us to choose what is right. Let us look for a moment at the way the Lord influences those who humble themselves and pray to him. He is able to place feelings and thoughts in their minds to help them.

Verse 10 describes what we desire when we are struggling with a problem: to have the Lord strengthen us and deliver us from evil. And how do we accomplish that? We pour out our souls to God in prayer. Verse 11 probably provides one of the best descriptions of how the Lord responds to us, again through thoughts or feelings. He seems to do these four things:

1. He visits us with *assurances* that he will deliver us.

2. He speaks *peace* to our souls.

3. He grants us great *faith*.

4. He causes us that we should *hope* for our deliverance in him.

What a tremendous way the Lord has of blessing us! He doesn't just solve our problems but he gives us assurance, peace, faith, and hope so that we will move forward to resolve our own problems under the direction of the Lord. Thus he makes us strong.

He helps us grow, and if we pursue the process over the years, we will ultimately become as God is. The effects of the influence of the Spirit are described well in verse 12. After we have been filled with assurance, peace, faith, and hope, we are then willing to *take courage* and have a *fixed determination* to conquer our enemies, our problems, our sins. Where does that courage and determination come from? From the Spirit of the Lord. The Lord actually provides additional power and strength because we have humbled ourselves and sought God.

Every time I read those verses or teach them to others, I think about where I learned them—during family scripture reading.

Two or three years after that experience, one of my sons was having a difficult time understanding an answer to prayer and was asking me about it. I opened up Alma 58, read those verses to him, and explained them. It was like a light turned on in his mind. He was so excited about these verses because they perfectly described his feelings and told him more clearly how the Lord answered prayers. Then we bore our testimonies to each other, and he said, "Dad, I'm surprised. Why haven't you ever shared that with me before?"

I just smiled and told him I had learned it *with him* three years before. It seemed that maybe just one of us had learned it, and we had a good laugh about that. A particular passage may not mean much to any of us unless we have a specific problem or need and then find the answer. That was a case where *he read the answer with the family but really didn't understand the question.* He had no personal need to know the answer.

It's difficult to be in tune with the Spirit day after day. Not all of our scripture readings are full of the Spirit, nor do we have great experiences every morning. Some mornings things are quite routine, but our scripture reading is *consistent*, and we have a good spirit together. When we find ourselves struggling and not having the Spirit, we have suggested to our family that we recount the mercies and blessings of the Lord to us. By so doing, many times we get the

Spirit back. The effect of that is recognizing the hand of the Lord.

We ought not to forget the seven principles discussed in chapter 2 about inviting the Spirit of the Lord. If things are a little slow in your scripture reading, consider singing, having another prayer, bearing testimony, expressing love to one another, or sharing a spiritual experience. All of these things will bring the Spirit of the Lord back into your meeting so you will not have such a routine scripture reading.

## INFLUENCING OTHERS THROUGH THE SCRIPTURES

A number of times when we have had serious sickness in our family, we have found great strength in reading the scriptures on such topics as faith, healings, priesthood blessings, and so on. I know of nothing greater that has helped us obtain healings and blessings in our family than reading the words of the Lord.

Whenever we doubted whether we could obtain such a blessing or healing, we just read and re-read the accounts of healings in the modern-day scriptures as well as in the New Testament. The words of the Lord fortified us to believe that anything is possible to "him that believeth." The scriptures have had as great an impact on our family in instilling faith and confidence in the Lord as any other thing of which I'm aware.

Joseph Smith's family seemed to understand that principle as well. The *History of the Church* records:

> Notwithstanding the corruptions and abominations of the times, and the evil spirit manifested towards us on account of our belief in the Book of Mormon, at many places and among various persons, yet the Lord continued His watchful care and loving kindness to us day by day; and we made it a rule wherever there was an opportunity, to read a chapter in the Bible, and pray; and these seasons of worship gave us great consolation (1:188–89).

Clearly Joseph Smith did not read James 1:5 by accident. He had been taught by his family to read the scriptures faithfully and to obtain answers therefrom. Had his family not taught him about the importance of the word of the Lord in the Bible, perhaps he would not have read the words nor believed them nor had the experience of the First Vision. What a great lesson that is to us from the parents of the Prophet Joseph Smith! They tutored their son to have faith in the words of the Lord. As a result, he had one of the greatest visions ever given and eventually brought *more scripture* to the world than any other prophet who has ever lived.

Sometimes when we've been upset with one of our children at night, they haven't wanted to come to scripture reading the next morning. I remember one such occasion when one of our sons didn't get up for scripture reading. I was tempted to really get after him for not coming, but fortunately I felt that would make him have negative feelings about me and about scripture reading. I think he was depressed about the negative experience he had had with his parents the night before when he had to sit in his room for half an hour for speaking harshly.

I knew he was discouraged, so before I went to work I called to him in his bedroom, "Son, what do you say we pray together. Do you remember the day I was having such a hard day and you prayed for me five times during the day?"

He said he did.

I said, "Well, I'm going to do that for you today. I'm going to pray my hardest that you'll have an excellent day. Why don't we start off with you praying right now, and then I'll pray." This approach totally softened his heart and changed his feelings about the day. The fact that he knew I was going to pray for him meant a lot to him.

I did pray for him six or seven times during the day. When I got home from work, the first thing I asked was, "Son, how did your day go?"

He answered, "Just great. It's been one of the best days I've had."

Not only in school was it great, but when he came home he wanted to clean and work for his mother. Everything was in good order. It gave me a chance to teach again the idea that the Lord really will help us if we will pray to him. I was not surprised to see him up and ready to go the next morning for scripture reading without our having to say anything to him.

Be careful when your children are resisting spiritual things, such as coming to scripture reading or prayer, that you don't bring in the Church or the gospel. If parents say something like, "You are going to offend the Lord" or "The Church teaches this or teaches that," it may influence the children to reject the Church or the gospel just to win the argument. They don't really intend to, but the parents set it up so that is their children's only choice, and thus they will.

At times one of our children will say, "I'm not going to church" or "I don't know if I believe that or not." Instead of trying to argue or defend the Church, we have often said, "Well, you will have to seek the Spirit of the Lord to determine what is really right. We are not going to argue about the Church or about going to meetings. That has nothing to do with it. That's between you and the Lord. We are talking about some things that are right. If you turn your heart to the Lord and have a prayer about it, you will know for yourself." In other words, don't allow the subject of the Church into an argument between you and your children. If you do, you may lose, your child may lose, and certainly the Church will lose.

Some parents wonder if it is more important to go to school and other activities with their children than to read the scriptures together. Of course, both are important, but there is no question about priorities. Some parents might be very good at camping and fishing and do nothing with the scriptures. But I believe that many mistakes we make in raising our families can be softened if the children have been involved in the scriptures. If you have to choose between reading the Book of Mormon with your family or doing other activities, remember that all the Scout outings, fishing excursions, athletic events, and so on will not even come close to what can be gained from the scriptures. While much can be learned from various activities, studying the word of the Lord has eternal consequences.

## THE SCRIPTURES BRING PEACE AND REMOVE EVIL

The scriptures can comfort us, give us peace, and even remove evil from us if we humbly read them. One friend of mine told me of an experience he had after an exhausting day of work away from home. In his hotel room, he flipped on the television. This is the story he told:

> For a while I watched a good show about the history of Will Rogers and what a great humorist he was. Afterward, an interesting movie came on. Unfortunately, part way through the movie a very bad scene came on. I should probably have turned it off but, feeling that I really needed to relax, I kept watching it. Then some other bad scenes came on. The movie had an excellent plot, but unfortunately these evil parts were in it.
>
> After I turned the television off, I had my prayers and tried to go to sleep, but I lay there with my eyes wide open. Every time I closed my eyes, the evil thoughts of the movie came in. The power of Satan became very real to me, and I could not go to sleep. Again I closed my eyes and tried to sleep, praying that this evil spirit would leave me, but all that came into my mind were scenes from the movie. I repented of not having turned it off earlier. It became evident to me that the spirit of the devil had entered into my heart the moment I gave in to the temptation of watching the show. I struggled for over an hour praying and trying to get back the Spirit of the Lord. I could not do it. In fact, the evil feeling seemed to increase.
>
> Finally, while praying, I felt I should read in the scriptures. Before opening the Book of Mormon, I prayed that it would open to a place that would teach me and give me relief. I opened the book to

Alma 40:13: "The spirits of the wicked, yea, who are evil—for behold, they have no part nor portion of the Spirit of the Lord; for behold, they chose evil works rather than good; therefore the spirit of the devil did enter into them, and take possession of their house—and these shall be cast out into outer darkness; there shall be weeping, and wailing, and gnashing of teeth, and this because of their own iniquity, being led captive by the will of the devil."

I was so impressed with this verse, which described what had happened to me. I began to feel better, and as I read the rest of that chapter and part of the next, the Spirit of the Lord returned. I felt the evil spirit leave. I closed my eyes and fell asleep.

How thankful I am to the Lord for his great power that is capable of overcoming that of Satan. How true the words the Lord taught: "It came to pass that the devil tempted Adam, and he partook of the forbidden fruit and transgressed the commandment, wherein he became *subject to the will of the devil, because he yielded unto temptation*" (D&C 29:40; italics added).

My friend learned a great lesson that night about the power of the scriptures over the devil. (It was similar to the experience of Christ quoting the scriptures in the three great temptations placed before him at the beginning of his ministry.) He also learned that he became subject to the will of the devil only because he yielded to temptation.

## THE SCRIPTURES AND GOOD HEALTH

When one of my sons was thirteen, I had fractured three of my ribs and was suffering somewhat from that. We had read one morning in scripture reading about the effect of praying for one another:

Is any sick among you? let him call for the elders of the church; and let them pray over him, anointing him with oil in the name of the Lord: and the prayer of faith shall save the sick, and the

Lord shall raise him up; and if he have committed
sins, they shall be forgiven him. Confess your
faults one to another, and pray one for another,
that ye may be healed. The effectual fervent prayer
of a righteous man availeth much (James 5:14–16).

We talked about how prayer can reach across time and
distance. That afternoon as I arrived home, this son said to
me, "Dad, I prayed for you about five different times at
school and at lunch that you would have a better day. You've
had such hard days lately. I prayed really hard that you
would get all your work done and that things would go better for you. I also prayed that your ribs would feel better." I
was quite moved by that, as it really had been the best day
I'd had for some time, and my ribs were feeling much better.

I think the faith of a child or a young man or woman
has great power. That son, particularly, seems to have a lot
of faith, and he is willing and happy to believe and to cause
things to happen.

As a result of scripture reading, my son was reminded of
the importance of prayer and saw it work with his dad.
That's how children learn the truth of the gospel. Little by
little their lamps are filled with faith through fasting, repentance, and prayer. In the process, their testimony becomes
unshakable.

Another time we were reading in Alma about the Lord's
having provided plants and roots as medicines: "There were
some who died with fevers, which at some seasons of the
year were very frequent in the land—but not so much so
with fevers, because of the excellent qualities of the many
plants and roots which God had prepared to remove the
cause of diseases, to which men were subject by the nature
of the climate" (Alma 46:40).

We were led in the scriptures to the Word of Wisdom,
and we discussed the importance of having our bodies function well physically as a result of what we eat.

Over a number of mornings, we discussed ways to
restructure our eating habits to focus more fully on plants,

grains, and fruits and to include meat sparingly only in times of winter or cold. As the years have gone by, we have truly counted our blessings as a result of our good health from living these principles taught in the scriptures.

Once again, this great blessing came not only from reading the scriptures but from the confirmation of the Spirit of the Lord that that was the thing to do. After a period of time of living this way and having readjusted our eating habits, the real evidence of the truthfulness of the words of the Lord was found in the great health that our family has had since that time. We thank the Lord for the revelations he has given. They are true, and they will make us happier and draw us closer to the Lord.

### THE SCRIPTURES AND THE LOST CABLES

Upon moving from Mexico City at the completion of a Church assignment, we made ample preparation to safely transport the two personal computers we were bringing, with disc drives, printers, and so on. We planned to hand carry most of the delicate equipment. We did put a few cables in our big suitcases, but most of it was in our carry-on luggage.

Back in the States, when we tried to set up our computers so we could print out our diaries, we realized that we were missing three computer cables, so we were unable to print anything. Over several days we did our best to search and pray for the return of those cables. We knew we could buy some more, but we hated to spend the money because we felt certain they were somewhere in the house.

We speculated that one of the children had put the cables in an unlikely place, and we hoped they had not been placed in an empty box and thrown in the garbage. As the days passed, all the boxes were finally emptied, but we found no cables. We searched again and again. Finally we borrowed some cables so we could print the things we needed.

After nearly two weeks, I felt impressed as I was reading the Book of Mormon to tell the family that we should search

to make sure we had done all in our power. We should have
a family prayer and then check in every corner, as I felt confident we would find the cables. As I read the scriptures,
the impression came to me to look again. *Reading the scriptures is one of the best ways to hear the voice and direction
of the Lord.* I went to work early that day, so my wife and
children prayed together. Most of them prayed throughout
the day while they searched, but they found no cables. They
searched in every cabinet, behind every curtain, in every
drawer—in the bedrooms, the kitchen, the family room, and
the garage. When they finished, there were still no cables.
When I came home from work that night, I felt quite disappointed, because I had felt certain they would find them.
The family was disappointed as well.

The next morning, doubts filled my mind: "The family
searched the whole house. The cables are lost in the hotel,
and you'll never get them." "You left them in Mexico. You
can't possibly find them. You've searched every piece of furniture, every closet, every room, and they are not to be
found."

To me, situations like this one where what is needed
seems impossible are always a great sign that they *are* possible. The Lord seems to work best in those things that are
impossible for us.

But my dominant thought that morning was, "Your family has prayed, they have believed they would find those
cables, and they have not. As a result, will they not lose
some of their faith?" This concerned me, since developing
faith in my family has always been one of my greatest
desires.

The thought came to me strongly, "Why do you want to
find the cables? Are you looking for a sign to prove to the
family, 'See, here are the lost cables; the Lord has done it
again'?" There seems to be a very fine line between obtaining answers to prayers like that and seeking for a sign.

As I recognized that, I tried to humble myself more and
intently prayed that the Lord would return the cables. I also

believed they would be found, in spite of the fact that this now seemed impossible, since my family had searched every single place. The previous night, I had even searched some more myself, asking, "Did you look here? Did you look there?" They had truly searched every single place.

After I had prayed intently and before continuing with my list of things to do that day, a peaceful feeling descended upon me, a feeling of confidence that the cables would still be found. When that feeling came, I prayed that the Lord would show me in my mind where the cables were so I could go find them. I did feel they might be in the garage or in a certain place in the house, but the Lord did not answer my prayer in that manner.

When I returned from work that day, I went downstairs into the boys' room to find the newspaper. While there, I noticed a suitcase that was on the bed, ready to be put up in the attic. We had already put up the other thirteen suitcases.

I opened the suitcase. It felt a little heavier than usual, but it was empty. Then I realized there was a zipper along its side. I opened the zipper, and sure enough, there were the three cables. I was overjoyed, and I immediately went up and told my wife.

The whole family had searched the suitcase, but apparently no one had thought to unzip the side because it was level and straight, and it was hard to see that anything was in there. If someone had spent thirty seconds to carry the suitcase to the attic, the cables would have not been found—at least not for many months to come.

Why were the cables not found when the family searched so thoroughly? Perhaps the reason is that the Lord really does, because of love, test us over and over again. Many times the answers to our prayers are delayed or brought about in unusual ways to see if we will still believe. After the test of not finding them, the real test was, "Do you still believe?" If we could pass that test, then we would receive an answer from the Lord.

I feel that the pertinent point in this experience was

when I determined I still believed in spite of what seemed to be the impossibility of finding the cables.

Some have asked, do you mean to say the Lord actually tests people in that way?" My answer is, "Yes, he does. Did he not know that he would never require the sacrifice of Isaac by Abraham? Yet he tested Abraham through all of that *to the very last moment* to see if Abraham would still believe. Before the Lord answered Abraham and Sarah's prayer for a son, years passed by. The Lord seems to have been saying, "Abraham and Sarah, do you still believe in the promise that you will have a child?" The testing in life is real. The Lord will test us over and over again to the ultimate degree to be sure that our unbelief is removed.

Why were the cables found? Perhaps for several reasons:

1. The family united in prayer. There was desire, hope, and faith that the cables could be found.
2. The family did all in their power to find the lost cables.
3. Ultimately, I had to humble myself even more, *submitting to the will of the Lord* in whether the cables would be found or not and removing any feeling of wanting a sign for the children. I had to believe against any hope that they could be found.

Through such experiences, the words of Isaiah take on greater meaning: "My thoughts are not your thoughts, neither are your ways my ways, saith the Lord" (Isaiah 55:8).

The Lord will surely choose how he will answer prayer. Our challenge is to find out how to present an adequate offering in faith, humility, and prayer so that the Lord can respond.

I find it interesting that reading in the scriptures is what really brought about this great experience. It was the "cause" that finally brought the result. We all learned much from this experience.

## THE IMPACT OF SCRIPTURE
## READING ON A FAMILY

A family that is close to me struggled for many years to get started in reading the scriptures. In fact, some of their boys were already raised when they finally decided they would begin trying to read the scriptures with their last two children. What follows is their account:

*Mother*: "Arriving home from general conference, my husband and I talked about how we could start, once again, to have regular family scripture study.

"After being in conference and receiving encouraging words from our BYU son and some extended family, our consciences had been pricked or rather pierced. We knew we needed to repent. This was very important to me, and I felt a great urgency to have this take place.

"We decided to present this idea to our two daughters, one Primary age and one teenager, at our next family home evening. I was worried about how the girls would accept it. One wasn't too fond of scripture reading, and both hated to get up early. We fasted and prayed and tried to invite the Spirit to witness that what we were saying was true. We also used scriptures and quotations from President Benson's conference talk.

"Well, it went beautifully. We expressed our love to the girls and to our Father in Heaven and the Savior. We said we needed to repent of not having had more spirituality and scripture study in our home. The Spirit was there and touched their hearts and ours as we bore testimony to the truthfulness of what we had said. The girls agreed, and we are now having scripture study early each weekday morning. I also want to tell you that we have had a wonderful spirit of peace and love come into our home that wasn't there before. I can see it is solving many of our problems without addressing the problems individually. The children are more patient and loving, and I also find myself being more considerate. More important, testimonies are growing, and there is a greater desire and effort to live the gospel.

"We are reading slowly and discussing each verse and how we can apply it to our lives. That is an important key. We are also trying hard to have the Spirit with us, as we realize that without the Spirit's bearing witness, real learning and doing do not take place."

*Daughter, age twelve*: "The night Mom and Dad gave us the lesson on their strong feelings that we should start family scripture study, I knew immediately they were right. My eyes were watering, and I felt all warm inside. The Spirit came so strong to me that night. I was afraid if I heard one more word about it, I would burst into tears. I don't know why except that my mom's words really touched my heart. Everything went smoothly that first morning. We decided on 6:00 A.M. Each morning I have a hard time getting up. I like reading in the scriptures. I just hate getting up in the morning. Although it's not easy, I go with the best attitude I have because I know it will save our family from the outside world, and I know it's right."

*Daughter, age fifteen*: "For family home evening my mom and dad fasted and prayed for the Spirit. They told us that they wanted to repent for lacking the spirituality in our home and family. They said they wanted to start having scripture study. So we planned to start the next week. It was hard getting up that early but I got used to it. We read a little and discussed it. I felt really good that whole day. Everything went really well. I didn't think I'd be ready on time for school because it took up part of my getting-ready time. But I was, and even a little early. I was in a happy mood the whole day. I went home from school that day feeling really good about this neat thing we started. And now I'm really grateful for it. It makes each day better."

*Father*: "I certainly agree with what my wife and daughters have written. Several weeks have now passed. It hasn't been a "flash in the pan" attempt and failure because the successes have continued. We have never missed holding our scripture reading. One daughter has missed two days in that time, one daughter missed one day, and the parents are full attenders.

"We do not force anyone to attend, although strong encouragement is given, such as turning on lights and giving "good morning" greetings. We sing a hymn promptly at 6:00 A.M. Some straggle in during or at the close of the hymn but always in time for a short beginning prayer.

"An important part of our success is that we are studying and experiencing the scriptures together, not just reading the Book of Mormon. We are not trying to complete the reading of the book. Rather, we are trying to have more family togetherness. We try to relate our family to Nephi's family: pride, murmuring, family contention, the importance of records (journals and genealogies), having a goodly family, and so on have all furnished interesting discussion topics. We have also drawn pictures of Lehi's vision of the tree of life and talked about its various elements, and we have discussed Nephi's revelation in relation to American history.

"We try to do more than just understand what the verses mean or how they should be interpreted or how to use the footnotes and cross-references. More important, we try to understand how it all *relates to us*. Have we had similar experiences to those in the scriptures? Have we thought as those people thought? Have we recognized the Lord's hand in our lives? Are we holding to the rod of iron? What do we observe at school and work in the lives of others as well as ourselves that relates to what we are reading? Are we pursuing the course of Lehi's older sons or younger sons? Are we really praying and living in the way the scriptures direct us? I believe these are the things that keep us on track.

"We always close with a family prayer, a hug, and kiss. We never go over twenty minutes. It doesn't matter whether we read one verse or one chapter. We sit at the breakfast table and use felt markers and scratch paper freely. The most important thing is spending this time together, sharing, and having Heavenly Father and his words with us.

"So far we feel successful and optimistic. We know that

each day and week will offer more challenges, but we feel that we will be up to them because we are united, and all of us are now in tune with the good things taking place in our lives and family relationships. As our sons return from mission and college, they will fit in and add more because they have constantly challenged us to hold our daily scripture reading and are extremely happy that we are doing so. Our married son and family are also eager to hear of our experiences. What a tremendous influence the scriptures are working on us!"

After four years, this family is faithfully going forward with their daily scripture reading. No matter your experience or your situation, it is never too late to begin reading the scriptures with your family.

## THE IMPACT OF SCRIPTURE READING ON A CHILD

Let me conclude this chapter with one last story that reflects the impact of scripture reading over a period of years.

Our son, nine years old, was asked to give a talk in Primary. His mother had helped him prepare it, and he had practiced it with me two or three times. Instead of his mother choosing the topic, she asked him to do so—to ponder and think of a story or one of the scriptures he loved the most, or something else he might want to tell. He finally settled on the story of David and Goliath.

In his talk he spoke of the faith of David and how he went to face Goliath. I was very touched by the Spirit as he read from 1 Samuel 17:46–47:

> This day will the Lord deliver thee into mine hand; and I will smite thee, and take thine head from thee; and I will give the carcases of the host of the Philistines this day unto the fowls of the air, and to the wild beasts of the earth; that all the earth may know that there is a God in Israel.
> And all this assembly shall know that the Lord saveth not with sword and spear: for the battle is

the Lord's, and he will give you into our hands (1 Samuel 17:46–47).

He bore his testimony of those verses and then told a story of his own faith in fasting and studying for a test on which he got an "A." The talk was about four minutes long. I could tell when he gave it to me that there was a lot of spirit in it and that it was from the heart. He was very moved by it because it was truly *his own talk*.

The day after his talk in church, my wife received a call from a sister in our ward who rather emotionally told her that she was overwhelmed by this young son's talk. She had sat through his talk weeping. In fact, my daughter, who heard part of the conversation on the phone, afterward said, "I know who it was that cried through his talk because I saw her crying." This was truly an indication that she was just totally taken aback by the spirit in which the boy had given his talk. It wasn't so much the content as the spirit in which it was conveyed. Somehow he had actually invited the Spirit of the Lord into the meeting.

"You could tell he really had a testimony of the scriptures by the way he read those verses," this sister said. "He read the passages with the Spirit of the Lord. When I saw that your son had such a sweet feeling and testimony about the scriptures, I had a great desire settle over me that that was what I wanted for my children. I talked over all these feelings with my husband and described the spirit I had felt. We want you to know, Sister Cook, that we had our first family scripture reading this morning."

She continued, "I just want you to know that your boy has affected our family tremendously. He has a special spirit. He is a very spiritual boy, and because he was touched by the Spirit so much, it touched us and has ended up blessing our whole family. We just want to thank you for having such a good son."

Yes, even a nine-year-old can speak with the Spirit of the Lord. What a great tribute to this boy that through the

Spirit he was able to influence this entire family to have scripture reading. I think there is no question that the power of example, as he showed in reading the scriptures, is what truly conveys the Spirit to others. By true testimony and spirit and by our acts as Latter-day Saints we will truly be known.

No wonder Jesus did so much service by example. It conveyed, it taught, it made an indelible impression on the minds of those around him. We can do likewise. Even a child can do it.

Scripture reading truly has great impact. If we have not been as faithful in holding scripture reading as we ought to, this is a good time to change our habits and to begin holding it as a family tradition. The Lord has said:

> I have commanded you to bring up your children in light and truth. . . .
> You have not taught your children light and truth, according to the commandments; and that wicked one hath power, as yet, over you, and this is the cause of your affliction.
> And now a commandment I give unto you—if you will be delivered you shall set in order your own house, for there are many things that are not right in your house (D&C 93:40, 42, 43).

Clearly, the Lord expects us to bring up our children in light and truth. One of the best ways is by teaching them through the scriptures. May the Lord bless us to faithfully read the scriptures as individuals and as families. We will then be able to hold to the iron rod and ultimately be guided back to our heavenly home.

CHAPTER FIVE

# TEACHING YOUR FAMILY TO LIVE
# BY THE POWER OF FAITH

At the turn of the century in Southern Utah there came a great drought. In the ward in a small town, the people had gathered together, and the bishop told them if rain did not come within the week, all of their crops would die. He asked the members to pray fervently that the Lord would send rain, and on a given day, after having fasted, they would gather at the church to offer a final prayer to break their fast.

After fasting, one family was leaving for the prayer at the church when their five-year-old daughter said, "Dad, I forgot something." She went back into the house and came out with something in a bag. Off they went to church. When the people had all arrived, they gathered in the courtyard behind the chapel to ask the Lord for help. The entire ward knelt and began to pray fervently, the bishop being voice, that the Lord would send rain upon their crops.

Before the final amen had been uttered, the drops began to come, first a few, then buckets full. The people ran to the chapel for shelter, except for the bishop and the little girl, who, reaching into her sack, said, "Bishop, would you like to share my umbrella?"

In this true story, what faith this little girl exercised—the faith of a child to know that if she would but pray, and all the ward members as well, the Lord would answer. And he did so. Who knows but what it was her faith, in good measure, that brought the rain?

How true are the words of Alma when he said, "Faith is not to have a perfect knowledge of things; therefore if ye have faith ye hope for things which are not seen, which are true" (Alma 32:21).

Alma also said, "If ye will not nourish the word, looking

145

forward with an eye of faith to the fruit thereof, ye can never pluck of the fruit of the tree of life" (Alma 32:40).

It is true that if we will look forward with faith to the fruit, having hope in the Lord in something not seen but true, according to our faith it will be done unto us.

Without question, we are here on earth leading our families in faith. President David O. McKay said it clearly:

> The most effective way to teach religion in the home is not by preaching but by living. If you would teach faith in God, show faith in him yourself; if you would teach prayer, pray yourself. Would you have them temperate? Then you yourself refrain from intemperance. If you would have your child live a life of virtue, of self-control, of good report, then set him a worthy example in all these things. A child brought up under such home environment will be fortified for the doubts, questions, and yearnings that will stir in his soul when the real period of religious awakening comes at twelve or fourteen years of age (*Conference Report*, April 1955, p. 27).

Truly, we must not only teach our family the principles, but we must also teach them to *live* the principles. So many of life's experiences, if handled correctly, can be turned into spiritual experiences. There is no question that the Lord has set things up so that, if we would, we could live better by faith than some of us now do. The Lord has not left us without instruction. Surely he might say to all of us: "Hearken all ye families of the earth—immediate and extended families—yea, every living soul, and the Lord will teach you of the sacredness of that heavenly organization called family, called home."

## LARGE FAMILIES

There are some in the world who make fun of large families and family life. Yet if we will live the principles of truth, we will fare well and in the process be able to teach others of the importance of families. I will never forget an experience we had while in a city in northern Arizona.

We had gone to one of those family restaurants that are not too expensive. With the size of our family, that was all we could afford. It was cafeteria style, and the family started through the line—all ten of us. I was the last one through. Just two people were managing the restaurant—the cashier, who was about eighteen years old, and the owner, who was about sixty. The cashier kept watching the children go by: one, two, three, four, five . . . She kept looking to see if there were more. By the time I finally got to her, I could see that she was really unsettled but was not brave enough to say anything. I paid the bill, and we sat down to eat just ten feet or so from where they were.

Then she and the manager began whispering. I knew they were talking about us. Not many people were in the restaurant, so I finally said, "May I help you?" They were a little embarrassed, but the manager finally asked, "Are all those children yours?" I paused a minute and then said, "Well, these are just the ones I brought with me today!" We all laughed. However, one of my older teenage boys said with some embarrassment, "Dad! Quit clowning around!" The owner even asked us if he could take our picture to promote his restaurant. We declined.

Families can really be fun—even in embarrassing moments and in trying times. However, there always seem to be times when we can teach true principles.

## THE LORD IS THE LEADER

One of the most important principles President Spencer W. Kimball taught me was to be more reliant on the Lord as the true leader. Even though President Kimball was the Lord's prophet, he would always, in his humble way, stay away from "center stage," seeking always to put the Master there. One of the most important things about leadership is to magnify the Lord in the eyes of the people. If we will lead that way, the Lord will give us power to lead. In my mind, the greatest thing leaders can do is turn the people over whom they preside to the Lord. Leadership, in the Lord's view, is the saving of souls. If a leader can turn a person to the Lord, the leader may have given the greatest gift possible. That is also true in families.

I will never forget a time when the presiding brethren approved the calling of a temple president. As I remember, President Kimball called this good man on the phone to inform him that the Lord had called him to be a temple president. The man was totally overcome. President Kimball told him he would arrive in his city on a certain day and that if the man would meet him in the temple, he would be pleased to set him apart as the temple president.

Some days later, President Kimball arrived at the temple. He bore testimony that the Lord had called the man, and he set him apart as the temple president. After he had finished, he told the new temple president that he loved him and that the Lord would bless him. Then he began walking toward the door. The man panicked and said, "Wait, President Kimball, what instruction do you have for me?"

President Kimball said, "Well, the Lord will bless you. You will do just fine," and began walking down the hall.

The man, now with great urgency, came trailing after the prophet, begging him, "President, what do I know about the temple? What if I have a problem with the cafeteria or the sprinkler system or with some of the temple workers?"

President Kimball said, "Well, if you have any problems like that, feel free to call the Temple Department."

This man now realized that President Kimball really was going to leave. In the parking lot as the prophet was stepping into his car, the man pleaded, "President, please, I don't know what I ought to do."

President Kimball said, "The Lord has called you and the Lord will assist you. Seek him and you will know what to do."

Not satisfied, the man continued, "Don't you have any specific counsel for me?"

Finally President Kimball said, "All right. If you want some specific counsel, I will give you some. It wouldn't hurt you to lose about thirty-five pounds. May the Lord bless you, president." Then he got into his car and drove off.

This new temple president was just flabbergasted. He went back into the temple struggling with his feelings and wondering why President Kimball had handled the situation that way. The man had no alternative but to do what he should have done in the beginning—fall on his knees and plead with the Lord for help. This good man, this humble man, did exactly that and became a most effective, loving, and spiritual temple president.

Could President Kimball not have given him much instruction about temple work? Surely he could have. Could he not have taught him much about leadership? Yes. But can you see that what President Kimball really did was turn this man to the Lord? If we can teach our families in that same manner to rely upon the Lord, who knows what blessings may come into their lives? Then they will know to whom they must look for the resolution of their problems.

When I was called as president of the Uruguay/Paraguay Mission, I might have done some things differently if I had known about that experience with President Kimball. But I didn't. I just knew I was to report to President Kimball's office to be set apart.

On the appointed day, I went with my wife and two of my young sons to the Church offices. After President Kimball had set me apart, I was anxious to receive any training he might want to give me, so I said, "President Kimball, you know I'm going among the Lamanites. You've spent much of your life among them. Do you have any counsel for me, any suggestions you would like to give me before I go?"

He said, "Well, I'd just suggest that you stay close to the Spirit of the Lord, and he will tell you what to do. "

I was a little disappointed that there wasn't anything else, so I pursued it further, saying, "President, I'd sure be pleased to have you teach us or give us some additional instruction."

Finally he said, "Gene, do you hold the Melchizedek Priesthood?" (I knew then I was in trouble.)

I said, "Yes."

He said, "Haven't you been set apart as a General Authority?"

I said, "Yes."

Then he said, "Adios."

I had the feeling he was saying, "Don't call us; we'll call you when it's time to return."

I testify that the effect President Kimball had on me as a new mission president was the same as the effect he'd had on the new temple president. What a powerful example of leadership training! "Rely on the Lord!" is what President Kimball was saying. He didn't want to get in the way between me and the Lord in terms of the training the Lord would give me. He didn't feel obligated to give me his best counsel or anything like it. He could have kept me there for days, teaching me about missionary work. Who among the Brethren knew more about it? No one. He was not diminishing the importance of our teaching one another in mission presidents' seminars and so on; he was just directing our attention to our first priority. He was a real example of a leader teaching people to rely on the Lord.

I had no alternative but to do what I knew I should have done—to humbly seek the Lord to find out how to be a mission president. I don't know of any principle President Kimball could have taught me that would have been more important. That single act of leadership helped me start my mission the right way, with more power and reliance on the Lord than would have ever been the case otherwise.

What President Kimball was teaching us was that we must learn to live by faith, to depend upon the Lord. We must remember that our children were Heavenly Father's children before they were ours, and that if we will faithfully turn to him, he will teach us how to lead them in righteousness.

If parents begin to teach as if they are the teacher instead of the instrument in the Lord's hands, things will not work as well. The Lord is the true teacher and we are here to assist him, not the other way around. How the Lord will work with us if we are faithful!

It is important to recognize that the responsibility for each family member rests:

- first, with the person;
- second, with the family;
- and third, with the Church.

If we will take the responsibility to learn for ourselves what our responsibilities are, we will learn much more quickly from the Lord. And we will be taught much *more* by the Lord. Let us as parents be sure we follow this counsel from President Spencer W. Kimball: "The gospel gives purpose to our lives. It is the way to happiness. Our success, individually and as a church, will largely be determined by how faithfully we focus on living the gospel in the home" (*Conference Report,* April 1979, p. 115). Let us follow his advice, teaching through precept and example.

## FAITH TO FIND A HOME

While we were living in Ecuador, we had a terrible problem with rats in our home. The first day we saw one, we realized what we were up against: they were nearly a foot long—not including the tail! They had a habit of chewing on the cantaloupes and bread in the pantry. They would even terrify us by coming up through the commode. We tried poisoning the rats. We tried catching them with traps. But nothing seemed to work. Soon we began looking for a different place to live, but we had about as much success in finding one as we had in getting rid of the rats.

Weeks went by, then months. My wife searched for a home nearly every day, although it was becoming most disheartening for her. House after house fell through. A number of houses were for sale, but because of our assignment, we could only rent. Finally we located a house and made an offer to rent, but it was sold out from under us. After general conference and a trip I had been on, I arrived home late one evening to find my wife in tears. She had gathered the family together for family home evening, and a big rat had come in and sat down to listen. "That's enough!" she had said to the children, and she chased him into the kitchen, bolted the doors, and for forty-five minutes fought the rat with a broom until she finally killed him. All the children were looking through the window and yelling, "Get him, Mom! Get him, Mom!" It was a real fight to the death.

After my wife finished the story, I sympathized with her and said we would do our best to solve the problem. As it was late, we decided to go to bed and talk more about it in the morning. I had just gotten to sleep when she awakened me to say, "There's a rat in our room."

I said, "No, honey, you're just imagining it. A rat wouldn't be in here."

Then we heard rustling in the paper in the waste basket. She jumped up and turned on the light, and, sure enough, there was a big rat right at the foot of our bed. She slammed the door so he couldn't get away, and I said, "You have experience in these matters, you get him." We both laughed. She got the broom and ended up killing that rat in our bedroom.

After that episode, we knelt down and fervently prayed to the Lord for help. We told him we had searched three months for a home, that my wife had looked almost daily, but that we had not been able to find anything for our family. In fervent prayer, which I realized later was truly a prayer of faith as described in the scriptures, we pled with the Lord for help.

The next morning we awakened the children early and told them of our experience. We then told them that as a family we would all have to pray fervently, and if we would, we were confident the Lord could provide us a house immediately, even that very day. After praying together, we got into the car and drove out to a nicer part of the city where we wanted to live.

We knew it might be difficult to find a home because owners of rentals avoided putting signs in the window; if they put up a sign, thieves would know the house was unoccupied. We asked a few people in the street if they knew of any homes to rent, but they all said no.

About half an hour after leaving home, we stopped in front of a house where a woman was standing out on the curb. We asked if she knew of any home for rent. She answered, "Well, no I don't. But frankly, we have been thinking of renting out this very home, although we have not posted it with a realtor or done anything about it. It is my son's home. He's having some financial problems and might be willing to rent it."

We looked at the home from the outside and thought it would never meet our needs. Nevertheless, she began to describe the interior, and we finally agreed to go in and take a look. The home was the best we had seen in three months. The rent was very reasonable, and, to our surprise, she said, "I think we could move within the week if you really want the home."

We told the woman we were very interested and would be back in touch. After a few hours, we decided to rent that home, and within twenty-four hours we had made an agreement with the couple to do so. We moved in about a week later. We were very impressed that in that one morning, in about forty-five minutes, the Lord had directed us to our new home.

My wife was a little disturbed to think that we might have gotten the house sooner if we had relied more on the power of the Lord and less on our own efforts. There seems to be a limit to what we have to endure before God will act. It is something like the principle that those who have faith to be healed can be healed; if not, we are to bear with them in their afflictions (see D&C 42:43–52). In other words, a better way exists if we have sufficient faith. Otherwise, the Lord will let us bear it on our own for a while. That is not to say that our family had not prayed about the house, but we had not done so as sincerely and strongly as the impression came to us that morning to do it, in a real prayer of faith.

It is amazing to me how the Lord, in a few hours, could solve a problem with which we had struggled for many months. It is a testimony to me that the Lord is willing to help us with any of our problems—spiritual or temporal. But the greatest blessing that comes from answers to prayer is an increase in faith, an actual spiritual blessing that the Lord gives us. No wonder the Lord said: "If ye then, being evil, know how to give good gifts unto your children, how much more shall your Father who is in heaven give good things to them that ask him?" (3 Nephi 14:11).

It's beautiful to see that greater gifts, many times, are given beyond what we are seeking while praying for a temporal blessing as we were on that occasion.

What has always impressed me in these experiences with faith is the impact they have on children. As children see, time and again, that the Lord will answer prayers, their own confidence in him is greatly strengthened. In each experience we learn something new about how to exercise our faith and obtain answers. That spiritual reward many times may be much greater than the specific answer to a prayer.

As we look back, we can see more clearly the impact of such spiritual experiences. It isn't that they have taught us more faith and reliance on the Lord or even how to better obtain answers to our prayers. Perhaps more important is that they have had a direct impact on the way we live the gospel. When family members really try to live by faith, they step up a level or two in their gospel living. They begin to set standards that are higher than some around them might be living. They tend to have a resolve that they will live these higher gospel standards. All of that seems to come not only to the parents but to the children as well.

## SETTING FAMILY STANDARDS

We have had an unusual experience as a family; three different times we have lived outside the United States for a total of just under eight years. In a way, it was a great blessing to be away from the customs, culture, and traditions of the United States. We were pressed to live in another culture and to provide most of the gospel teaching and activities for our family. We could also see more clearly the strengths and weaknesses of the society from which we came. When it was time for us to return to the United States the second time, we determined that we would do our best to maintain the closeness we had experienced while living away from the U.S. culture, which tends to divide families and send children off with friends.

We wanted to maintain the good we had learned by living in some third-world countries and also the good found in the U.S. culture. We had tried not to absorb any of the evils of the third-world countries' cultures and were determined that we would not absorb the weaknesses of the culture in the United States. Because we had lived in areas with such dire poverty, we were somewhat overcome by the great material blessings the Lord had given to Latter-day Saints and others in the United States.

We determined in a family council that we would maintain the following four goals:

1. To not be absorbed into materialism and selfishness or to give in to financial social pressures.

2. To not yield to pride in any of its forms by aspiring to the honors of the world, and so on.

3. To avoid worldliness at all costs.

4. To not allow our family to be divided by anyone, including peers and friends, nor to lose our closeness as a family.

We determined we would set some family standards so we could monitor these objectives. It should be stressed that these are not meant to be Church standards but just standards for our family:

1. We would use our money for basic needs—clothes, equipment, furnishings, food, and so on, but would make no elaborate or luxurious purchases. We would save money for future needs; however much we earned, it would never be so little that we couldn't save some. We would use our money for family-oriented activities. Finally, we determined that our children who were old enough would obtain jobs; the younger ones would try to earn money on the side.

2. We determined as a family to control television and video watching. Basically it would be allowed only on weekends, and then only when we could all watch it together. Furthermore, we would control what we watched by renting carefully selected videos, especially older ones. As a result, the children also became vigilant regarding which videos they watched at friends' homes.

3. We determined that our family would not waste away time, and that if our children were involved in activities, they would be good wholesome ones with a purpose. For example, we felt that our teens ought not to spend too much time on the telephone. Also, they shouldn't walk the malls and engage in other activities that promote idleness and thus bring them under the influence of the evil one.

4. We committed to continue eating all our meals at home, *together*. We would continue our nightly activities, as a family, of reading, knitting, sewing, singing, working on the computer, building, visiting, gardening, playing musical instruments, providing service, and so on.

5. We would maintain modest, basic dress standards no matter what others wore, staying away from revealing clothing, extreme clothing, or clothing that would not be appropriate for someone who had been endowed.

6. We decided that, at least for our family, there would be no sleep-overs. That was difficult to maintain in the beginning since nearly all our neighbors allowed them. But we had seen enough problems, moral and otherwise, from sleep-overs that we were determined to hold that standard in place.

7. We determined to continue our family outings, parties, and so on, and at times to include other families as well.

8. We determined to maintain our family music standard of Church music, classical music, or other good general music, but no light or hard rock or anything like unto it.

9. We determined we would hold firm against any peer or social pressures, and that we would all be willing to talk them out with the family when we began to feel them.

10. We encouraged our children to bring their friends *to our home* for ice cream, pizza, dinner, games, and so on. Our home was always "grand central station," but we were happy with that, and the children felt comfortable bringing their friends there.

It is all-important that young people select good friends. If they do, they will be influenced to keep the commandments. They will be involved in wholesome relationships that will help them grow and develop. If they choose bad friends, they will quickly become involved in bad activities and fall under the influence of Satan. He will teach them to be disobedient to parents, to break the family curfew, to use bad language, to watch bad television programs, and much more. They will then be much more receptive to unrighteous peer pressure.

11. We were committed that our family would come first and our friends second, and that when Dad was home, because of his many travels, in large measure that would be family time. Time with friends would be spent mostly on the weekends when Dad was traveling.

12. We encouraged our children to date, but we were committed that they would abide by some safe rules when doing so. For example:

- They could not date before age sixteen.
- They could not go out with the same person several times consecutively.
- There could be no steady dating.

- They could not go out alone with someone of the opposite sex but had to go out in groups of four or more.
- They could not typically be out beyond midnight.
- They could not date nonmembers or even members who were not worthy.

13. All in all, we committed as a family to continue to have the Spirit of the Lord with us, especially by using the seven ways to do that as suggested in chapter 2 of this book. Children who have the Spirit of the Lord with them will maintain not only the family standards but also the standards of the Lord.

Lest anyone misunderstand, to come to an agreement on all of the above, we first discussed as a family the great blessings that had come to us individually by living as we had in Latin America. Each of us listed the things we liked best about it. We then felt such an overwhelming commitment to keep these things that it was relatively easy to come up with a list of standards we could all agree on.

Back in the United States, we faced some real challenges over two or three years. However, as we look back, we can see we were able to keep about 90 percent of our standards in place. While this is not perfect, think of the blessings it has provided as compared to the problems we might have had if we had not developed the standards.

Even with our standards, we have faced many of the same challenges you have in your neighborhood: children who feel they have to be doing something exotic all the time or they're not "having fun"; adults who want to sit on the back row of the chapel; people who don't want to sing in church; Aaronic Priesthood young men who don't wear white shirts and ties while officiating during the sacrament; adults who do much in the church that the youth could do; an inordinate emphasis on style, hairdos, and dress; lack of reverence in the chapel; young people staying out until 2:00 in the morning for parties and roaming the street; summer dates and parties nearly every night; lack of Sunday observance; casual dress and TV sports on Sunday; some who watch soap operas daily and PG-13 or R-rated movies; parents with loose rules; teens whose parents have bought them their own car; all-night marathon dances to raise money; girls wearing immodest clothing; a general attitude of play, fun, and leisure but no need to work at home or have a job; families not doing things together but largely letting their children go with friends where they are exposed to inappropriate music, swearing, bad language, vulgar jokes; and so on.

With problems like these around us, how can we maintain standards like those mentioned above? I don't believe it is possible unless the relationship between parents and children and the Lord is strong. If the standard in the family is to be the Lord's standard and it is witnessed by the Spirit to all, then it is not difficult to set those kinds of standards.

## RESPONSIVENESS TO THE SPIRIT
## IN DATING STANDARDS

When one of our daughters was fifteen, a budding romance began between her and a young man from a good member family who lived nearby. He was actually a fine young man, and thus we were pleased about their friendship, but she was only fifteen and could not date.

They sat on the bus together day after day on the way to school, talking and having fun. It was a healthy, wholesome relationship. However, as the months went by, we realized it was becoming more serious, culminating in the fact that this young man, whom we will call Bill, held hands with our daughter at a dress rehearsal for a talent show at the church.

She was quite embarrassed because all the other kids saw them and teased her about it. But secretly she was very happy, because she really liked this young man. Fortunately she had a close enough relationship with us that she told us about it that very evening. She wasn't sure what she should do. Janelle and I talked with her about it that night, since we were leaving the next day for a church assignment that would last three or four days and did not want to leave the matter unresolved. We also knew that there was going to be a church dance that night and the next day a youth activity where they would be going on a hike. Thus, she would be spending a lot of time with this young man.

We had talked a lot about these kind of things before, so we just reminded our daughter of the seriousness of things if they continued to go along, and that it really wasn't right at that age. We further suggested that it could cause others to have an image of her that she would not want them to have. She said, "But I like him so much, I don't want to hurt his feelings."

We gave her a few ideas of what she might say and told her that we were not going to tell her what to do. She should follow the Spirit, and then she would know what to do to handle the situation correctly. We were confident because of her closeness to the Lord and felt certain that she would know what to do.

We were very pleased when we got home a few days later to find out how things had turned out. At the dance that night he took her hand again while they were sitting together. She said to him gently, "You know, Bill, I really don't think we should do this."

"Why?" he asked.

"Well," she replied, "I'm too young. I really do like you, and we do have a fun time together, but I think we should wait and not do this now. I just don't think that it is right."

He said, "Are you sure?"

And she said, "Yes, I really am."

Thus, she had nipped something in the bud that could have grown into some difficulties for her later. She told us how bad she felt to have to tell him that, but she knew it was right and was relieved that she had done it.

He was still very nice to her the next day on the hike, and she tried to be attentive and speak kindly so he wouldn't be offended. Because she followed the Spirit and kept the gospel standards in faith, she may have prevented problems that could have come later, not only with this young man but with others who would court her in the future.

Our daughter learned, I think, that it was best to choose the right even when she would rather not. Children need to learn to act in faith, following the promptings of the Spirit, even when there is pressure from others to have relationships like this one, and even when many of their peers are doing much more than that.

We must teach our children in the home to choose the right, to follow the promptings of the Spirit. If parents have properly planted the gospel seed in the hearts of their children, many problems will resolve themselves.

Parents need to remember that being home isn't just a time to rest and take it easy, although that is a part of being at home. Rather, it is mostly a time for faith, a time to search for ways to strengthen the family. We may struggle sometimes at work and other places to exercise our faith fully and keep our priorities in place, but if some priorities have to suffer, let it not be at home. With the family is where we really must be at our best. We must not let our guard down. We must truly show our children how to live by faith.

The average family faces many challenges at home. Some surveys show that in the United States people are watching television seven and a half hours a day. Videos and television shows actually bring the world into the home. Thus, if we are not on guard, the faith of the family may be destroyed through these worldly influences.

Having experiences where all the family is united in faith helps prepare children for the time when they will need to act on their own, to exercise their own faith in resolving a particular problem. I suppose we all take great comfort in the words of the proverb: "Train up a child in the way he should go: and when he is old, he will not depart from it" (Proverbs 22:6).

Many experiences with faith come by heeding the promptings of the Spirit, which we must sincerely desire to receive. If we simply expect to receive instruction from heaven and are prayerfully going about our lives, many times promptings will come that will be of great benefit in raising a child or even protecting the family from danger.

## LISTENING TO THE PROMPTINGS

Some years ago on a Sunday morning a husband was berating his wife for making the family late for church again. That had been a common theme in their marriage for some time: "Honey, are we going to be late again? Can't you get ready earlier? Why can't you assign out more responsibilities to the children so they have something to do? Why do you have to do it all? We're late every time. It embarrasses me to go marching in to church late. We ought to be setting a better example." On and on went the husband's chastisement.

Finally they were in the car on the way to the chapel, but the chastisement continued. As they prepared to enter the chapel, the wife said, "I know this is going to make you mad, but I've got to return home."

"What?" responded the husband. "We're already late. Why do you have to go home?"

"I don't know," she responded, "I just have to go." And she left before he could respond any further.

As the husband sat through the meetings, his irritation increased. He had to tend the kids, and his wife never did come back to the chapel.

He finally got home after the meetings, ready to chastise his wife further, until he saw her sitting in the kitchen weeping. The kitchen had nearly burned down. Had his wife not returned home when she did, their house would have burned to the ground. He was greatly humbled that his wife had heard the voice of the Spirit and he was repentant that he had not and that he had chastened her so. Why had the husband not heard the Spirit? I suppose because he was angry and argumentative.

One of the problems for many of us is that we are just

too busy to listen for the voice of the Spirit. We're too busily engaged and thus fail to notice some of the significant things that are occurring around us. I have always loved the words in D&C 5:34: "Yea, for this cause I have said: Stop, and stand still until I command thee, and I will provide means whereby thou mayest accomplish the thing which I have commanded thee."

This is the only verse I know where the Lord has told us to stop and stand still and that then he will command us and provide means to help us accomplish what he has told us to do. In other words, at times we've got to stop and stand still and ponder and determine where we really are. Then we will be more susceptible to inspiration from the Lord.

The voice of the Spirit really is a whisper. If there is any kind of contention, pride, or other sins, we will not hear the voice. How many times have instructions been given us from the heavens and we have not heard them? If we will follow the impressions and do as the Lord prompts us, we will have greater guidance in our families.

## FAITH AND UNEMPLOYMENT

An earlier chapter included a story of one of my sons who prayed for employment at school. On a different occasion he had a similar experience that more fully taught us the kindness of the Lord in responding to our faith. This son had worked hard during the spring to have enough money to attend Ricks College during the summer and fall semesters. He did so, and all went well until the end of December, when he found himself running out of money. He had been able to do some work at Ricks to help sustain himself, but by Christmas vacation, he was pretty much broke. He was worried about how he would be able to go to school the next semester. He wanted a loan from his parents, I think, but we did not give him one. Instead, we told him we were sure the Lord would provide if he would be faithful.

He came home with about two weeks of vacation before

Christmas and wanted to find a job. He made a number of contacts. He went to personnel department after personnel department. He could not find anything and was quite discouraged after his first day of searching. He knew also that every day that passed by during the Christmas break would mean that much less money he would have to sustain himself in school.

He talked with one company's personnel department the second morning. They told him there were no openings at all and that during Christmastime jobs were always filled. He came back home quite discouraged and talked to me about it. I tried to get him to exercise his faith, testifying that the Lord knew of his serious situation and that he would have to pray more fervently to convince the Lord he really needed help right then.

About that time, he went to his car, ready to do some more searching, when the telephone rang. I called him back in to answer the phone. After the call, he came to me with tears in his eyes and told me that one of the personnel managers had called. She had said, "You must really have someone upstairs who likes you. In the past half-hour we've had an opening come up out at our distribution center. If you want the work, it's full-time during the Christmas holidays."

He was overjoyed. He felt that his prayers had truly been answered. Then he told me that just five minutes earlier, after I had talked with him, he had gone down to his room and pled with the Lord to find him a job, that he needed it urgently or he could not go to school. I sensed that he had really exercised his faith. He was so touched by the fact that within a matter of minutes the phone rang and he was offered a job.

This son then went back to Ricks College with the thought that he would find employment there immediately and thus be able to sustain himself through the spring semester. But after searching all through January and up to the middle of February, he could find nothing. He was really discouraged. We talked to him a number of times on the phone. He finally told us that if he couldn't get some money soon, he would just have to quit school. We loaned him a little money to help pay for the insurance on his car. He doesn't like to ask for those loans, and we know it's best for him that we not provide them, but we did assist him for about a month. He finally reached a point where he called us to say that if he couldn't somehow obtain more money in the next week, he would have to come home.

We suggested again that he exercise his faith. My wife and I fasted for him. We encouraged him again about really praying for work, and we began to pray fervently as a family as well to help him. Within a week he had a call from a motel in Rexburg. They were looking for a night manager. The man interviewed him, learned that he was bilingual and had worked in the hotel business before, and hired him. My son then began to earn a good income, enough to sustain himself in school.

The hours were a little more than he had planned on, but he sustained himself with excellence. He was later able to pay us back the money he owed us and to have some money in his pocket. He was really pleased to have the work and the money and to be able to do his schoolwork at the same time.

It's surely evident in his life that whenever he has really exercised his faith humbly and forcefully, the Lord has responded to him in rather dramatic ways. As poor as he was, "keeping the commandment" helped him sustain himself through school. A month or so after this experience, we received a call from an extremely happy son. He had felt impressed to ask the college if he could get some sort of a grant to help him with his finances for the rest of his schooling at Ricks. To his surprise and delight, he was approved for a grant of five hundred dollars. The blessings for this young man went on and on as he tried to be faithful and do what was right.

## PRAYER FOR A SON IN DANGER

A mission president's wife recounted to me an experience where the faith of a mother had great impact on her son.

A young teenage boy had permission from his parents to take their pick-up truck into the mountains to ski with his friends. They told the parents that they would be back by about six o'clock in the evening.

As the day progressed and the mother watched the clock, she saw six o'clock pass by, seven o'clock, and then eight o'clock. Her fears and doubts began to mount. She became greatly concerned that her son was having problems. She offered a silent prayer for his safety. Nine o'clock, ten o'clock, and eleven o'clock passed by. She and her husband talked about the situation and finally went to bed, their hearts filled with anxiety and fear for their son.

After the husband fell asleep, the wife got up, went into the family room, and on bended knee poured out her heart to the Lord to protect her son. She felt a great peace come over her, and she went to bed and fell asleep.

About six o'clock the next morning, the son and his friends finally arrived home. The mother threw her arms around him. His first question to her was, "What were you doing about midnight last night?" She then told him of her heartfelt prayer.

The son said they had been stuck in the mud for several hours. Then, after getting unstuck, they had begun driving down the mountain in the late evening, but about midnight their truck began to slide off the road. It was headed to the edge of a dangerous precipice; if they had gone over the edge, they would surely have been killed. The boy bore his testimony that as they were sliding to the edge of the cliff, it was if someone had stood in front of them and pushed the car away from the edge and back onto the road. He saw it as a direct intervention from heaven, especially considering the prayer of his mother.

Such examples show the great power of faith and prayer,

especially the faith and prayers of parents for children, or of children for parents. The Lord seems especially to honor the fervent prayer of a good mother in behalf of her children. This young man surely knew his mother's faith well and held her in deepest esteem.

Are we exercising the same kind of faith and prayers in behalf of our own families? As we set that kind of example, day by day, our children will surely follow. I am sure this boy will never forget what his mother did for him that evening.

## A PRIESTHOOD BLESSING FROM A SON

We will know our example and teaching has borne fruit when we are able to call on one of our children for help in a spiritual matter. We had an interesting experience with a worthy son who could give me a priesthood blessing. It reminded me of the words in Alma 38:2–3: "And now, my son, I trust that I shall have great joy in you, because of your steadiness and your faithfulness unto God; . . . I say unto you, my son, that I have had great joy in thee already, because of thy faithfulness."

Some years ago while living in South America, our family came back to the United States for a visit. While here, we spent some time at a water resort. After coming down one of the water slides, I had a pain in my right foot. However, while walking around the rest of the water park, it didn't bother me.

Later that day, we returned home, and I took a nap. When I woke up, I had a terrible pain in my foot. I drove the car to have dinner with some friends, but I could hardly push the gas pedal. Finally, at our friends' house I took off my shoe and sock to examine my foot. It was really swollen and hurt more and more.

I ate dinner with great difficulty, trying not to complain. After dinner, the pain was so bad that I thought we should go to the hospital.

By this time, I couldn't even walk on my foot. It hurt

terribly, even with no weight on it. My daughter and wife, who were with me at the dinner, helped me down the stairs and into the car, and we drove to the hospital.

In the very moment I was entering the hospital doors, a doctor friend of ours appeared. He said, "I didn't have any patients here at the hospital. I just felt perhaps I was needed and came." We felt he had been inspired. An X-ray showed that the foot was not broken or fractured but badly sprained. The doctor found an orthopedic surgeon who took us to his office to treat my injury. Instead of putting the whole foot and leg in a cast, he gave me a removable cast and some crutches. I experienced a lot of pain going home, and I was quite depressed and discouraged because I had suffered from so many health problems in the previous few months. Some had been life threatening, and I just didn't feel I could handle one more.

We got to the house where we were staying at about one o'clock in the morning. I was in a lot of pain and was very concerned about it, so I asked my son to give me a blessing. He was a newly ordained elder and had assisted me a few times in anointing. But he had never sealed an anointing. This was his first time, and he blessed me that I would recover quickly and be healed. He gave me a fine blessing that was full of faith.

I tried hard to exercise my faith in the blessing but went forward assuming, as the doctors had told me, that I would have to have the cast on for probably a month or six weeks and use the crutches from ten days to two weeks until all the swelling had gone.

What a great blessing this son gave me. I slept through the night with no problems at all, even though my leg was in the cast and outside the covers. The next morning I kept my leg up and stayed home the whole day. Some friends came to visit, but I just tried to take care of myself and not do much.

That night when I finally removed the cast, I found I could walk without it. The next day I took the cast off and walked normally. My foot was well! It was hard to believe, but I had experienced a total healing. The six-week recovery time had been done away with. In total kindness the Lord had removed this ailment. The next morning, with a lot of faith and trying not to doubt, I left behind the crutches and the cast, walked onto a plane, and flew home to Mexico.

I was surely thrilled and humbled by the fact that the Lord had answered our prayers and honored this blessing from my son. I don't know that I could have handled one more ailment at that time. It was a great thing to have my own son perform the blessing, and I'm sure it strengthened his own faith in the priesthood that he held.

## PRINCIPLES OF LIVING BY FAITH

Such experiences as those in this chapter, when examined carefully, can actually teach us how to exercise our faith as a family. As I have thought about them, I have identified certain principles that can help us do it again and again:

1. Believe beforehand that you will obtain the thing you desire. If it doesn't occur, double your faith (see D&C 18:18).

2. Prophets receive direction, but so do parents—as do all who sincerely *ask* (see D&C 41:3; 42:61).

3. In exercising faith, many times you will receive answers to questions you didn't ask and blessings you didn't seek.

4. Answers may come more frequently while you are "about the work" than while you are your knees.

5. Many answers will come from reading the scriptures—the Lord may already have given the answer there (see D&C 32:4).

6. Some answers may not come for years. You must patiently wait and trust the Lord.

7. In trying to make decisions in faith, frequently two difficult choices come at the same time to increase your power of discernment.

8. Answers will come more easily if you are doing what the Lord has asked you to (see D&C 79:2; 100:15).

9. The Lord will never tell you to do something wrong in answer to prayer (see D&C 46:7).

10. Compare answers to prayer with the fruits of Spirit so as not to be deceived (see D&C 11:12–13).

11. Pray as fervently in gratitude after your faith is rewarded as you did while asking for the thing you received.

12. The more grateful you are for what the Lord has given you, the more you will receive.

13. Learn patiently to distinguish between the Lord's will and your own, and to avoid submitting to the will of Satan (see 2 Nephi 28:22).

14. Exercise faith more for the good of others, and answers will come more quickly.

15. Answers to personal prayers seem to come best while a person is serving others.

16. Be sure always to sanctify the Lord in the eyes of the people as answers come; magnify the Lord, not yourself (see Numbers 20:12; D&C 115:19).

17. Answers at times seem to come in half-steps. If you take a step forward in faith, the rest will be revealed.

18. The Lord reveals in prayer and in the scriptures many answers and conclusions. Seek to understand the original questions and problems being addressed.

There are many principles we can learn and then teach our families about how to live by faith. However, in general the idea is simple: if we will have faith in the Lord, humble ourselves, and repent of our sins, the Lord truly will bless us with the things we desire.

Lest anyone misunderstand that these principles will work only in an exceptionally good family, let me stress again that we have a very average, normal family. If anything is different about it, it may be an attempt on the part of the parents to try hard to help our children have spiritual experiences.

To the degree we can take advantage of the routine experiences in life and turn them into experiences in faith, we will find one of the secrets to raising up a family to the Lord. If we can show our children who the leader really is, meaning the Lord, and turn them faithfully to him, *he* will raise up our children. He will turn their hearts. He will humble them. He will teach them from on high.

Many of the stories in this book were just small, everyday experiences. But because we wrote them down, thought about them, and discussed them, they *became* spiritual experiences. Part of the key to having spiritual experiences is simply to recognize them, value them, and treat them with enough respect to record them. Surely the Lord taught us well through the Prophet Joseph Smith, who, after his great vision of the heavenly kingdoms said, "This is the end of the vision which we saw, which we were commanded to write while we were yet in the Spirit" (D&C 76:113).

Think what would have been lost if Joseph Smith had not recorded those revelations at the time they were given, while he was yet in the Spirit. Surely we would have lost most, if not all, of the revelation.

That is so in family life as well. When we have a spiritual experience, if we do not take time to record it, it will shortly be lost. We think we will always remember it, but shortly thereafter we will not. The facts become clouded, the memory becomes shortened, and before long we forget the great blessings of the Lord to us.

May I recommend strongly that you record your experiences and then recount to your family the great blessings the Lord has given you over and over again. Many families have the experiences but do not record them. Thus they must go on learning anew instead of benefiting from the lessons of the past.

In order to have spiritual experiences and to turn routine experiences into such, we need to have the Spirit of the Lord with us continually. We need to ponder the significance of the events in our family, many of which appear, at the time, to be very small and unimportant but which are actually great experiences if seen in their proper perspective. As Alma wrote, "By small and simple things are great things brought to pass; . . . and by very small means the Lord . . . bringeth about the salvation of many souls" (Alma 37:6–7).

May the Lord bless us to do our best, to ponder more, and to be more susceptible to the promptings of the Lord. Then we will better teach our family to live by the power of faith.

# CHAPTER SIX

# TEACHING YOUR FAMILY REPENTANCE AND DISCIPLINE

Upon arriving at home a few years ago, I met my wife as she was going out for an appointment. She said, "Honey, we've got a problem, and you'll have to solve it. *Your* six-year-old son has been a party to killing some expensive tropical fish at the neighbors' house. I've got to leave right now, so please solve it with him. He probably ought to go down and apologize."

This six-year-old and I had a little father-to-son talk. He said that he and his friend Tony, the son of a neighbor, had been in Tony's brother's room playing. This older brother raised tropical fish, which he had received from his father from several places around the world. The two boys thought the fish were probably hungry, so they decided to feed them. Not knowing any better, they gave the fish all the food they wanted—in fact, four or five times as much as they needed—and the fish began to die. They also caught some of the fish with their hands and moved them from one tank to another. Of course, several of them slipped through their fingers and fell on the floor. From what I gathered there were dead fish all over—about ten in all.

After my son explained what had happened, I said, "Well, what do you think we ought to do?"

He gave the typical six-year-old's response: "I don't know."

We talked about it some more and finally concluded, with Dad doing most of the concluding, that he should go to the neighbors, apologize, and make restitution.

Over several weeks he had saved seven dollars, part of which he had received for his birthday just four days earlier. That was all the money he had. I suggested he had better bring it with him.

He cried and didn't want to give his money away, but I finally said, "You go into your room and pray about it; then you come and tell me in a few minutes what you think you ought to do." About five minutes later he came with his crinkled dollars all in a pile, saying, "I guess we'd better go down. I'll have to pay him the money."

We walked down the street, my son really not wanting to go. In fact, he tried to convince me it would be better to solve the problem some other way. But I persisted, and we went to the neighbor's house.

I had him knock on the door. It was a very quiet knock. I'm sure he was hoping nobody would come. He knocked again. Finally the door opened, and there stood the older brother. We could tell he was quite upset and was probably thinking, "What are you doing here?"

My son and I just stood there. I tried to coax him, saying, "Come on, Son, tell him why we came."

Finally, in a quiet voice, he said, "I'm sorry I killed all your fish."

The neighbor boy responded quite sternly, "Well, I'm really mad and upset. Those fish were special to me. My dad gave them to me, and now they're dead."

My boy said again, "I'm sorry," and it seemed to humble the older boy's heart.

He said, "Well, okay. But don't ever do it again."

My son pulled the seven crinkled dollars out of his pocket and said, "I want to pay for your fish."

The older boy graciously said, "No, that won't be necessary."

I winked at him, telling him he should accept some money. Finally he said, "Well, all right. How about if I take two dollars?" A big grin came across my boy's face.

I said, "Well, maybe three dollars. What do you think, Son?"

He quickly said, "I think that would be fair" and handed three dollars to the owner of the fish. My son was really relieved he didn't have to pay the whole seven dollars. Again he apologized, and we left.

As we walked back up the street, I sensed that my companion was walking about a foot taller than the young boy who had walked down the street with me. He seemed pleased with himself and thankful he had repented. When we got to the house, he said, "Dad, I'm glad we went down there. It was right, wasn't it?" A hug around the neck, a thanks, and he was off to play.

It would have been easy to have been angry and upset at our son. Our reputation as a good neighbor was somewhat at stake, and our neighbors' son was angry with us. Fortunately, because my son knew inside what he should do, and because he received encouragement from his father to follow the promptings even though he didn't want to go and confess, it ended up being a great blessing to him. It increased the love between the two of us and reinforced the rightness of always following the Spirit. I was also pleased because:

1. He recognized his sin.

2. He confessed it to the Lord and to me.

3. He asked forgiveness.

4. He tried to make things right with the one who was offended.

5. He resolved never to do that wrong thing again.

Again, I think the reason things worked out so well was that the Lord was in it. Thus our son's heart was softened. My heart was also softened so I was not angry. Instead, I could handle the situation spiritually so it would be a good growing experience for him.

## THE POWER OF LOVE IN DISCIPLINING

Love in all forms, including discipline, can be a great blessing to children. They must learn obedience from their family. They must learn the principles of the heart from the examples of family members. If they so learn, they will then assimilate further lessons from the Lord and fare much better in life. Yes, love that comes through lovingly administered discipline brings the Spirit of the Lord.

Is there any greater power than love? Is there any greater commandment? The Lord commanded us that we must first, above all else, love him, and secondly, love one another. On this hangs all the law and the prophets (see Matthew 22:35–40).

Love is a divine motivation; it motivates the Lord and thus must also motivate us. Particularly is that so in dealing with our families. Joseph F. Smith once said:

> Fathers, if you wish your children to be taught in the principles of the gospel, if you wish them to love the truth and understand it, if you wish them to be obedient to and united with you, love them! and prove to them that you do love them by every word or act to them. For your own sake, for the love that should exist between you and your boys—however wayward they might be, or one or the other might be, when you speak or talk to

them, do it not in anger; do it not harshly, in a condemning spirit.

Speak to them kindly; get down and weep with them if necessary and get them to shed tears with you if possible. Soften their hearts; get them to feel tenderly towards you. Use no lash and no violence . . . approach them with reason, with persuasion and love unfeigned. With these means, if you cannot gain your boys and your girls . . . there will be no means left in the world by which you can win them to yourselves (*Gospel Doctrine*, 5th ed. [Salt Lake City: Deseret Book Co., 1939], p. 316).

Truly, love is a great power for good. President Smith was teaching the importance of softening children's hearts, getting them to feel tenderly toward us and us toward themselves. President David O. McKay said it this way:

Earnestly we urge parents to gather their families around them, and to instruct them in truth and righteousness, and in family love and loyalty. The home is the basis of a righteous life, and no other instrumentality can take its place nor fulfill its essential functions. The problems of these difficult times cannot better be solved in any other place, by any other agency, by any other means, than by love and righteousness, and precept and example, and devotion to duty in the home (*Family Home Evening Manual*, 1965, p. 111).

This book has tried to focus on the importance of teaching our children love of God and love for one another. That truly cannot be overstated. However, sometimes our understanding of love is somewhat one-sided. Thus, we cannot understand how our children could do wrong when we have loved them so much.

When you think of Jesus Christ, what image do you have? Most people remember him healing the sick, forgiving the adulterous woman, and loving the little children. They think of him as a loving, kind, and tender God.

All of that is true. But we must remember that genuine

love is motivated by what is best for another. At times, the softness, tenderness, and loving care of the moment may not be what is best for the one being loved. We need to remember that it was the same Jesus who drove the ungodly from the temple; chastened Peter, James, and John; and chastened Joseph Smith and even the Saints as a whole in Missouri.

How could that be for one who loved his people so much? We have to understand that the Lord will always do what is best for his people, even if that means removing them from the earth lest they bring themselves deeper and deeper into sin. In truth, then, the chastening is really an act of mercy on the Lord's part, motivated by his divine love.

The Lord explains this principle in a beautiful way in D&C 95:1–2: "Thus saith the Lord unto you whom I love, and whom I love I also chasten that their sins may be forgiven, for with the chastisement I prepare a way for their deliverance in all things out of temptation, and I have loved you—wherefore, ye must needs be chastened and stand rebuked before my face."

It's interesting that the Lord says those whom he loves he also chastens. Since he loves all his children, we can assume we will receive some of that chastening. The true purpose of the chastening is that our sins might be forgiven. I am so impressed with the fact that he also says he will prepare a way for our deliverance from our problems if we will follow him as his disciples. He then reasserts, after speaking of chastening, "And I have loved you."

Isn't that the same spirit with which we must discipline our children? Let no one misunderstand the "chastening" as harsh words, unkind responses, or severe physical punishment. The Lord would not act that way, and neither must we. We must love our children with all of our heart, with kindness, tenderness, and a loving touch. And at times, if they need it, we must chasten them as well. Remember that we are showing love when we discipline our children, every bit as much as when we hug them. The children who receive the discipline will love the parents who discipline them even more if it is done in the spirit of love.

## THE POWER OF REPENTANCE

Let us remember that our reason for disciplining children is to help them humble their hearts and repent of their sins. In other words, if they have hardened their hearts and are doing something wrong, they have to be helped, on occasion, through chastisement, to humble themselves and thus receive the Spirit of the Lord. If that is our purpose, we will not make very many mistakes in disciplining our children. If we truly love our children, we will be willing to do whatever is honorable and right to help them turn their hearts to the Lord.

While the word *discipline* has something of a negative connotation, it comes from the word *disciple*. The Lord will discipline us, and if we are willing to receive it with the right spirit, we become his disciples.

The word *repentance* denotes a change of heart or mind, or, in other words, a conversion. Perhaps it's the "mighty change" that the Book of Mormon speaks of (see Mosiah 5:2; Alma 5:14; Matthew 3:2, footnote).

The Hebrew word for *repent* means "to turn or return to God." Thus when we talk about repentance, it is a very positive aspect of the gospel. When I repent, I am returning my heart to God. I am seeking to undergo that mighty change. Similarly, when I administer discipline to my children, I am seeking to turn their hearts to God.

In Spanish, as well as in some other languages, the word *chastisement* is difficult to translate. It is usually translated into Spanish as *castigo*, meaning punishment. However, that word has too negative of a connotation. When the Lord chastens someone, it is always with a righteous purpose. It is never punishment for punishment's sake. It is to turn people to the Lord, to humble their hearts, and thus to bring about growth and development from the mistakes they have made. If that is our purpose in disciplining our families, we will know we are on the right track.

If we start with the correct spiritual premise about discipline, we will have fewer problems in disciplining others or in receiving discipline ourselves from the Lord. It is essential to teach children as they grow older to say, "Thy will be done, O Lord, not mine."

All of us are selfish, and children especially so, in seeking their own will. Sometimes children want to tease their brothers and sisters. They try to compete with one another. All these kinds of activities will bring contention into the home. Children many times do things for the wrong reasons—to please their parents or to avoid punishment—and not so much because the things are right.

Those who seek to please only themselves are very selfish. But the will of the Lord must be supreme in all things. We must learn to do things we don't want to do, simply because we ought to. The key, then, is to nourish in children the desire to respond to the feeling "You ought to." If their motivation is merely external, they will never be well-disciplined or submissive to the Lord.

For example, when we first started reading the scriptures as a family, we had a rule that the children had to be up by six o'clock. If they didn't comply, they had to go to bed an hour early that night, on the premise that they must need more sleep if they weren't able to get up for scripture study. Then one of my sons said something that really caught my attention: "Dad, the only reason I come to scripture reading is so I won't have to go to bed early." We realized then that we were unrighteously pressuring our children to obey, and we rescinded the rule. Children will respond outwardly to that kind of discipline, but then they will not learn to obey for the right reason—an inner desire to follow the Lord.

Perhaps the paramount description of what it means to be humble before the Lord is found in Mosiah 3:19:

> The natural man is an enemy to God, and has
> been from the fall of Adam, and will be, forever

and ever, unless he yields to the enticings of the Holy Spirit, and putteth off the natural man and becometh a saint through the atonement of Christ the Lord, and becometh as a child, submissive, meek, humble, patient, full of love, willing to submit to all things which the Lord seeth fit to inflict upon him, even as a child doth submit to his father.

Truly, we must submit to our Father in Heaven, all of us. And our children, particularly when they are young, will submit to their earthly parents because they want to, if those parents have disciplined them correctly.

Let us look at some statements from the Lord himself from which we can learn some principles to use in administering this kind of love to our children. Some parents who are a bit "laissez faire" feel they should not intervene when their children are having problems or quarreling. However, the Lord clearly said, "Ye will not suffer your children that they go hungry, or naked; neither will ye suffer that they transgress the laws of God, and fight and quarrel one with another, and serve the devil, who is the master of sin, or who is the evil spirit which hath been spoken of by our fathers, he being an enemy to all righteousness" (Mosiah 4:14).

Clearly, we are not to allow our children to fight with each other or to transgress the laws of God. Furthermore, the Lord says that a bishop should be "one that ruleth well his own house, having his children in subjection with all gravity" (1 Timothy 3:4). The same is true in any good family.

In Proverbs we find much counsel about discipline:

Withhold not correction from the child: for if thou beatest him with the rod, he shall not die (Proverbs 23:13).

Chasten thy son while there is hope, and let not thy soul spare for his crying (Proverbs 19:18).

Correct thy son, and he shall give thee rest; yea,

he shall give delight unto thy soul (Proverbs 29:17).

The New Testament also teaches us to not provoke anger in our children:

> Fathers, provoke not your children to anger, lest they be discouraged (Colossians 3:21).

> Fathers, provoke not your children to wrath: but bring them up in the nurture and admonition of the Lord (Ephesians 6:4).

I am always impressed that when children are given time to turn to the Spirit and follow it, the Lord will tell them what to do, and they will choose the right. Sometimes they need their parents to help them have enough courage to face their mistakes, but as they face them time after time, they will learn to do what is right on their own.

On one of the first days of elementary school, one of our boys and his friend were caught climbing up a wire-mesh baseball fence during lunch break. They didn't know that was against the rules. Nevertheless, the teachers took them in and made them work through recess for several days. In fact, they were probably a little harder on them than they should have been.

This boy came home mad at the teachers—he felt very rebellious, with the attitude of "We'll teach them" and "Just wait until we figure out how to get back at them." In other words, he and his friend did not receive the punishment with humbled hearts but with hardened hearts.

My wife and I started working on this son to convince him that he ought to go apologize to the teacher even if he was only partly in the wrong. He resisted, embarrassed about what his friends might think. Instead of deciding the issue for him, I finally told him to go into his room and pray, and if the Lord told him that he didn't have to apologize, that would be all right with me. But if the Lord told him that he did, then he ought to be man enough to do it. After being alone for twenty minutes or so, he came back with a humbled heart, determined that, whatever the cost, he would apologize to the teacher. And he did so the next day.

I am convinced that if we give our children a chance to choose, having taught them correct principles, the Holy Ghost will lead them to decide for themselves what they ought to do, without someone else dictating or controlling their lives. They, themselves, must decide.

## PRINCIPLES CONCERNING DISCIPLINE

Over the years I have learned several principles of discipline that have made it easier to turn our children to the Lord:

1. Don't discipline when angry or out of control. Wait until later.

2. After disciplining, be sure to show forth an increase of love (see D&C 121:43).

3. Love, love, love all, but especially those who seem to deserve it the least.

4. In disciplining, apply logical consequences (consequences that have some relation to the sin committed). Many times just letting children "face the music," the natural consequences of their own acts, is the best possible discipline, as long as it will not harm them in some way.

5. In disciplining, be sure to not "pick up the pieces." Sometimes after parents have disciplined, they try to snuggle up and show love to their children too early. There is correct timing in showing an increase of love. If it is done too early and the parents try to make up with the child instead of letting the child come to them, the child may misinterpret that affection as a weakening of the parents' resolve. Don't try to mend a temporarily frayed relationship until the time is right.

6. Don't be too merciful on the transgressor when a law is broken. Your love must be greater than that. We must not allow the Lord to be offended because we lacked the resolve to help our children follow a true principle.

7. Love children enough to cause them to face the con-

sequences of their own behavior. Do not shield them from the result.

8. Plan out, before the heat of the moment, the consequences that will be paid for breaking family rules. Be sure they are clearly understood, and children will then largely discipline themselves.

9. When administering discipline, do not allow discussion of discipline or give explanations or reasons for it. If you do, it will water down its effectiveness.

10. Physically hold and love your children. The physical contact breaks down numerous barriers. Kiss them and hug them.

11. Commend, praise, and recognize good performance. Commend for the intrinsic value of the task, not for manipulative reasons on the part of the parent ("You pleased me").

As I have watched parents discipline children, they often seem to fall into two different patterns. In my judgment, one is incorrect. The other is correct.

## INCORRECT PRINCIPLES
## OF DISCIPLINE

1. Sometimes parents' discussions with children center only on the problem and not on how the children are feeling about the problem. Thus the parents give advice, counsel, criticism, condemnation, and so on, and the children tend to rebel, fight back, or clam up. Then nothing is solved.

2. After such a discussion, the parents impose discipline upon the children. Because the discipline is *external* to the children, they again rebel, feel resentful, and reject the discipline. Even if they conform outwardly to the parents' wishes, they will have these inward tendencies, which will eventually come out.

3. The parents feel better because they have unloaded their feelings. But the children continue to do wrong in the future because they haven't learned anything except to avoid the parents who disciplined them. Also, they no longer like their parents as much as they did, and the relationship is

diminished or destroyed. Perhaps most important, the problem that was to be corrected remains uncorrected and will be repeated.

4. Because of the nature of the discipline given, things don't remain in a neutral state. The children either accept counsel and change and humble themselves and repent, or they reject the counsel, and the discipline administered to them is damaging to themselves and their relationship with others.

Parents cannot go on giving that kind of discipline without harmful results, and it will eventually result in the destruction of their children or of their relationship with them.

## CORRECT PRINCIPLES OF DISCIPLINE

There is a more enlightened way to discipline.

1. The parents will pray before and (silently) during the discussion with their children. They will pray to humble their own hearts and to be an instrument in the hands of the Lord to humble the hearts of his children. The parents will also be receptive to the promptings that come to them.

2. The parents will center the discussion on the *feelings their children have* about the problem, not just on the problem. They will try to understand why the children did what they did, allowing them to describe the problem from their own point of view. This creates an open atmosphere where honest feelings can be expressed. This is vitally important, because unless the children express these feelings, no lasting change will occur. Parents might say such things as "What did you feel at the time you were doing it?" or "I sense you really have some deep feelings about this. Help me understand why you're feeling the way you are." If parents omit this step, the children may try to hide what really happened and not admit to their errors. It is *paramount* that children be encouraged to share their feelings about what happened.

3. The parents will create an environment where the

children can humble themselves and ask for counsel. The goal of the parents should be to prepare the atmosphere so the children will be willing to learn. If they are not willing to learn, whatever is said to them will be destructive. Then they will lose respect for the parents because the discipline has been "unfair" or they will lose respect for themselves because the parents think they are "no good." Even if the parents are *right* about what happened, if they give their counsel at the wrong time, it will end up being offensive.

The relationship between parents and children must be in order. It is not enough for the parents to feel good about their children; the children must also feel good about their parents. Then the discipline will work.

4. After the children have talked about what happened and expressed their feelings about it, the parents can ask a few questions for clarification and give inspired advice or counsel so the children can learn.

5. When children understand *why* what they did was wrong, they will discipline themselves. The discipline will come from within.

6. Because the discipline comes from within, the change is permanent and adds to the children's growth and development. The children see it is in their own interest not to do the thing again.

7. Because of the way the discipline was handled, the relationship between parents and children will be strengthened, and their love will be deepened. In addition, the children will be more inclined to listen to the parents in the future. Finally, the children will be more inclined to turn to their Father in Heaven and to repent of their sins because their hearts have been softened.

There are many other principles of effective discipline that might be discussed. For example, parents must be careful not to try to resolve a serious problem in the moment that it happens. They are better off to wait until a little later—a few hours or the next day—before getting involved, especially if they are feeling the emotion of the moment.

Sometimes this same seeming lack of involvement by the Lord is used as evidence by nonbelievers to "prove" the "nonexistence" of God.

The world criticizes the Lord for allowing evil to occur. They wonder why he allows little children to be killed, women to be raped, violent deaths to occur, and so on. While these things are difficult to understand, we must have faith that the Lord knows what he is doing. As Isaiah recorded, "My thoughts are not your thoughts, neither are your ways my ways, saith the Lord. For as the heavens are higher than the earth, so are my ways higher than your ways, and my thoughts than your thoughts" (Isaiah 55:8–9; see also Alma 14:8–11). In truth, it may be one of the greatest characteristics the Lord could possess to know everything, to have all the answers and all the power, but still not intervene, even when the world would intervene.

Many parents are not disciplined enough to hold back and let their children learn at their own speed, to experience things for themselves. Instead, the parents are anxious to jump in and tell the children what to do, because, after all, the parents "know." Then they try to manipulate the children to go in that direction.

The Lord seems to work in the opposite way. If we ask him, he will help us. But he does not seem to openly control or direct things. His seems to be a "laid back" way of operating that allows maximum growth and development for the individual. Sometimes when parents see clearly what needs to be done, they find it difficult to refrain from intervening or conveying information that will solve their children's problems. But standing back may be the greatest love of all, and it gives us new understanding about the majesty of the love of God. It makes us humbly recognize that we know very little about the Lord.

We could do everything for our children, but the only real safety for them lies within themselves. We can set up restrictions to guide them and put every protection around them, but when all is said and done, the final test is what is inside of them. They *must* be able to stand alone and to follow the promptings of the Spirit.

When disciplining your children, remember that people are usually doing the best they know how to do. They may have incorrect motives and make mistakes, but they usually have a reason for doing what they do.

If parents and children know they will not intentionally offend one another but seek to understand one another, through time that trust will pay many other dividends.

## TRUST BETWEEN PARENT AND CHILD

One of our daughters was quite anxious for her eleventh birthday to come. She wanted us to commit that she could have one of her friends over for her birthday on Friday night. We didn't say yes or no, but as the time grew closer, we learned that her friends were planning a surprise party for her.

Knowing this, we told her it would not be possible to have anyone over on Friday night. She was really disappointed, and she cried and pestered us about it for some time. We kept telling her, "Honey, it will be okay. Don't worry about it." She had a hard time understanding why.

I finally said, "Listen, do you believe in your dad?"

"Yes."

"Do you believe he would do anything to hurt you or have things go badly for you?"

"No."

"Then trust me, and things will resolve themselves by Friday night. Okay?"

She finally did believe and was somewhat calmed by our discussion. When Friday came, we made up a reason for going to her friend's house. When we walked into the room, her friends were all there, holding a big sign and shouting "Happy birthday!"

Our daughter was very emotional and taken aback. She was so pleased by the love of her friends in having a party for her. She was also pleased in the trust she had placed in her parents, which had been rewarded. She stayed for the evening and had a wonderful birthday.

How children need to trust their parents! Parents know the end from the beginning on certain things, and if their children will believe and trust, things will turn out well for them, usually even better than they anticipated. Trust is never built in a moment; it is built through many weeks and months and experiences of parents and children seeing each other respond in true love. Again, if parents will teach their children to pray and read the scriptures and respond to the voice of the Lord, the accounting will occur internally with the children and the Lord. Then the parents will not have to be "the sheriff," directing their children's lives.

## SELF-DISCIPLINE

One day at school, a boy was pushing around one of my sons. He had even punched him because he and some of the other LDS kids were dressed in their nice Sunday clothes. They had planned on going to the temple right after school to do baptisms for the dead and were taking some real razzing from the other students because of their clothes.

A boy who was smaller than my son kept pestering him. My son was very strong for his age, and he had the tendency to be quite physical with everyone. He could easily have made the other boy stop, but he refrained from hurting him even though the boy was really giving him a hard time. A couple of the LDS girls were very impressed with that and told him they admired his discipline in refraining from hitting back. My son replied, "I couldn't punch him. I'm going to the temple."

I was impressed by the fact that down deep he knew it was wrong to "punch people out," especially if he was going to the temple. Somehow that message had taken hold in his heart and helped him to discipline and control himself. I found it interesting that even after that experience was over, he had better control over himself and stopped being so physical with others.

The same kind of self-discipline can be exercised by adults in speaking out when they know something is wrong. One time my wife attended a luncheon with several other women. Some were active Latter-day Saints; others were less active. A few nonmembers were also present. The subject turned to abortion and birth control. For several minutes, one of the women voiced her strong feelings that nothing was wrong with abortion and that no restriction should be placed on birth control.

My wife was faced with the difficult challenge of whether to talk about the weather or speak out in favor of the truth. She chose to do the latter, explaining that under most circumstances abortion is a serious sin with the only exceptions being in cases of rape or incest. Even then, the matter should be decided only after careful counsel with priesthood leaders and under the direction of the Spirit of the Lord. She then bore testimony about her feelings on the subject. As you might expect, the luncheon concluded rather abruptly. However, afterward one of the inactive women approached my wife to say that she had never before understood the Lord's view on those issues and had felt the truth being spoken on that day.

A few years ago one of my daughters found herself in a similar circumstance. She was just going to class when one of her friends said, "Let's ditch class." The girl made it sound very tempting to my daughter. But my daughter thought about it and felt the Spirit say to her that she should not do it. She then said to her friend, "No, I can't. It wouldn't be right. I have to go to class." And she did.

Later I asked her what had happened to her friend. She thought about it a minute and said, "Oh, I didn't realize it at the time, but she went to class too."

How thankful I am that she heard the voice of the Spirit and had the self-discipline to follow it. This experience told me that she was truly progressing spiritually and would merit increased trust from her parents.

All of us, children and parents alike, need the courage to

follow the voice of the Spirit, for the Lord himself is the true disciplinarian. I know of no pain greater than having disappointed the Lord. Doing so often requires intense repentance to regain the privilege of having the Spirit return and give instruction.

## REQUIRING ACCOUNTABILITY

Some parents have a difficult time obtaining an accounting from their children about such things as what time they will be home, where they've been, what they've been doing, or especially whether they have finished an assignment. As important as planning and doing the work is, providing a proper accounting for what was done is most important and is taught clearly in the scriptures.

Parents can help their children be more accountable by following certain principles. Please consider the following:

1. If children are not required to make an accounting to their parents, they will have no respect for their parents.

2. If children have no respect for their parents, they will not respond to them when their parents expect them to be obedient.

3. If no accounting is required, there will be no improvement because there is no correction, guidance, or direction.

4. The Lord holds parents responsible to have children account to them and discipline them.

5. To require a proper accounting for work done, parents must be sure that the assignment is clear and specific and that their children know beforehand what will be expected.

6. When parents give assignments, they must follow up to see that their children report back.

If children are having difficulty with a reasonable assignment, parents must not be too quick to get involved. Some of us make the mistake of trying to jump in and solve all of our children's problems. One thing I've noticed about the Lord is that he does not seem overly eager to take over. He lets me struggle, feel frustrated, humble myself, work through the problem, and finally see the fruits of my labors and the personal growth that follows. Parents need to follow the Lord's example in that thing. They should be involved with their children, caring about what is happening in their lives and in their hearts, but they should not be too involved in helping them solve every problem through their "great wisdom," their "great resolve," or their "great discipline." Otherwise, how will the children ever learn to develop their own strengths and turn to the Lord for help?

Parents must be responsible to enforce the rules of the family. If parents are delinquent in enforcing a valid rule over a period of time, they should not be surprised when children frequently break that rule. It is not proper for parents to penalize children for their own neglect in enforcing the standards. In such cases, the problem is a default in the leadership of the parents, not in the disobedience of the child.

## A LESSON IN ACCOUNTABILITY

One morning I could tell that one of my sons was really "blue" about something. I got him alone, and we began to talk about what was concerning him. After some hesitation, he said, "Dad, I let Patches go." Then I knew he was talking about the neighbors' pet rabbit, which they had been trying to find for more than a month. I thought, "Those folks are going to have some bad feelings about us as neighbors."

When I asked him why he did it, he said, "I don't know. I guess I was just angry with my friend." I remembered then that our boys had seemed extra concerned about finding the neighbors' rabbit. Now I understood why.

We talked for a few minutes about what it all meant. I asked if he needed to talk to his friend about it, but he had been praying and had already decided to do so.

He was mainly concerned that the other boy might not like him anymore. The other boy would surely wonder why he had let the rabbit go and why he hadn't told him about it over those many weeks. The parents had felt bad enough about it that they had purchased two other rabbits to replace the one that was lost.

My son wondered if it would be all right to call his friend and discuss the problem over the phone. I told him that it was usually better to tell people to their face what had happened, and that maybe he could invite his friend to come over. I gave him the option of having me present or telling his friend alone. A little later, he told me he would do it alone.

I told him that besides clearing the matter up with his friend, he would also need to clear the matter with the Lord. He told me he had already prayed about it and asked forgiveness. He had surely followed the promptings on that matter.

My son invited his friend to come over, and they went downstairs to watch a video together. I went down two different times to see what had happened, only to learn that he still hadn't brought the matter up yet. I felt he was stalling because he was really worried about his friend's response. Finally I called him aside and told him that he needed the courage to do what needed to be done, and to do it now.

In short order, this good boy was back to me with a big smile, saying everything was okay. A little later, I got him and his friend together for a minute and told the friend how bad my son had felt about it, that he was hoping it wouldn't affect their friendship, and that he hoped he would forgive him. His friend smiled and said that things were fine. My son volunteered to buy him another rabbit, but he said they didn't really want another one because of their two new ones.

I was surely pleased to see that my son had been responsible enough to face up to what he had done and to "clear the air" with his friend and with the Lord. He had pretty much done it on his own, although someone had been there to help him be accountable and to help him follow through with what he had already determined was right. That is a much different thing than *telling* him what to do and *making* him do it.

## DISCIPLINE TECHNIQUES

When we hold our children accountable for their actions, they will interpret that as love. When we are loose and let them do whatever they want, they will interpret that as a lack of love. Children need direction, guidelines, and parents who love them enough to enforce the proper discipline for the breaking of rules. Remember that empty ultimatums are doomed to failure, and rebellion will usually follow.

President Kimball used to say about someone who was not doing right: "He is *entitled* to discipline—not as a punishment, but as an aid to his growth. It's because we love him so much. Let us, therefore, seek him out and discipline him." I believe that is a great principle.

Several techniques for administering discipline have worked well for us, especially the following:

1. Do your best to turn your children to the Lord.

2. Help your children have repentant, humbled hearts. Then they will:

- recognize their sins.
- confess their sins.
- ask for forgiveness.
- desire to make good what they have done.
- resolve to sin no more.

As you can see, those are the five steps of the repentance process. Repentance is what we want for our children, because it brings about a humbled heart.

3. After the discipline, with the proper timing in mind, be sure to show your children an increased amount of love—physical, verbal, and emotional.

4. Be sure to not bring up the sin again. Sometimes parents or families continue to bring up a past mistake, trying to remind the person not to fall into that error again. But in essence that shows they have not truly forgiven and forgot-

ten in their own hearts. Thus, it is better to *forget it,* as the Lord promised he would do.

5. Use the seven suggestions made earlier in this book for inviting the Spirit. If you will do that, it will have as much impact on humbling the heart of your children as anything else I know.

6. Make good use of family councils. Problems that affect more than one family member need to be discussed openly with the family. Be careful that everyone's feelings are honestly expressed and that each person is heard from. Usually everyone will give a bit in order to compromise and come to an agreement. (Of course, that would not be the case if it meant bending or adjusting a commandment of the Lord.) Family councils should always begin with prayer, perhaps some testimony, expressions of love, and maybe even singing that will bring the Spirit of the Lord into the meeting before sensitive matters are discussed. After decisions are made by the council, the conclusions should be clearly stated to all so there can be no misunderstanding about what was decided as a family.

7. Personal, private interviews can be very valuable in helping with discipline problems. We've handled those differently over the years. Sometimes we've had a fixed schedule for each child. Sometimes we've had interviews at the table, sometimes in a tree, sometimes while on a walk. Lately we have been holding less formal interviews without a schedule. We've usually had a word of prayer together if it's been a more formal setting where I have interviewed them for worthiness. If it has been more just checking to see how they were doing, we have often just walked around the block for an informal talk.

Early in our marriage, I used to conduct the interviews on my own as the father. Later we found it much more productive for my wife and me to hold them jointly. We try to learn the children's feelings about themselves, their progress in school, their friends, their spiritual progress, and so on. This seems to have more impact than when one of us would interview them alone. That does not mean, of course, that they won't occasionally need an interview with an individual parent, especially to talk about worthiness.

This focused attention on an individual child has gone a long way to help keep them on the straight and narrow. Often we have sensed needs that would otherwise have gone unnoticed. Sometimes we have been able to discuss serious questions about spiritual or sexual matters. These interviews have also been valuable in deepening the love we have for one another. Many times the interviews have ended with a priesthood blessing, but always with a prayer, which, again, greatly increases our love for one another.

8. Priesthood blessings can be very effective in disciplining children. If you can help children humble themselves so that *they* will seek the blessing, it will increase their faith and give them added power over themselves. It will also give their father an opportunity to humble himself in providing the blessing and will greatly increase the love between children and parents.

We ought to be careful not to give blessings only when there are problems. We should encourage our children to ask for blessings when they're going away from home, leaving for school, starting a new job, or at any other appropriate time. Sometimes a father may just feel prompted to give a child a blessing of commendation. If the family wants to record these for the child's future benefit, that could surely be done.

## RULES

Part of providing discipline for children includes setting good rules, especially for younger children. But even older children need some rules. We have tried hard not to have very many rules, but some things should be completely clear in the minds of the children. If rules are made and presented in kindness and respect, with the Spirit of the Lord, the children will see them not so much as rules as guidelines for their own benefit.

For example, we've had rules about modest clothing, makeup, jewelry, and so on. There have been some rules for the younger children about bedtime, and even the teenagers and adults are usually in bed by ten-thirty or eleven. We have agreed as a family on different curfews, depending on the age of the children. When the older children were on dates, they could not stay out beyond midnight. We didn't allow sleepovers or overnight parties. We tried to maintain some control over friends, music, TV, radio, videos, proper language, and use of the telephone.

We have also had some clear understandings about schoolwork, chores, and music lessons being completed before playtime. There was also some clear direction about eating meals together as a family, and especially about avoiding contention at all costs.

If children learn to discipline themselves, they will abide by family guidelines as coming from the Lord. The more mature the children, the less their need for rules as they guide themselves by the Spirit. And if children are busily involved in constructive projects, developing their talents, working, and so on, they will not have much time to get into many problems or difficulties.

## PUNISHMENTS

I believe that sometimes punishments are a necessary part of discipline. But before administering any kind of punishment, parents should consider their motives for so doing. They should do it because they love their children and with the intent that it will humble them and turn them to the Lord. If it will do these things, the punishment should be administered. If not, the parents should seek a different form of discipline.

Punishments, of course, will vary greatly depending on the age of the children and what those children need. We have always sought to find something the children hold dear, that would be a sacrifice for them and really "get their attention" if they were deprived of it. But what is an appropriate punishment for one may not be for another, and thus it is very individualized.

We have not been too prone to spank our children. When they were younger and we were not getting their attention on something, we occasionally did spank them. We used an old racquetball paddle that the kids gave me for Christmas one year. Later the children wrote "paddle whacker" on it, with lots of other funny comments. We determined to use it when it was needed to get someone's attention. And on those occasions, it was very effective, especially with the younger ones. Fear and respect for the "paddle whacker," however, were always more effective than the pain from the "paddle whacker."

Sometimes, when children are rebelling about something, they want to "grandstand" or to have an audience. The worst thing you can do is let them do so. Thus, an effective discipline is to isolate them, to send them to their room where they can think things out on their own.

We've actually had fun over the years with a room we called the "cooler," an uncomfortable room, such as the bathroom, where we have sent children to wait until they were ready to humble their hearts and talk to us. One of our sons used to call himself "the cooler king" to remind us that he had been sent there more often than any of our other children.

With smaller children, sometimes just having them sit on a chair while they calm down and get control of themselves is sufficient. The important thing is to have them prayerfully consider what has happened and, when they are humbled, to seek you out.

On occasion, the little ones, especially, would come out and *say* they were humble. Sometimes they were, but other times they were not and needed to be sent back again. But once you feel that they are truly repentant and humble, then you will know the discipline has been effective.

Another particular technique that has worked well for us is to have our children stand against the wall for twenty minutes. That, too, is a form of isolation. It's also a difficult position, and our children didn't like it, but it surely brought about the desired results.

Another traditional approach that is good, depending on the age of the children, is to ground them—in other words, to withhold privileges that for them really matter. For this to be effective, you must really know what it is your children hold dear, and that is what must be withheld. It takes real discipline on the part of the parents to withhold something that really matters to children when they cry and beg for it. But you still must say no. One or two of those experiences will teach more respect and obedience than a hundred attempts to do so when you give in to the cries of a child.

Use logical or natural consequences with your children. If you can find a way to make your children "face the music," that will be much more effective than just pulling a punishment out of the air. A bit of creativity in this area will result in some effective chastisements.

Always remember that punishment must be administered with a cool head, with detachment from the situation. When you are emotionally involved in something, that is not the moment to discipline. You might want to have your spouse handle it or wait until you can discipline without emotion. Especially remember to always be gentle in your words and gentle in your ways and to avoid any kind of abuse.

There is a critical moment in disciplining when children beg and cry and say, "I'm sorry! I won't ever do it again." That is the time to go forward with the discipline, not listen to explanations or promises or excuses (assuming you have the facts). The time for talk is not at the time of discipline but after the discipline is over.

When your children know you hold the gospel dear, don't allow them to get the Lord or the gospel into the issue. A child might say, "Well, if that's how you're going to be, I'm not going to pray anymore" or "I'm not going to church" or "I'm going to go play ball on Sunday." Our response has been, "Well, that has nothing to do with this matter. If you want to do that, it's up to you. That's between you and the Lord. But this has to do with . . . " and then we restate the real problem. Under no circumstances have we allowed children to bring the Church into issues about discipline. If they do, it becomes a bargaining chip. In time, that may destroy faith and testimony or keep them from attending church.

Often parents can have success with such tangible rewards as an apple, a cookie, a star on a chart, a trip to the zoo, a day with a friend, and so on. Rewards might also be social—hugs, kisses, and pats. Or, more important, you can teach your children to recognize the good feelings that naturally come from doing what is right. To the degree you can do that, your children won't need other rewards. They will instead provide their own.

## PRINCIPLES OF SELF-ESTEEM

In disciplining children, parents must be careful to maintain the children's self-esteem. We should never put them down or destroy their image of themselves. Here are some ways we can strengthen the self-esteem of our children:

1. Build on the strengths and abilities and gifts of each individual child.

2. Commend children frequently in an honest expression of love and admiration for their having magnified some talent or having done something good. If you are watchful, you can always find some things to compliment them on. A good rule is to compliment four or five times for every correction you make.

If you can't think of anything good, pray that the Lord will help you see some things upon which you might compliment them. That will always work. Remember the rule to *commend in public* and *correct in private*. Always be careful to reject children's bad actions but not the children themselves.

3. Remember that the worth of souls is great in the sight of God (see D&C 18:10).

4. Esteem your children as yourself (see D&C 38:24; Matthew 22:39).

5. Look to the heart rather than the outward appearance (see 1 Samuel 16:7). Help your family appreciate the importance of both.

6. Self-respect seems to be based on feeling lovable and worthwhile. Be sure you do nothing to destroy either of those feelings in your children.

7. Your belief in the person is the most important thing to be conveyed.

8. Remember that body language, many times, speaks louder than words.

9. All children have an overpowering need for love, acceptance, and approval. Seek to provide that, especially when you're disciplining. Be sure and give not only attention but *focused attention* to your children. Children especially need focused attention when they are under stress. It isn't enough just to be with your children; they must also feel involved and important and loved. In many families children misbehave because of lack of attention. They try to get attention by doing things they know are wrong but that will attract their parents' notice. If we will truly listen to our children, not by just knowing they are around but by focusing clearly upon them and their needs, wants, and feelings, many problems will be resolved before they ever develop.

10. Be sure to do things with your children not just on your schedule and on your "turf" but also on theirs.

11. Be honest in your own feelings about situations. Share conflicting feelings. If you share only part of your feelings, you may confuse your children, and they may see it as dishonesty.

12. It's not enough to just love children. They need to be cherished just because they exist, just because they are children of our Heavenly Father.

13. Be sure to treat your children as separate and

independent people with a right to their own feelings, ideas, and attitudes.

14. See yourself as a "feeling releaser" rather than a fact finder or a judge of evidence. Withhold your preaching until a later time. First find out what your children are feeling. Remember that negative feelings always precede negative acts.

I will never forget the impact a particular man had on me in damaging my self-image in athletics. I was in the seventh grade, was a little taller than the other boys, and was doing quite well in basketball and track. However, as the year progressed, the coach began saying to me, "Gene, stay on the bench. You're no ball player. You're too clumsy! You can't run. You can't shoot. You're not fast enough." This treatment continued for a number of months.

I finally began to believe what the coach was saying, and in coming years I did my best to avoid sports altogether. I set aside running. I determined not to play basketball with the young men at church or school.

This negative conditioning followed me into my first year of college. Some athletics were required, but I minimized my involvement as much as possible.

A year later I served a mission in a distant land. In that country the buses did not stop to let passengers board; they just slowed down. We soon learned to board the bus while on the run. One afternoon as a missionary companion and I looked down the street toward the bus stop, we saw the bus coming. We took off running to catch it so as not to miss our next appointment. To my great surprise I beat my companion to the bus stop. Later that day, I purposely arranged a few runs for the bus, and each time I beat my companion. I was shocked and amazed, especially because my companion had received a number of awards in college for being one of the fastest runners in northern Arizona. It was then I realized I had wasted all those years. I could have excelled in athletics, but I had believed what someone else had planted in my mind.

I was totally taken aback by this experience. That very day I spent some time considering what had happened to me and whether I had created this image in my own mind or the coach had inadvertently done it. It didn't matter; the effect was the same. As a result of that experience, I reexamined my life in a number of other areas, trying to determine if by chance I could have been "fooled" by myself or someone else into believing things about myself that were just not true.

Some people believe they are not good in music, and thus they are not. Others believe they are not good in math, and thus they are not. Of course, some have gifts in certain areas, but all can improve upon what they have. Whatever you sincerely believe about yourself becomes true, even if it is false in the beginning. We would all do well to stop and examine the beliefs we hold about ourselves, because many are true and probably many are not.

Many of us go through life believing ourselves capable of a lot less than we really are. Be careful in dealing with your children to help them believe the very best they can about themselves and the gifts the Lord has given them. Be careful not to inhibit them in the great growth and potential of which they are capable.

We must discipline our children in love, considering their eternal welfare. Our main purpose must always be to turn their hearts to the Lord. If we do that, our discipline will always be effective.

# CHAPTER SEVEN

# TEACHING YOUR FAMILY TO KEEP THE COMMANDMENTS

My wife's great-great-grandparents, Edward and Caroline Amelia Owens Webb, were among the Latter-day Saints who were driven out of Nauvoo. Brother Webb was a blacksmith, and when he arrived in Council Bluffs, Brigham Young asked him to stay there for a time to help outfit the pioneers going West. One year, two years, three years, four years, and finally five years passed before word came for Brother and Sister Webb to move their family to the Salt Lake Valley. They were thrilled that at last they could join the rest of the Saints.

By 1852 the Webbs were outfitted to make the journey, and they traveled with the last company to leave Council Bluffs. When their company reached the Platte River, an epidemic of cholera struck the camp, and several people died of it.

Amasa Lyman, writing about this disease, said: "The cries and moanings of those suddenly attacked were truly terrific—to see one stricken down in a moment and in a short hour the ruddy glow of health displaced by the pallor of death and to know that the sufferers were the forms of loved ones endeared to us by the tenderest ties that bind the heart and soul, was heart rending. To most of those sufferers there was no rest but the grave. However, some were healed, through administration, by a servant of God."

A young woman who was suffering with this disease sent for Brother Webb to administer to her. Though his wife tried to persuade him not to go, a thing she had never done before, he felt he should go and perform this duty when called upon. In faith he administered to the sick girl. She was healed and was able to go on to the Salt Lake Valley. However, he was struck with the disease and died that very night. From a box nailed to the end of his wagon a rude coffin was made, and he was buried at night near the Platte River. In the sketch of her life, his wife wrote, "He died in full faith of the gospel."

We can only imagine how Sister Webb must have felt. In helping another, her husband had lost his own life. It would have been easy for her to challenge God, to be upset, to be angry, and to turn her family from the Church. Instead, she was obedient to the commandment of the Lord and took her family alone to the Salt Lake Valley. She was faithful to the end. Now many years have passed. What does the Webb family have to show for this sacrifice in faith? Hundreds and hundreds of their descendants have been endowed and sealed in the temple and are faithful in the kingdom.

How important it is to keep the commandments of the Lord! How far-reaching is the impact of faithful parents! That faithfulness can be traced through generations of Saints.

Clearly, we must teach our children to keep the commandments. If we have taught them to turn their hearts to the Lord and to feel the promptings of the Spirit, teaching them to keep the commandments of the Lord will be relatively simple. Also, as children watch their parents living the commandments, they will *see, feel,* and *know* the importance of so doing. They will experience the blessings that come from keeping the commandments in a faithful family and thus will not have to be convinced or go through a period of rebelliousness. Still, they do need to be taught.

Parents sometimes think their children will learn to keep the commandments by osmosis or learn them on their own. They say, "Well, I was never taught by my parents, and I suppose children have the freedom to choose on their own." However, the Lord has instructed us that parents are to teach their children:

> Inasmuch as parents have children in Zion, or
> in any of her stakes which are organized, that
> teach them not to understand the doctrine of

> repentance, faith in Christ the Son of the living God, and of baptism and the gift of the Holy Ghost by the laying on of the hands, when eight years old, the sin be upon the heads of the parents.
>
> For this shall be a law unto the inhabitants of Zion, or in any of her stakes which are organized.
>
> And their children shall be baptized for the remission of their sins when eight years old, and receive the laying on of the hands.
>
> And they shall also teach their children to pray, and to walk uprightly before the Lord.
>
> And the inhabitants of Zion shall also observe the Sabbath day to keep it holy (D&C: 68:25–29).

Alma was taught by the Spirit of the responsibility to teach his children to keep the commandments:

> The Spirit of the Lord doth say unto me: Command thy children to do good, lest they lead away the hearts of many people to destruction; therefore I command you, my son, in the fear of God, that ye refrain from your iniquities (Alma 39:12).

The Lord will hold us responsible if we do not teach our children. President Heber J. Grant said it well:

> The Lord has said it is our duty to teach our children in their youth, and I prefer to take His words for it rather than the words of those who are not obeying His commandments. It is folly to imagine that our children will grow up with a knowledge of the Gospel without teaching. . . . I may know that the Gospel is true, and so may my wife; but I want to tell you that our children will not know that the Gospel is true, unless they study it and gain a testimony for themselves. Parents are deceiving themselves in imagining that their children will be born with a knowledge of the Gospel (*Conference Report*, April 1902, p. 80).

Church leaders need to be careful not to take over this responsibility from parents. Elder Boyd K. Packer has said:

Bishops, keep constantly in mind that fathers are responsible to preside over their families.

Sometimes, with all good intentions, we require so much of both the children and the father that he is not able to do so.

If my boy needs counseling, bishop, it should be my responsibility first, and yours second. If my boy needs recreation, bishop, I should provide it first, and you second. If my boy needs correction, that should be my responsibility first, and yours second.

If I am failing as a father, help me first, and my children second. Do not be too quick to take over from me the job of raising my children ("Solving Emotional Problems in the Lord's Own Way," *Ensign*, May 1978, p. 93).

## TEACHING CHILDREN TO RECEIVE THE ORDINANCES OF THE GOSPEL

Parents should make a special effort to prepare their children for baptism and the reception of the Holy Ghost. They should also prepare them for ordination to the priesthood, missions, temple marriage, and so on. As children learn to follow the Spirit, they will naturally want to receive the ordinances of the gospel.

There is great power in the ordinances. President Brigham Young said:

> Let the father and mother, who are members of this Church and Kingdom, take a righteous course, and strive with all their might never to do a wrong, but to do good all their lives; if they have one child or one hundred children, if they conduct themselves towards them as they should, binding them to the Lord by their faith and prayers, I care not where those children go, they are bound up to their parents by an everlasting tie, and no power of earth or hell can separate them from their parents in eternity; they will return again to the fountain from whence they sprang. (In Joseph Fielding Smith, *Doctrines of Salvation*, 2:90–91).

## TEACHING THE LAW OF TITHING

A few years ago, one of my sons got his first paycheck from his job at a cemetery. The check was for $245, and he was very excited about buying some things he wanted.

We went to the credit union, where he put a third of the money in his mission fund and held out the rest for tithing and for a bicycle. While we were driving back home, this son put his envelope with the money in it in a cubicle in the back of our station wagon.

Suddenly another driver began honking at us, rather rudely, I thought. We moved ahead, thinking he wanted the passing lane. He continued to honk and acted very excited. Finally at a stop light he yelled through the window, "Don't you know your boy is throwing money out the window? Twenty-dollar bills were flying all around."

While we had been driving, one of our younger children had found the money and proceeded to throw it out the back window. We were all very upset. We drove off the highway and had a word of prayer. Then the whole family searched for a quarter of a mile along both sides of the highway but didn't find one single bill. (The total lost was about sixty-five dollars.) The bills must have blown away or been picked up by other people. My older son cried and was very upset, as we had been on our way that very moment to buy his bicycle.

This son finally said that if he used his tithing money, he would still have enough to buy the bike. We told him we didn't think that was a very good idea. He said, "You've always told me that the earth is the Lord's and the fulness thereof. Well, now he's got his money." He was determined that we should take him to buy the bike, using his tithing money. We finally said we would talk about it a day or two later after he had cooled down and prayed about it. After that, if he still wanted to do it, we would sustain him in his decision. If not, he ought to pay his tithing to the bishop.

We were very pleased a few days later to see him walk into the bishop's office and pay his tithing. He had turned to the Lord and received an answer and was obedient to those promptings. We told him he would surely be blessed for having done that.

However, as is often the case, he began to face some tests. The owner of the cemetery where he worked said he would have to terminate his employment. The cemetery had been purchased by someone else whose son was going to do his job. My son was very hurt by that and said to us somewhat kiddingly but with a bit of seriousness, "I wonder if it really does pay to pay your tithing?"

He struggled a few more weeks trying to get a job somewhere else but could not. Finally, a doctor who was a member of the Church called him to say that he had a cleaning job to be done in his office and that if my son wanted the job, he would employ him. My son was delighted.

Interestingly, though the janitorial work didn't pay quite as much as the cemetery job had, the doctor took a personal interest in our son and did much to help him mature and prepare for his mission. The gain to our son was much more than just a financial one.

This experience in keeping the commandments was a blessing to the whole family, and it especially served our son well as he went on his mission and was able to preach from first-hand experience the importance of paying an honest tithing to the Lord.

## TEACHING CHILDREN TO PROCLAIM THE GOSPEL

When one of my daughters was ten years old, we had been talking as a family about how to use the Spirit to influence other people.

One day while she was talking with her nonmember piano teacher, who came to our home to provide lessons, she felt an inspiration come to her. She said to her teacher, feeling this would bring the Spirit to her, "Let's sing together." The teacher was agreeable, so my daughter purposely gave her our hymnbook from which to play. The teacher easily played the hymns, and they sang together. After singing a few numbers, our daughter felt the additional impression to sing "In Our Lovely Deseret." The lyrics of this hymn talk about not using tobacco, tea, coffee, or alcohol—all of which the teacher used. This good daughter started to sing the words with the teacher, but the teacher choked up and couldn't continue singing. As a result of our daughter's initiative, we were able as a family to teach more of the gospel to her.

Some weeks later, this same girl challenged a group of teachers at school to quit drinking coffee (they were on their coffee break). She told them it was against the commandments of the Lord. A teacher, with a chuckle in her voice, called to inform us of our daughter's activities. These kinds of experiences build real faith in a child. It was interesting to see how courageous she was, and now, as a teenager, what a great missionary spirit she still has. Those experiences served her well.

We need to be sure that in training our children to keep the commandments, we do not neglect missionary work. Children can have a great influence in bringing people to Christ, and as they have these experiences, they will develop a desire to serve formal missions when they are older. We must teach our young men and, as appropriate, our young women to go on missions. All young men should be prepared to go. We have always felt that our daughters should be prepared to go on a mission or be married in the temple, whichever comes first. All of our children have been taught to save for both mission and marriage. As you teach your children to prepare for missionary service, you might consider the following:

1. In family prayer, let your children hear you pray about the time they will go on a mission, and pray that they will prepare for one. Some parents have said, "We will pray them there."

2. Remind your children of the covenants they made in

the premortal life to "labor in [the Lord's] vineyard for the salvation of the souls of men" (D&C 138:56).

3. Remind young men particularly that missionary service is inherent in the priesthood. When they receive their ordination, they also receive a calling to call the world to repentance.

4. Be sure that your children, at the appropriate time, receive a patriarchal blessing. That blessing will be of tremendous guidance to them through the years. For many it will give specific instruction about missionary service.

5. Share missionary stories from your own experiences and those of others.

6. Teach children that a mission is just another stop on their way to exaltation. It will prepare them for the rest of their lives. If we will truly teach our children the importance of missionary work, they will be greatly blessed.

There is a mission of the family as well as a mission of the Church. The mission of the family is also to proclaim the gospel, perfect its members, and redeem their kindred dead. Teach your children by example as well as by precept, and they will be great missionaries—in each of these areas.

## CONTROLLING TELEVISION AND MOVIES

In my judgment, we must be careful not to let television rob us of time with the family. We have had varying rules about television, but the result over the years is that we've watched it very little in our family. Sometimes we have gone for months or even years with the television unplugged. Normally, during the school year, the television has not been on from Monday through Thursday. We have watched some on Friday and Saturday as a family. Sometimes the children have watched cartoons.

Too much television gives children the idea that they should always be entertained, often at the expense of learning about more important things. Although we can't hide from television and the world, we can certainly teach our children to be selective and disciplined about what and how much they watch. We should be careful to help them pick programs that will be educational and uplifting. Some families have found it beneficial to simply disconnect the television.

Teaching our children to keep the commandments when they're with us will bring great payoffs when they're alone and have to rely on themselves and the promptings to know what to do. My wife and I were so pleased to hear from some friends about the faithfulness of one of our sons.

This nonmember family had tried on occasion to get our son to do things with them on Sunday, but he had always told them that Sunday was a family day, that it was the Lord's day, and that he didn't do those kinds of things on Sunday. He had always refused in a polite way. They were very impressed with the fact that even under some real influence from them, he would tell them no.

What added more to their experience with him was when they decided to go to a movie on a weekday and asked him to go with them. He said, "I can only go if it is a good movie, if it doesn't have swearing and sex in it." They said that would be all right. He asked what movie they were planning on seeing. When he learned what movie it was, he told them he didn't think he should go. They didn't pressure him, but they did try to persuade him.

They were somewhat surprised that his convictions about the quality of the movie were enough to turn down a friend, their son, who wanted him to go. They were even more impressed with the fact that he would stand up to two adults and tell them that.

I'm thankful that my son did what was right on his own, with his parents nowhere in sight. As a result of his example, my wife and I were able to introduce the gospel to this family.

I remember another time when I decided to take two of my sons to a certain movie. We had heard good reports about it from neighbors, but the first few minutes had a lot of very bad language. The three of us commented to each other that it was surely bad but assumed it would pass. The language continued but so did our interest in the show.

I asked the boys a couple of times, "What do you think we should do?" perhaps more to see where they were in their thinking than anything else. (To be honest, I was really enjoying the show and, except for the language, would have liked to stay.) The language became even more severe, and finally the younger boy said, "Dad, I don't think it's right that we should stay here." The older one quickly agreed. They both sat there staring at me to see what I would say. I choked out, "Well, you're probably right. I think you're right. Let's go." So, with some reluctance, and yet knowing that we were doing what was right, we walked out of the movie within fifteen minutes of its beginning.

We ended up going somewhere else and doing something fun together. As I left the movie, I had some interesting feelings:

1. I have good sons.
2. They were really sensitive to the Spirit and were anxious to do what was right at all costs.
3. They looked to their dad to see how he would respond.
4. I felt pleased that all three of the "Cook boys" had walked out of the show and not stayed to watch it even though the temptation was great.

This was a case where dad really wanted to see the movie and might have been tempted to do so, but his children were more disciplined at that moment than he was.

## KEEPING THE SABBATH DAY

Sometimes children have real questions about what they can do on the Sabbath Day. Following is a list of some activities that might be appropriate on Sunday; at least they have been of assistance to our family:

1. Read the scriptures.
2. Read Church magazines.
3. Write letters.
4. Do family history work.
5. Go to a Church visitor's center.
6. Visit the sick and the lonely.
7. Read good books.
8. Play quiet family games.
9. Write in a journal.
10. Pray.
11. Fast.
12. Hold family discussions.
13. Memorize scriptures.
14. Play and sing hymns.
15. Do missionary work.
16. Quietly walk through the neighborhood visiting neighbors.

What is most important is for a family to learn together from the scriptures what it really means to keep the commandments and then work together to do so. That's a much better approach than just "laying down the law." If children participate in helping to determine what's right, they will usually make things more strict than the parents would anyway.

Once when we were struggling with what it meant to keep the Sabbath Day holy, we determined to turn to the scriptures and see what the Lord had said. Consulting the Topical Guide, we looked up and read aloud the following passages:

> *Exodus 31:13–17:* Speak thou also unto the children of Israel, saying, Verily my sabbaths ye shall keep: for it is a sign between me and you throughout your generations; that ye may known that I am the Lord that doth sanctify you. Ye shall keep the sabbath therefore; for it is holy unto you: every one that defileth it shall surely be put to death: for whosoever doeth any work therein, that soul

shall be cut off from among his people. Six days may work be done; but in the seventh is the sabbath of rest, holy to the Lord whosoever doeth any work in the sabbath day, he shall surely be put to death. Wherefore the children of Israel shall keep the sabbath, to observe the sabbath throughout their generations, for a perpetual covenant. It is a sign between me and the children of Israel for ever: for in six days the Lord made heaven and earth, and on the seventh day he rested, and was refreshed.

*Nehemiah 10:31:* And if the people of the land bring ware or any victuals on the sabbath day to sell, that we would not buy it of them on the sabbath, or on the holy day: and that we would leave the seventh year, and the exaction of every debt.

*Nehemiah 13:15:* In those days saw I in Judah some treading wine presses on the sabbath, and bringing in sheaves, and lading asses; as also wine, grapes, and figs, and all manner of burdens, which they brought into Jerusalem on the sabbath day: and I testified against them in the day wherein they sold victuals.

*Isaiah 58:13:* If thou turn away thy foot from the sabbath, from doing thy pleasure on my holy day; and call the sabbath a delight, the holy of the Lord, honorable; and shalt honour him, not doing thine own ways, nor finding thine own pleasure, nor speaking thine own words:

*Matthew 12:8:* For the Son of man is Lord even of the sabbath day.

Our observations as a family:

1. The Sabbath is a sign of faithfulness, a perpetual covenant between us and the Lord.
2. We are not to work but to rest on the Sabbath.
3. We are not to buy or sell on the Sabbath.
4. We are not to do our pleasure on the Lord's holy day.
5. Christ is Lord of the Sabbath.

*D&C 59:9–14:* That thou mayest more fully keep thyself unspotted from the world, thou shalt go to the house of prayer and offer up thy sacraments upon my holy day; for verily this is a day appointed unto you to rest from your labors, and to pay thy devotions unto the Most High; nevertheless thy vows shall be offered up in righteousness on all days and at all times; but remember that on this, the Lord's day, thou shalt offer thine oblations and thy sacraments unto the Most High, confessing thy sins unto thy brethren, and before the Lord. And on this day thou shalt do none other thing, only let thy food be prepared with singleness of heart that thy fasting may be perfect, or, in other words, that thy joy may be full. Verily, this is fasting and prayer, or in other words, rejoicing and prayer.

We observed that we may:

1. Offer our sacraments on the Lord's holy day.
2. Rest (a nap is okay).
3. Pay our devotions.
4. Offer our oblations (time, talent, means, and service).
5. Confess our sins.
6. "Do none other thing."
7. Fast.

*D&C 59:15–20:* Inasmuch as ye do these things with thanksgiving, with cheerful hearts and countenances, not with much laughter, for this is sin, but with a glad heart and a cheerful countenance—verily I say, that inasmuch as ye do this, the fullness of the earth is yours, the beasts of the field and the fowls of the air, and that which climbeth upon the trees and walketh upon the earth; yea, and the herb, and the good things which come of the earth, whether for food or for raiment, or for houses, or for barns, or for orchards, or for gardens, or for vineyards; yea, all things which come of the earth, in the season thereof, are made for the benefit and the use of man, both to please the eye and to gladden the heart; yea, for food and for raiment, for taste and for smell, to strengthen the body and to enliven the soul. And it pleaseth God that he hath given all these things unto man; for unto this end were they made to be used, with judgment, not to excess, neither by extortion.

We observed that as we keep the Sabbath, the Lord will give us the fullness of the earth, including food, clothing, houses, barns, and so on.

As we read together, we listed the main points of each verse, watching for the things the Lord expected and the wonderful promises he had made. We reviewed the commandments in some detail and thus learned with the Spirit what the Lord would have us know about the Sabbath Day.

It is interesting that when a family takes that kind of approach, the Lord's values pass from the older generation to the younger generation. If parents teach and testify by the Spirit, their values pass into the younger generation's hearts. I believe that is what happened that day in our family. When we were finished, we felt that we understood more clearly what it meant to keep the Sabbath Day holy, and we felt a renewed desire to do so. *This is a powerful way to teach your children (and to learn yourself) any principle of the gospel.*

## TEACHING HONESTY

Parents should make a special effort to teach their children to be honest with others and with themselves. They should teach them to honor the laws of the land, including traffic laws, tax laws, and so on. In these things, especially, children will follow their parents' example.

One morning one of my sons, a nine-year-old, and I took a three-mile walk, and he talked almost the whole time as I asked him questions and prodded him along.

In the process, he told me he had passed a pre-test in school on Monday with a score of 100 percent and thus would not have to take the spelling test on Friday. I commended him for it and we went on talking.

A little while after we returned home, my wife sought me out privately and said, "Your son has something to talk to you about." His conscience was bothering him badly because he had told me a lie about his spelling test.

He'd felt really bad about it and gone in immediately to confess to his mom. The truth was that he didn't get 100 percent on his test; he had misspelled one word and gotten 99 percent. He had spelled the word "Friday" as "Fryday" but had corrected it anyway and submitted the score of 100 percent. He was very embarrassed to tell her and then later confessed to me through his tears.

To make matters worse, his teacher had put his name on the board with the other star students whose names stay on the board all week when they pass the Monday spelling test. He felt very repentant and guilty and yet relieved that he had confessed it to his mom and then later to his dad.

He asked what he should do. We asked him what *he* thought he should do. He said he had to tell his teacher, but he said, "I'm so embarrassed. She'll wipe my name right off the board, and all the kids will ask, 'How come your name's not on the board?' " He was really worried about having to face up to the truth and especially the public humiliation that might be forthcoming.

In addition, he was worried about when he would even tell his teacher. He said, "She's always in the room, and there are always students around." We suggested that he try to seek her out in the hallway before she arrived in class, or afterward, and maybe he could solve it that way.

We told him that he needed to face the music and put things right, and that if he did it humbly and prayerfully, perhaps his teacher could figure out a way to handle it so that he wouldn't be unduly embarrassed. We all three had a prayer together. He seemed relieved, and I know he prayed about it that night. We bid him farewell the next morning and wished him good luck with his teacher.

He came back from school very happy. He had caught his teacher before she arrived in the classroom and talked the problem through with her. She was very happy that he had been honest with her, and while all the kids were out to recess, she erased his name, and no one ever noticed that his name was gone from the board.

He was greatly relieved that his teacher had received his confession well, and he was thankful that he had been honest. He told us three or four times the next night that he would never lie again. He said, "I've learned a hard lesson about telling the truth."

I'm always amazed at how the punishments that the Lord has for disobedience to his laws seem to be built right into the laws themselves. If we are dishonest, we will pay the penalty sooner or later. The guilt that is associated with disobedience is often sufficient to bring about repentance.

It's amazing that even with a child, guilt is the signal from the Spirit that something is wrong. I'm thankful that this son was a boy of integrity in this incident and that he was willing to tell the Lord, his parents, and his teacher.

## TEACHING THE WORD OF WISDOM

We must teach children to avoid the use of tobacco, alcohol, coffee, tea, and all inappropriate drugs. We must teach them to keep their bodies healthy and strong before the Lord at all times.

I once interviewed a young priest who had been going out with some friends who were not such a good influence on him. These young men smoked, and they had been working on this young man (we'll call him John) to smoke. He'd told them no many times, but he finally caved in and said, "Well, I think a little bit won't hurt. Just one." And he started smoking a bit. He went to the priests quorum one Sunday morning, and one of the priests began to sniff and said, "Aha! You've been smoking, John." John was terribly embarrassed and turned red-faced in front of everybody. As he left the meeting that day he thought, "What should I do?

Should I continue to be friends with these priests, or should I go off with my other friends?" Unfortunately, he decided to go with his other friends.

I met him six months after that "little decision" to smoke one cigarette. By then he had also broken the laws about drinking alcohol and using drugs, and he had even broken the law of chastity two times when he finally came to confess what he had done. He said to me through his tears, "Elder Cook, all for a dumb cigarette. That's what did it to me. If I had just not done that . . . "

I said, "What do you mean?"

He said, "Well, I didn't realize that my friends were doing a lot more than smoking. Then I found out that they were drinking, too. And I found they were doing other things worse than that. Before I knew it, I was ensnared in it." And then again he said, "For one dumb cigarette." That is a very telling story.

I remember another young man who had resisted his friends on an athletic team who had pressured him to drink. He had done well in resisting them, but they continued to harp at him. He finally thought (erroneously), "If I go out with them and drink just one time, I'll get them off my back. At least they'll leave me alone and quit teasing me about being a Mormon." And so he believed that lie.

Now, if you want to get a drink, where do you go? You don't go to the church or to the bishop's house, do you? You go to a bar. And there are a lot more things going on in a bar than just drinking. There may be people who have more on their minds than just having a drink. Well, this eighteen-year-old didn't think too much about that and went in to have a drink with the boys. An hour or so later he came out, an unchaste person.

Once again, having confessed to his bishop and stake president, he wept in an interview with me. He sorrowed over the fact that he had been ensnared by "one dumb drink." He said, "Elder Cook, if you ever have a chance to talk to young people, tell them how dumb I was so they won't fall into the same trap." And it all began with just one drink.

## TEACHING CHASTITY

Chastity is one of the most important of the Lord's commandments, and in many ways it has the most far-reaching effects. We should carefully teach our children to avoid pornography, inappropriate videos (especially at friends' homes), being alone with someone of the opposite sex, filthy language, dirty jokes, bad stories, improper dress standards, close dancing, kissing, petting, masturbation, and improper thoughts. We must teach them that Satan continually says, "A little bit won't hurt," and that he will do all in his power to tempt and try them and cause them to fall into sin. Teach them clearly that all such sins come from Satan himself, and that he is behind the teaching of these evil practices. They must be taught that if they meddle with these things in the least degree, they will get burned. Of course, our own example is paramount in teaching children to avoid these things.

It's often good to role-play with our children how they might handle temptations that arise. For example, if someone offers to let them look at pornography, what will be their response? What if someone offers them a drink or a cigarette? If they have worked this out with their family beforehand, they will know what to do when the reality hits. Parents can use this technique in teaching any area of the gospel.

We should emphasize the positive in teaching moral cleanliness, stressing especially the blessings it brings. We must spend many a family home evening teaching children the importance of keeping themselves chaste throughout their lives. The world would have them believe that all young people are involved in immorality. We must teach otherwise. We must teach the Lord's standard about moral cleanliness. Where should children learn about sexuality? Who should provide sex education? Without question it must come from their parents. From the time children are small, parents should teach them about their bodies, about cleanliness, and about the proper relationship between boys and girls. This should be done naturally over the years so there won't need to be a "crash course" on "sex education" when they become teenagers.

If these matters are built on a spiritual foundation, they are easily understood by children. Parents need to be frank and direct in letting their children know that sexual relations that take place between parents are good and appropriate, not only for the important purpose of conceiving children but also in regenerating and strengthening love between husband and wife. Parents can show children that they love each other through appropriate displays of affection. Then the children will have little difficulty understanding these things.

Parents must be very careful never to cross the line of propriety with their children. Parents who are involved in any way with child abuse whether physical, mental, emotional, or any other kind, will certainly be held accountable before the Lord. Few sins are more serious. Children must be taught to be careful in their dealings with other adults as well. They should be quick to talk to their parents if any kind of abuse occurs.

## TEACHING REPENTANCE
## AND FORGIVENESS

The Lord has commanded us to repent and to forgive one another, and children especially must be taught these important principles of the gospel. Often the sweetest experiences in life have to do with forgiveness, and it is parents who must set the example. In disciplining children and helping them learn to repent, some of the greatest lessons of all are taught. These experiences allow us to truly teach our children to keep the commandments and to rely more fully on the Lord. If parents and children seek to follow the Spirit, they will forgive one another, and they will also receive forgiveness from the Lord.

When I arrived home from work one day, I found my youngest son in a very sober mood. He came up and put his arms around me, and I could tell he was upset about something. My wife and daughters all knew what he was doing and signaled me to give him a lot of love. He was very, very sad and took me into the bedroom.

There on the bed was my outdoor thermometer—now broken—with about seven dollars in bills and coins—all the money he had. My boy told me through his tears that he had accidentally broken the thermometer by kicking his ball. He particularly felt bad because he had broken the one in the front yard the week before. Also, he felt even worse because he knew I had worked to calibrate the thermometers with each other and with the thermostat. He was sure I was going to be really upset.

I put my arm around him and told him that I forgave him. He was so repentant that I didn't have the heart to make him pay for the thermometer, or even for part of it, although ordinarily I would have. I was glad I didn't, as I learned later that the accident had happened that morning and he had been sorrowful the whole day. He was *really* repentant.

He told me later that evening that he had prayed fervently to the Lord that I would not be mad at him. For some reason he had been really worried and was very relieved when I told him I forgave him.

The next morning in scripture reading, we were reading in John 3 about how the Spirit comes to us and how we can be born again and have spiritual experiences throughout our lives. What made this experience especially sweet was that when I asked the children, "When was the last time you really felt like the Spirit helped you?" this youngest son said, with great feeling, "It was just yesterday." He related how he had prayed fervently that I would not be angry about the broken thermometer. He also said that after we had settled things between us the previous night, he had truly thanked the Lord for answering his prayer.

He said, "I really feel like the Spirit inspired me and that I was able to get my prayer answered. I also told the Lord how thankful I was, and I'm glad I did that." He was strongly confident that he had had an answer to prayer and that he had been inspired to follow the promptings of the Spirit to give thanks for the answer thereafter.

Without question, if we will properly teach our children faith in the Lord Jesus Christ and repentance as the first two basic principles of the gospel, those principles will lead our children to the ordinances of the gospel. They will learn of the Lord's forgiveness of sin and of his atoning sacrifice for all of us. If we keep those things in mind as we are teaching the principles, we'll be better at disciplining our children and teaching them obedience to the Lord's commandments.

The Lord really will bless our families if we turn the hearts of our children to us as their parents and even more so to their Father in Heaven. The same will be true if parents turn their own hearts to their children. May the Lord bless us to teach our children with profound love and thus turn all of our hearts to God.

CHAPTER EIGHT

# TEACHING YOUR FAMILY ABOUT WORK AND FINANCES

After we moved to a South American country to preside over a mission, we realized that our food budget was in serious trouble. We started talking about where the money was going. What was happening? Were we feeding all the missionaries, or what?

Then we began to realize that we were feeding four or five extra people a day who came begging at our door. They were very compelling cases, like the woman who would come with a three-year-old and say, "My son needs to have an operation. I don't have enough money, and without it he'll be dead within the month. I'm trying to get the money." You know how that would tug at your heartstrings, and my wife had responded from her heart.

We talked about that and thought, "Well, we can't support this whole city. We can't even support this neighborhood. In fact, on a mission budget we will have a hard time supporting ourselves." So we wondered what we should do. We decided that any time we really felt inspired to give, we would do so. However, we also came to understand that we were "on the beat." In other words, some people were sustaining themselves month after month by making the rounds of certain houses, and ours was one of them.

We had a piece of ground right by our front door, and I said, "Honey, when they come by, why don't we say, 'We'd be glad to give you a full dinner. We'd just like you to put in one hour working in this little plot of ground. We're thinking of putting in a garden.' "

Guess how many people in a full year took us up on the offer? Not one. Isn't that surprising? They had been taught an easier way. I don't know how many hundreds came to our house, but not a single one was willing to work to obtain

225

the money, medicine, or food for which they were asking. How thankful we should be for inspired principles of welfare that allow us to maintain our dignity and self-respect by working for what we receive.

Do these principles apply also in our families? Yes, they do. We must be sure to teach our children "how to fish" and not just "give them a fish." We must be careful not to provide an easy life-style for our children; rather, we must help them provide a life for themselves. If children are raised with a poor attitude about work and do not learn to sustain themselves, they will be weak and dependent as adults. They may ultimately become a liability to society instead of making a real contribution.

The Lord was speaking to us all when he said: "Cursed shall be the ground for thy sake; in sorrow shalt thou eat of it all the days of thy life. Thorns also, and thistles shall it bring forth to thee, and thou shalt eat the herb of the field. By the sweat of thy face shalt thou eat bread, until thou shalt return unto the ground—for thou shalt surely die— for out of it wast thou taken: for dust thou wast, and unto dust shalt thou return" (Moses 4:23–25).

The commandment to work was one of the first commandments given by the Lord to his children. I believe the Lord knew that if we were idle, we would be more prone to discouragement and temptation. If we were given something concrete to do, we would be closer to the Lord and more fulfilled in life. Nothing else is quite as disheartening as being idle and not having work enough to do. I believe this is why the Lord would have us work all the days of our lives, as we are physically able, to sustain ourselves by the sweat of our own brows.

The old proverb "Idle hands are the devil's workshop" is certainly true. The Lord has commanded us to be busily engaged in a good cause and to not idle away our time:

> It is not meet that I should command in all things; for he that is compelled in all things, the same is a slothful and not a wise servant; where-

fore he receiveth no reward. Verily I say, men should be anxiously engaged in a good cause, and do many things of their own free will, and bring to pass much righteousness" (D&C 58:26–27).

Cease to be idle; cease to be unclean; cease to find fault one with another; cease to sleep longer than is needful; retire to thy bed early, that ye may not be weary; arise early, that your bodies and your minds may be invigorated" (D&C 88:124; for other scriptures on work and related subjects, see the Topical Guide).

The Lord gave special instruction on this subject to parents: "I, the Lord, am not well pleased with the inhabitants of Zion, for there are idlers among them; and their children are also growing up in wickedness; they also seek not earnestly the riches of eternity, but their eyes are full of greediness" (D&C 68:31).

## TEACHING CHILDREN
## TO WORK AT HOME

Where will children learn the principles of work? They must learn them at home. These principles are not necessarily learned because parents try to teach them. They must be *experienced* by children in doing the work itself.

Parents must take the lead in determining what work must be done around the home and then dividing that work among their children according to their age and abilities and any special needs. This division of responsibilities will change over the months and years as the family grows older and as needs at home change, and it will depend on the children's physical, mental, and emotional ability.

A few years ago we divided up work responsibilities with a rotating job chart made from two paper plates, a large one and a small one, fastened together in the middle with a pin. On the larger plate were written the family chores; on the smaller plate were the names of the children. Each week the smaller plate could be turned and the duties rotated among family members.

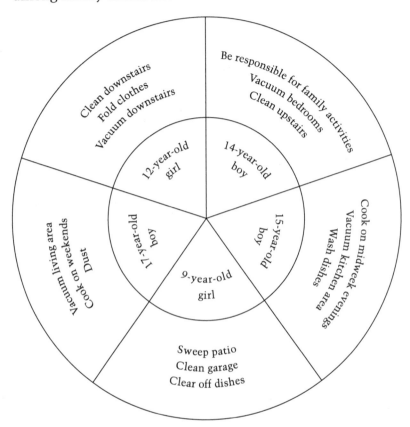

Of course, we made sure the children understood how to perform the duties on the chart before requiring them to follow it. We also followed up to make sure the children had done their work correctly. My wife checked the work inside the house, and I checked the work outside.

We also found that we needed a less formal list of things that had to be done around the home from time to time. It needed to be a flexible list that could be added to from day to day so the children would know daily what was expected of them. The list was helpful year round, but it was especially handy during the summer when children would ask over and over, "What can I do?"

We also used lists and charts to keep track of repairs, major purchases to be made, family home evening assignments, issues we wanted to discuss as a family, family activities, and so on.

Yes, to be successful, families must be well organized. But that kind of organization doesn't happen on its own. It requires plenty of planning and hard work.

As Elder L. Tom Perry has said:

> Eternal families don't "just happen." To enjoy this greatest of all gifts, we must earn it through our accomplishments here in mortality.
>
> First, I would be certain that sufficient time was calendared each week for a family executive committee meeting to plan family strategy. The executive committee, composed of a husband and wife, would meet together to fully communicate, discuss, plan, and prepare for their leadership role in the family organization.
>
> Second, I would make the family home evening times on Monday night a family council meeting where children were taught by parents how to prepare for their roles as family members and prospective parents. Family home evening would begin with a family dinner together, followed by a council meeting, where such topics as the following would be discussed and training would be given: temple preparation, missionary preparation, home management, family finances, career development, education, community involvement, cultural improvement, acquisition and care of real and personal property, family planning calendars, use of leisure time, and work assignments. The evening could be climaxed with a special dessert and time for parents to have individual meetings with each child.
>
> Third, Saturday would be a special activity day divided into two parts: first, a time for teaching children the blessings of work, how to care for and improve the home, the yard, the garden, the field; second, a time for family activity, to build a family heritage of things you enjoy doing together.

Fourth, Sunday would become the special day in each week. Careful preparation would precede the three hour worship service time at the chapel. The family would arrive at church rested, relaxed, and spiritually prepared to enjoy the meetings together. The balance of the day would be spent in a climate of spiritual uplift. We would dress to fit the occasion—boys in something somewhat better than levis and t-shirts, girls in comfortable, decent dresses, not in shorts or slacks. It would be a time for our family scripture study, genealogical research, personal journals, family histories, letter writing, missionary contacts, and visits to extended family, to friends, and to shut-ins ("For Whatsoever a Man Soweth, That Shall He Also Reap," *Ensign*, November 1980, p. 9).

## THE SPIRITUAL BENEFITS OF WORK

Why is it necessary for children to work, and work hard, around the home? I believe there are many reasons, both spiritual and temporal, for the Lord's commandment that we must work all the days of our lives:

1. Work causes children to be more disciplined.

2. Work causes children to feel a part of the family, part of a team.

3. Work helps the family fulfill family objectives. Keeping up a home requires lots of work: cleaning, repairing, painting, gardening, and so on. Children benefit from that work, and they also have a responsibility to help accomplish it.

4. Work teaches children responsibility. It teaches them that they must do their part in the family as well as in society. Work will also help children become responsible Church members, and it will be of great assistance to them when they must go into the workplace and sustain themselves in the world.

5. Work teaches children to be disciplined enough to "finish the job." They learn patience, perseverance, disci-

pline, and many spiritual characteristics that cannot be learned otherwise.

I'll never forget how my Father taught his children as we worked in a citrus grove in Arizona. It was hot work, in temperatures up to 110 degrees, and we really wanted to go inside for a drink. He would always say, "Let's do just two more rows and then we'll go in." That taught us to discipline ourselves and to make sure the job was finished.

6. Work allows children to have a job inspected and approved and corrected if need be. Proper follow-up from parents allows children to give an accounting of their work.

One father used to have his children straighten old nails that could not be used again. When asked why, he said that work is more than producing a result; it is a discipline. If parents focus on the outcome of their children's labors, they will become frustrated at how inadequately children do things. However, if they realize that the true outcome of the work is what the children *learn*, they will have more patience. They would realize they are building attributes and characteristics in their children that cannot be built in any other way.

7. Through work, children learn to be independent and self-reliant. Parents will not need to worry about them. They will do their responsibilities without being asked, nor will there be a need to follow up much. For example, I never liked spraying fruit trees. As my older sons learned how to do that, it was a great blessing to me not to have to worry about it. Each few weeks the trees were sprayed. They relieved me of that responsibility and thus became more responsible themselves.

I'll never forget a sweet note one of my daughters gave to me after we had some difficulty with her not wanting to work. After some counsel, she did the work and felt really good about her accomplishments. She tucked a note into my suitcase when I was leaving for one of my conference assignments. Part of the note read:

> You mean so much to me and you do more
> than I know or than I can repay you. I hope I will
> never disappoint you, and that I'll always be a
> good daughter to you. You deserve the best! I hope
> I can come close to what you deserve. And if you
> ever think you're not handsome or compare your-
> self, don't say it to me because it makes me cry.
> You are the best dad there is! I love you for every-
> thing. Have a good night's sleep. I love you!

How happy that made a father feel that night, but especially because he had loved his daughter enough to discipline her when she didn't want to do her work. She learned.
I learned.

8. Work teaches children to have confidence in themselves. They will know they can work, and work effectively.
Then when the parents are gone, the work will go on anyway. This will give parents even more confidence in their
children and treat them accordingly—a pleasant cycle for
any family.

9. Work teaches a family to be together, work together,
and accomplish good things together. We must be sure we
don't just send our children out to work but that we *work
with them*. Besides getting the work done and building good
relationships, spending this time together provides an opportunity to discuss prayer, scripture reading, and other important principles. Time spent together with children provides
many "teaching moments."

Work also provides many fun times. I will never forget
one little boy who saw his father drive up to the garden with
a truck full of manure. The boy said, "What is that for?"
The father said, "It's for the strawberries." The boy said,
"Well, if it's just the same to you, I'll just keep having sugar
and cream on mine."

## LEARNING SKILLS THROUGH WORK

Through their work at home, our children have learned
some unusual skills. One of our sons, for example, has

developed an uncanny mechanical aptitude that will be useful to him throughout his life.

When we were called to live in Mexico, we were quickly confronted with the fact that Latin Americans love keys. I thought that our home would have eight or ten keys for the various doors and cabinets. After we moved in, we counted sixty-two keys. There was a lock for everything—bedrooms, bathrooms, closets, kitchens, cabinets, and so on. Every lock had its own key, and all the keys were different.

The practice in that area was to leave the keys in the locks inside the house so they could be more easily managed, and we had been told by the "professionals" that our house was as secure as any in the area. After just a day or so, my fifteen-year-old son had learned how to unlock any of those locks from outside the house in about fifteen seconds using a coin, a pen, or a potato peeler. When I asked him how he had learned to do that, he said, "I just noticed that when a key is left in a lock, it frees the lock to turn, and it can easily be opened." He could get into any of the doors from the outside as long as the key was in the lock on the inside. Of course, we immediately stopped leaving the keys in the locks.

A building contractor for the Church came a few days later. He said, "I consider myself an expert on locks. We've put these locks in hundreds of places. We have always felt they were secure." He stood there in amazement as a young boy showed him how to open a door from the outside when it was locked on the inside.

Although we laughed about this incident, I realized that this young son had some unusual mechanical talent. He has always been quite ingenious in figuring out how things work and fixing them when they are broken. A lot of that, I think, has come from working on things around the house.

## GARDENING

The prophets have often counseled Church members to have a garden. We have always found a garden most useful in teaching our children to work. We have found that besides producing food, gardens strengthen family unity—we have really had to learn to work together to produce a large garden. It was so large at times that the children would claim we were trying to become farmers. They used to say, "Dad, we're nothing but slaves." It may have seemed so to them, but it was certainly a great way to teach them the value of work. To be continually responsible, as a garden requires, will certainly help children when they reach adulthood.

Gardening also teaches many spiritual lessons. It lets children see that the Lord's creations, things of *great value*, cannot be rushed. There is a process that must be followed patiently. They learn that besides doing the work, we must wait upon the Lord to finally see the fruits of our labor. Finally, children can see the hand of the Lord while working on a garden. The miracle of life in all its varieties is manifested. These are some of the jobs that can be delegated to individual children or done as a family.

To have an effective garden, families must plan the garden out, prepare the soil, and plant the seeds. Then, when the seeds begin to sprout, they must weed and weed and weed. At times we have had our children take responsibility for a particular part of the garden; at other times we have weeded together as a family. To succeed, we had to water regularly, spray as needed, and weed some more. This process takes work but develops discipline, patience, and endurance. Then the family begins to harvest, store, and eat the food, and they begin to appreciate the value of their work.

We have always found it a great blessing to have a year's supply of food. We have tried to store more than just the basics of wheat, sugar, and so on, and to have a year's supply of bottled fruit and canned goods. That meant one or two of our children had to keep a count of the inventory and suggest to their mother what we needed to purchase to maintain the supply. (We are constantly eating and replenishing our food storage.) Not only did our storage provide security for our family; it also gave them quality work to do, taught them useful skills, and helped them become more responsible. We also hope they will carry these characteristics into their adult life.

Finally, we have found that one of the great benefits of a garden is that we always produced more than we were able to eat. This gave us an opportunity to share with others in and around our neighborhood and develop good relations, except, may I say with a smile, in "Zucchini sharing." Actually, sharing vegetables always gave us a reason to go visit someone, and again some great principles were learned in the process.

I bear testimony that gardening is a tremendous way to teach the family many principles of the gospel. The Lord often mentioned planting and harvesting in his parables, with good reason, I think. Gardening teaches the true value of work—that we must plant and cultivate and then we can harvest. Watching plants grow also provides many spiritual lessons. In addition, gardening provides a lot of talking, sharing, and fun time together while the work is going on.

Of course, gardening has not always been fun and games. At times children had to be disciplined because they didn't want to work. Sometimes they let their duties go in order to go play with friends. But even though things haven't always gone smoothly, having *something worthwhile to do as a family* has been of invaluable assistance in raising up a family to the Lord.

## TEACHING CHILDREN
## TO WORK OUTSIDE THE HOME

President Wilford Woodruff once said:

> It is one of the greatest blessings that God ever bestowed upon children that they have had parents who were in possession of true principles in relation to their Heavenly Father, salvation, eternal life, and were qualified and capable of teaching and traditionating their children in the same that they may be qualified to fulfill the object of their creation. . . . Ninety-nine out of every hundred

children who are taught by their parents the principles of honesty and integrity, truth and virtue,
will observe them through life (*Discourses of
Wilford Woodruff,* ed. G. Homer Durham [Salt
Lake City: Bookcraft, 1990], pp. 266–68).

It is important for children to be able to learn principles
of honesty, truth, integrity, and virtue and to learn them at
home. Those children then go out in the world to work and
to begin to learn to sustain themselves. If those principles
are in place they will have a successful experience, in large
measure due to a good family who taught them those principles from the Lord.

It has been our experience that children must learn not
only to work at home but also to work in the world so they
can sustain themselves as they become older.

Work outside the home, of course, depends somewhat
on the age and ability of the children. We have always tried
to teach our children to earn money on their own as soon as
they were able. Some have been able to get paper routes at
age eleven or twelve. Before age sixteen, when most young
people can work, young children can work for neighbors in
mowing lawns, washing windows, washing cars, cleaning
garages, and so on.

We have also had fun teaching our younger children to
sell things. Some of their best money makers have been
cookie sales.

One of our sons was struggling to earn money. He had
tried to mow lawns around the neighborhood, wash windows, and so on but really couldn't find anyone who wanted
to employ him. His mother and I talked to him about learning how to make cookies on his own and sell them. He was
desperate enough that he determined to do so. His mom
taught him how, and he immediately made about ten dozen
cookies and went out to sell. I tried to coach him somewhat
before I went to work about what to say and felt that perhaps he would be able to do it.

When I came back home, a little earlier than usual that

afternoon, I found a very negative and discouraged young boy. He had gone to many homes but had only sold a dozen cookies. I told him that if he was going to be so negative and discouraged, the Lord could not help him. I told him that the Spirit would help those who exercised faith, believed they could do it, and believed that the Lord would help them.

I asked him if he believed that. He said, "I want to believe, but I've been out there. I was the one out knocking on all the doors, and nobody wants any cookies."

I said, "How would you feel about having a prayer together? Then I'll drive you around to see if we can exercise our faith more and help you sell the cookies."

He was relieved at that and said, "I think that would be very good."

He prayed and then I prayed. Each of us tried our best to exercise our faith in the Lord that he would be inspired to know what to say to touch the hearts of the people so they would purchase the cookies from him.

He was more encouraged as we left home but was still struggling a little with what he had faced earlier in the day. We reviewed very carefully what he was saying at each door. At the third home, he made a sale, and then again at the fourth, and at the sixth. Within forty-five minutes, he had sold nine dozen cookies and was twenty dollars richer. He was thrilled and humbled. His father was also humbled. We both realized that because he had set aside doubt, fear, and negativity and was trying to exercise faith in the Lord, that spirit was contagious to others. They sensed his sincerity, his earnestness, and his good spirit at the door, and thus they purchased the cookies.

The real object of all of this wasn't so much for him to earn money or even to learn to bake cookies, although that was valuable, but to learn the more important spiritual principles relative to work.

He learned determination and persistence. He learned how to respond to other people, to look them in the eye.

He learned to answer their questions directly, to speak with confidence, and to handle objections. Above all, he learned how it *feels* to succeed. He learned the satisfaction and fulfillment that came as a result of his own accomplishments, of fulfilling what he had set out to do. I might add that this boy, some years later, became one of the best cooks in our entire family. He is well known in the family and in the neighborhood for his pizza, his homemade ice cream, and, of course, his cookies.

One year, some weeks before Christmas, we told our younger children that they could earn some real money if they went around gathering up Christmas trees after Christmas and disposing of them for a fee. We thought if they called people on the phone, they could get a number of commitments. They could also try knocking on doors.

Two sons and a daughter made the major attempts and went down the street talking to the neighbors. They had some real discouragement, as they approached thirty or forty homes but signed up only three or four people. I told them they really had to sell their product, not just take orders. They challenged me, saying, "Oh, that can't be. We've tried it and people just aren't interested."

I took one of my sons aside, as he seemed the most interested, and gave him a persuasive talk to give on the telephone. He practiced it but tried to change some of the wording. I said, "No, you've got to say it exactly this way. If you'll say it this way, that will counter any objections they might have. If they say no because of a certain reason, then you must say this."

In about half an hour he had made twenty dollars. He then started to change his approach, adjusting the carefully measured words I had given him, and he started having less success. He quickly went back to the original wording and then continued to receive commitments to pick up Christmas trees.

A week or so after Christmas, I convinced a younger son and daughter to go with us and knock on the doors of houses on both sides of where we were to pick up the trees. They were to persuade the people to give them two dollars to haul away their trees. The children were agreeable but were not sure it would work.

After a while, the one son was really discouraged as he had not made a single sale. He came weeping into the car and said he was quitting. I finally convinced him to humble himself and to say what I had told him to say. Then he would have success. He said he would. Then he too began making sales.

I'll never forget the delight on my younger son's face when the first two dollars was placed in his hands. He came dragging the tree across the snow like lightning. His smile would have reached from the west coast to the east coast. What tremendous self-confidence he exuded!

One woman came to the truck and said to our older son, "I'm not really interested in having you haul my tree away, but you can do it. I'd pay two dollars anytime to see a boy working. Most young people just want a free ride. I commend you for earning your own way."

Our younger boy had gone to a door where the woman went to get the two dollars, but her husband came out and rather brusquely scared my boy off. He came back to the truck and said, "I'm sorry. He wouldn't buy."

"Well," I said, "did you tell him you would do it for one dollar?" He hadn't and wouldn't go back.

The older boy came to the truck, and I said to him, "This guy thinks he's winning. Go back and tell him we'll take his tree for one dollar."

This boy went to the door and said, "We've reconsidered; we've decided we'll take your tree for one dollar." The man didn't know what to say at this boy's determination. Finally he said, "Okay, you've got a deal for fifty cents." We hauled the tree away and all got a good laugh out of it.

Toward late morning my daughter was not having much success and was a little discouraged as it was so cold. When we went home for lunch in a warm house she decided not to go out again.

While she was there, she had a talk with her mom, and in the afternoon she went out again and made quite a bit more money. When we were alone she said, "Dad, do you know why I've done so well this afternoon? Mom told me I should pray to the Lord and that he would help me. I really prayed when I was home and have been praying. Look what the Lord has done! Look at all I've sold."

Sometimes the children were embarrassed when they came to a house where they knew children their age. Once one of the trees rolled off the truck and right into the middle of the street. I went out to grab the tree only to face the first counselor in the bishopric, who laughed at what we were doing. A counselor in the stake presidency also drove by and laughed in good spirits with us about what we were doing. We were in a fairly well-to-do area, and some of the neighbors probably thought that was not the thing to do, but I saw great growth in these three children that day.

They gained more confidence that the Lord would help them in whatever they were doing. They gained more confidence in themselves. They learned how to meet people and talk with them and counter their objections. They learned more about how to handle their money and figure out their tithing and mission funds. Above all else, we felt a great amount of love and unity. Together we had devised a plan in our minds, something we had never seen anyone else do, and made it successful. They were so pleased that they began looking for other projects to make money, and the next year they wanted to collect Christmas trees again.

This time I talked to the children about how to persuade people. They had learned this skill in part the year before, so they knew what to say and could pretty much do it without my help. The real difference between merely average "persuaders" and those who accomplish their goal most of the time is what they do when people say no.

If the people initially said they weren't interested, the

children would say, "Well, because we're already here, I'll take your tree for just one dollar. May we throw it on the truck?" Most of the people would say yes. If they said no, the kids would say, "I'm trying to earn this money for my school clothes, and I sure would appreciate your business. It's just a dollar. We'd sure be pleased to take it to the dump."

If the people still said no or said, "Well, the city will come by and pick it up," then the children would say, "This very morning we called the sanitation department [which we had done] and confirmed that they would pick up trees, but it won't be until the third week of January. Meanwhile, your tree is going to lie out here on the curb, spread needles all over, and make a real mess. We'll take it for just a dollar." At that point almost all of the people gave in and delivered up their trees.

I made sure the truck was sitting right in front of the door so the people could see us. Sometimes I would honk the horn so they would see the truck. I told the children to point to the truck so people could see the trees that were already on it. Then they would feel we were offering a good deal and would want to get in on it. Those little things make a big difference. In fact, little things like that make all the difference between an average "persuader" and one who can persuade almost anyone.

I taught the children not to talk in their normal voice but to put some feeling and enthusiasm into it. I couldn't hear what was being said because I was too far away, but I could watch the reaction of the people and tell almost exactly what the children were saying. It was fun to watch a no turn into a yes and see the children come dragging another tree out to the truck.

The gift of persuasion is one we ought to transmit to our children, as it will greatly help them throughout their life. It will be of tremendous benefit in the mission field and in their teen years when they begin searching for employment. (That is why I have shared the details of these experiences.) I believe that this process is nothing more than removing doubt and fear and uncertainty from our words and approaching a situation in pure faith. As Joseph Smith taught, faith is the moving cause of all action.

## EXCUSES FOR NOT WORKING

How important it is for children, especially as they move into their teen years, to find employment and learn to earn money on their own. Great blessings will come to them as they learn how to deal with people beyond their family and to live in the world but not be of it. Children need to be taught to give of themselves, of their own time, to sacrifice and learn to work. The very sacrificing of some of the things they desire will teach them much and help bring the Spirit of the Lord to them. "Sacrifice brings forth the blessings of heaven."

It is not always easy to convince children that they ought to have a job. Some have felt inclined to, but in our community many of the families were well enough off that their children didn't have to work, so many of them did not. We have always felt that children should work whether it was necessary or not. Children learn much from having to be dependable and regularly respond to an employer.

We have found that the excuses for why children don't want to work are all about the same:

• "I don't want to use up all my free time. I have lots of things to do with my friends."

• "How can I get a job when I have homework after school, piano lessons, and chores around the house?"

• "How can I get a job when there are so many after-school activities? I wouldn't be able to be a member of the pep club or the choir or just have a good time in all the after-school activities."

• "I don't want to work because I would be embarrassed to have my friends see me working. After all, about the only place you can work are those fast food places. None of my friends want to work there, and neither do I."

Through your own faith, you will have to teach your children the principles of hard work. Testify to them about the value of work, and lovingly convince them to put aside their fears and "with all their getting, get going."

## FINDING A JOB

Children who want to find work will be more successful if parents teach them how to go about it. The following suggestions may be of help:

1. Children need to dress up when they go out to look for employment. Many teenagers just go out in their grubby old clothes and thus do not attract much attention from an employer. If children will dress in their Sunday best or something close to it, they will really stand out from the competition.

2. Children may need help in preparing a short biography or resume. If they hand that to an employer, particularly if they have had another job or two, it will be very impressive.

3. Most children need some assistance in preparing an introduction to present themselves to a potential employer.

4. We found it helpful particularly when children were younger to go with them, wait in the car, and talk with them after each approach. Most children become discouraged after being rejected a few times. Having a parent there to encourage them has been most helpful. This is also a good time for the parent to invite the Spirit of the Lord through prayer or other means discussed earlier. Also, in times like this children need to know how to have the Spirit with them and how to cause others to feel that. Then employers will be more likely to offer employment.

5. Teach children not to fall into the practice of just "leaving applications." Many employers suggest that as a way of placating the one asking for employment but have no real intention of hiring.

6. If possible, teach children to tell a quick story or

example to illustrate their maturity and confidence in themselves.

7. Children should enter a business establishment with a positive attitude and act with confidence. They are not there to beg for a job. The employer is fortunate to have someone as good as they are offering their services. The attitude of the young person will make all the difference.

8. Find ways to show that the child has special talents and abilities. They can say things like, "I have worked regularly for four years in our family garden. I am dependable." "I am willing to get up early and work late." "I am willing to do whatever you need to have done." "I will do my best to anticipate what you need." Such statements generate a feeling of trust in a potential employer and suggest the self-confidence of the job seeker.

These kinds of experiences truly helped our children develop. They learned to be more bold and to take better command of the environment around them.

When I was a young man, I saw the means my father used to motivate his children to work. When I reached age eleven, he told me he was not going to buy my clothes anymore, and that I would have to. I knew he meant it, as he had done the same thing with my older brother. My father was very determined that his children would be economically self-sufficient, and he did all he could to teach us to bring that about. So, when I was eleven, I obtained a paper route and began to earn and save some money. Five years later, I was still delivering papers. One day the manager of the newspaper, said, "Young man, you have been so loyal and done so well in delivering your papers and selling subscriptions that I'm going to appoint you as assistant manager of circulation of this newspaper. You'll supervise the other paper boys and teach them how to sell subscriptions. After school, upon finishing your route, you'll be able to come to the office to work two or three more hours. You'll be able to do some homework while you're waiting to answer complaints on the phone. All in all, it will be a great job for you. And by the way, your pay will be tripled."

I was delighted because I was saving money for a mission, and this pay increase would help me reach the goal much more quickly. This was an ideal job, at a time when many teenagers had no work. I said to myself over and over again, "The Lord truly does bless those who keep the commandments." I had been trying to faithfully pay my tithing, keep the Sabbath Day holy, and honor my priesthood.

After a few more years, the newspaper manager approached me one Saturday with another opportunity. "Good news!" he said. "One week from now, we're going to begin delivering the Sunday paper. You will not only have a Sunday route to deliver early in the morning, but you'll be able to stay in the office from about seven until two in the afternoon. You'll also receive a 30 percent increase in pay."

When the manager saw my countenance fall, he said, "I know you're a Mormon, and you may be thinking of not accepting this extra responsibility. But if you don't take the job, you'll lose your paper route and be fired from your weekday job as well. Many of my other paper boys would give their right arm to have your job. I haven't trained you all these years for nothing. Well, what's your answer?"

I said somewhat emotionally, "I'll answer you on Tuesday."

As I rode home on my bicycle that day, I was despondent. I prayed over and over, "How could this be, Heavenly Father? I have kept the commandments. I've tried to do what is right. I've paid my tithing. I'm trying to save for my mission. Now I may lose my job. Shall I work this added job on Sunday or not?"

I explained the problem to my father, who wisely responded, "I don't know the answer, but I know someone who does." (He was referring to the Lord.) I talked to my bishop, who told me much the same thing that my father had told me. For two full days I prayed and struggled. I knew that I could attend sacrament meetings on Sunday in another ward later in the afternoon, but then I would miss all the meetings in my own ward.

When my boss asked for a decision the following Tuesday, I replied, "I love my job and my route, but I cannot work on Sunday and miss all my church meetings. It's not right."

"You're fired!" he said angrily. "Come in Saturday to pick up your last check. You're a very ungrateful young man!" And he stomped out of the office.

For the next several days the manager hardly spoke to me. But whenever I wondered if I had decided correctly, the answer seemed to be the same: "There may be some who have to work on Sunday, but you don't have to, and you should not."

When I went to pick up my last check on Saturday, I found the manager waiting for me. "Young man, please forgive me," he said. "I was wrong. I ought not to have tried to make you go against your beliefs and the commandments." Then he confessed to me that he was an inactive member of the Church. He said, "I have found a young man of another faith who is willing to do the extra work on Sunday. You can keep your job. Will you?" With a thankful heart, I answered yes.

The manager then added, "By the way, you'll find the extra 30 percent I was going to pay you for the work on Sunday included in your paycheck from now on, even though you'll not be working in the office on Sundays. That will be so for as long as you work for me."

What great joy I felt in my heart as I went home that afternoon. I said to myself over and over, "It *is* worth it to keep the commandments of the Lord. The Lord will bless those who do." Of course, it would have been worth it even without the tangible reward. A year later, when I gave my final talk before leaving for my mission, I was overjoyed to see my manager in the congregation. I felt even greater joy when, not long ago, I learned that, after all these years, he is now a faithful high priest group leader in his ward.

Decisions about employment and careers truly are difficult ones. But if young people are taught to look to the Lord and keep his commandments with exactness, he truly will cause all things to "work together for [their] good" (D&C 90:24). We must teach our children never to compromise the principles they believe in. They must remember to always trust in the Lord.

Life is a struggle, but the promises from the Lord are sure. Major problems and decisions face all of us. But they are all solvable if we will rely on the Lord. The Lord really is the answer to everything. He's the one who can unleash our potential and that of our children, who can teach us who we are and what we ought to do.

We must teach our children that the Lord will ultimately prosper those who keep his commandments. As Nephi said, "If it so be that the children of men keep the commandments of God he doth nourish them, and strengthen them, and *provide means whereby they can accomplish the thing which he has commanded them*" (1 Nephi 17:3; italics added).

I bear testimony of the fact that if we will teach our children to keep the commandments, the Lord will provide for their needs and enable them to accomplish all that is required of them. He will help them find a job. He will bless them for working and applying the principles he has taught us.

## CREATING A DESIRE IN YOUTH TO WORK

At times parents will need to help create a desire in young people to work. Sometimes that is difficult to do. What follows are some suggestions that might create a desire in a young person and also some thoughts on how the Lord does it with us. For example, it is interesting that the Lord tells us we must earn our own way by the sweat of our own brow and literally leaves us in the world to fend for ourselves. He leaves us to find employment, to find a home, to fend for ourselves each day. That is a tremendous challenge. The Lord will be of assistance, of course, but only as we work and do our part. Do not those same principles apply to our children?

When I was a boy, people used to throw puppies in the canal to teach them to swim. They all then began to swim of necessity. I never saw one drown, although each time it was most upsetting to watch. But, out of necessity, every one of them began to swim.

Are not we much like that? If we have a real need for something, then will come the desire to achieve it, but usually not before. Thus to create that desire in their children, parents must help them to recognize a real need. Children can often be motivated to help out financially when there is sickness, a death in the family, a serious economic problem, or other problems. The same is true of spiritual things; when the need is there, so will be the desire. Then if our children are properly directed, they will turn to the Lord for help in resolving the problem.

Sometimes a need can be created by giving a child a difficult calling or assignment. For example, my father originally told me he would not pay for my mission, that I would have to do it myself. I'm sure he was trying to create a need, and he did so. I worked for eight years to have enough money to sustain myself on my mission. However, a few days before I left for my mission he informed me that he had "no intention of being robbed of the blessings of paying for my mission." He said I could use my money for marriage and college when I returned home. Whatever his reasons for doing it, he surely created a need in me. He helped me accomplish a most valuable goal and at the same time develop my character well beyond what it would have been otherwise.

At times we have suggested to our children that by a certain date they must have a certain amount of money in place to be on target for their mission, college, or marriage. That kind of specific goal has helped create a real need in the children. The same is true when they have no money and want us to buy something for them. We have usually said we would not (except with very small children) and that it was up to them to earn their own money.

Another way needs are created is by seeing something exemplified in someone else. Many times a good friend may be working and earning money and thus help create the desire in a child to do the same. If parents are able to start out their first or second child correctly with respect to employment, the rest of their children will almost automatically fall in line and follow that powerful example.

One last suggestion about creating a need: Many times children can create a need within themselves. If young people are approached spiritually and taught what the Lord expects them to do, they will create the need within themselves and will stretch to do what is right.

## LESSONS FROM WORKING
## OUTSIDE THE HOME

Working at a job teaches children many important lessons:

1. They learn discipline. They learn to work regularly, day after day. They learn to respond to an employer. They get a broader perspective on life by being away from the family and seeing how other families operate or do not operate. In our experience, working at a job has always brought a greater appreciation of our own home.

2. At a job, children are faced with people who are breaking the commandments, and with the world itself. They are faced with difficulties about the Word of Wisdom, chastity, honesty, and so on. It is good for them to face those things while living at home where parents can talk them through the problems and help strengthen them. That is much better than being launched off to college or somewhere else and having to face those problems for the first time alone.

3. They learn how to deal with people, to open up and

not be so selfish. They learn how to persuade others and to use good human relations skills.

4. Steady work makes young people reliable. They know it, and thus have confidence in themselves, and that confidence is quick to show up in many other endeavors in life.

5. They learn how to manage their finances. They learn to save, to put away money for large expenditures in their future, such as missions and marriage, and especially to pay their tithes and offerings.

6. A job teaches children the real value of a dollar so they are less likely to want to spend money on big expenditures like cars or other things they can't afford if they are saving for the future.

7. A job helps children develop a healthy self-image, a feeling of self-reliance, of making it on their own, of earning their own way. It aids greatly in their overall maturity and development.

8. Having a job strengthens relationships among other family members as younger brothers and sisters see young people going to work. It develops respect in the younger brothers and sisters for the older ones and sets the example for future years when it will be the younger ones' turn.

It is not always easy for parents to help their children be employed, as it creates additional demands on the parents. But then again, it is certainly worth it. Parents sometimes have to be the taxi drivers who take their children to work at odd hours. Or the sharing of a car may be a major challenge. Many times children begin to miss family activities because they are at work. That is always hard on the family, but these children are preparing to leave home anyway, and it is time to assist them in that preparation. Sometimes it is hard for the parents to let go, but employment in the world helps children make the transition from youth to adulthood.

May I bear testimony one last time of the importance of young people working. It will build into them honesty, integrity, faith, diligence, determination, and many other characteristics of a good, well-developed person.

## TEACHING CHILDREN
## ABOUT FINANCES

When children are employed, parents face the additional challenge of teaching them to properly manage their finances. As with most other areas, children learn about finances best from their parents. If the parents are diligent in budgeting, saving their money, being careful in distinguishing between needs and wants, and staying out of debt, so will be the children. If children see that example, they will learn the proper relationship between spending and saving and how to control their finances.

Children must learn the difference between the things they would like to have and the things they can afford. Most important, they must learn the financial laws of the Lord regarding tithing and fast offerings.

Parents must decide whether to give allowances to their children. There are some strengths in so doing and also some weaknesses. Some families have found it beneficial to pay smaller children for work around the home. This enables the children to earn some money, learn to pay their tithing, and save for the future.

Other families have not paid allowances to their children. They have felt that work around the home is an obligation of all family members and that children should not be paid for routine labor. They might be paid for special work that has to be done but not for day-to-day chores. These families have been more inclined to encourage their children to work in the neighborhood or do odd jobs for other people in order to earn money. Perhaps it doesn't matter much whether children receive an allowance or not as long as they are learning to work.

As young people begin earning money, parents should introduce them to a simple budget that allows them to plan their expenses. It is important that they be taught that a budget is not just a way to keep track of their expenditures but also a way to plan them. Then they will learn to stay within their budget.

We have always felt it essential that children budget a regular amount of money for savings, no matter how much or how little they are earning. In addition, we have always suggested a priority of expenditures:

1. Tithing and fast offerings.
2. Savings for mission, college, marriage, and so on.
3. Money for ongoing personal expenditures.

We have always felt that children should not be given a car in their teen years or even purchase one, as it eats up too much of the money they are saving for the future. It has been a challenge to have children share the family car, but it has saved them from many unnecessary expenditures. This principle has surely helped our older children, who have been able to pay their way through college without loans, money from parents, or other help. It also took away some of the temptation children face to come and go as they please, with whomever they please, at any time.

Whenever the family was planning a vacation, we made sure that the children saved some money to help out. That not only lessened our burdens financially but also made our children more aware of the cost involved. They were thus more helpful in reducing the cost and in suggesting what we should do on vacation.

In family councils we have regularly reviewed parts of the family budget over which the children had some control, such as utilities, food, music lessons, educational costs, and so on. That has helped them realize that they couldn't just have whatever they wanted in life but had to live within a budget. As they saw their family do that month after month, they naturally wanted to do the same. Then they found it easier to do so when they were on their own or married.

One of the most important things children must learn is that there is a direct relationship between keeping the commandments and being financially stable over the years. If that concept can be taught when they are young, then they will have fewer financial problems when they become adults. The Lord is certainly willing to be involved in our temporal problems if we will do our best to humbly involve him.

## SPIRITUAL ANSWERS
## TO TEMPORAL PROBLEMS

A friend of mine has a Mexican friend who used to drive his old car from Mexico to Utah to attend each general conference. Year after year he would come and stay with my friend.

After one of those conferences my friend got kind of upset and told him he must never come again in that old car. He said, "That car is so old it is going to fall apart right on the California freeway. I know that you drive back home through Los Angeles, San Diego, and Tijuana. You are not to come up here again in that old car and endanger your life." My friend gave him quite a talking to.

This good Mexican man listened and then went on his way. The next general conference he arrived once again in the same old car. My friend again began to counsel him a bit, but this good Mexican brother said, "Wait a minute my friend, listen to me. Sure enough it was as you said. When I left here last time and was driving on those freeways in Southern California, right in the middle of all the traffic my car stalled. There my brother and I were, sitting on the freeway with all the cars honking about us.

"We did not know what to do. Neither one of us is a mechanic. We finally went around to the front of the car and looked under the hood, and as I looked at the engine I thought to myself, 'What this car needs is a blessing.' My brother and I bowed our heads and prayed that the Lord would bless the car and help it function well for us. After we finished we closed the hood and went around and got in the car. With a humble heart I turned the key, and the car started again and has worked exceptionally well ever since. Thus, with my car having been blessed, it won't be necessary for me to get a new one. It is working just fine now."

One can see the humility in this good Mexican man. He truly had a need to keep his car and not buy a new one, and I believe the Lord did bless him and his car.

I bear testimony that there are spiritual answers to all temporal problems, and that our children must learn that lesson early in life. There will be times in the years to come when they will be faced with unemployment, debt, or other difficult economic problems. If they clearly see the connection between the spiritual laws and the temporal laws and experience them when they are young, they will know how to face those problems as they get older. The laws are eternal. They work every time if we will humbly submit ourselves to them and thereby to the Lord.

While I was on a conference assignment in a Latin American country, some things occurred there that really taught a lesson and began to help the leadership of that country teach the attitude that people must be self-sustaining as individuals and as a country. The start of this change began with a humble bishop and a man whom I will call Brother Garcia.

At a stake conference, Brother Garcia came to me in private and said, "I have a serious problem. I'm unemployed. I'm an engineer." He then told me about his career and the money he had made earlier. He said, "I've been a good member and I've been to the temple. But I have been unemployed for a long time. I went to my bishop for help, and my bishop told me that what I needed was more *faith* and *diligence* and to *humble myself.* Can you believe that?" And then he laughed somewhat sarcastically. (The bishop had helped him and his family with the necessities, but he wanted more.)

This humble bishop, uneducated but most inspired, had given him the correct answer to his problem of unemployment. But he expected some sympathy from me. He was talking to the wrong man.

I could see his was not a humble heart. I told him, "Brother Garcia, you have misunderstood. The Church doesn't plan to help you out at all. In fact, I'm going to tell you that the bishop gave you the right answer right from the scriptures." I was really very blunt with him. Then I tried to give him some direction as to what to do. He said, "As you know, in this country one-third of all men are unemployed. You talk as if with faith and humility all could have jobs. That isn't possible, is it?" I said, "There may be some unemployed from other faiths, but there need not be one among the Latter-day Saints." I bore testimony that the Lord would help him and shared the passages just mentioned: "Verily I say unto you, concerning your debts—behold it is my will that you shall pay all your debts" (D&C 104:78).

I asked him if he was out of debt. He said no and that he never really had been since he had been married. I told him that he couldn't expect the Lord to be of much assistance if he didn't plan on obeying him. We then read verse 79: "And it is my will that you shall humble yourselves before me, and obtain this blessing by your diligence and humility and the prayer of faith."

I asked, "Brother Garcia, what are the three keys?"

He answered rather sheepishly, "To humble yourself, be diligent, and the prayer of faith."

I then said, "Now, the Lord doesn't usually repeat himself immediately in the next verse, but he did in this case, perhaps because he thought we wouldn't get it," and then we read verses 80 and 81: "And inasmuch as you are diligent and humble, and exercise the prayer of faith, behold, I will soften the hearts of those to whom you are in debt, until I shall send means unto you for your deliverance.

"Therefore write speedily to New York and write according to that which shall be dictated by my Spirit; and I will soften the hearts of those to whom you are in debt, that it shall be taken away out of their minds to bring affliction upon you."

"Brother Garcia," I said, "the Lord will soften the heart of the one to whom you are in debt or the heart of the one who does the employing. Who will send the means for your deliverance?"

He answered, "The Lord."

I said, "Brother Garcia, you will notice that the Lord summarizes it all again in verse 82: "And inasmuch as ye are humble and faithful and call upon my name, behold, I will give you the victory."

I expressed my love and testimony to him and then left him.

I returned to that same city about a year later. In a priesthood leadership meeting, for some reason I began to say something about this fellow, not remembering I was in that very same city. (If I had remembered, I probably wouldn't have been bold enough to talk about it.) I started to say something, without using his real name. Suddenly a man stood up right in the middle of the congregation. He said, "Elder Cook, the man you're talking about is my friend, and he is sitting right here next to me. He's too modest to tell you this, but I will." And then he told this story.

He said Brother Garcia had been so taken aback by our earlier conversation that at first he was offended. Financially things became worse for him. For a month to six weeks, things just went downhill. He then began to think about what the bishop and I had said about *humility, diligence,* and the *prayer of faith*. He began to realize that the bishop's counsel was correct and that he should follow it.

He humbled himself to the dust and finally told the Lord, "I will receive *any* employment you give me."

Sometimes in unemployment situations, we are not humble enough to take whatever work might come as a "starter." But the process won't begin unless we remove our prejudices and conditions and humble ourselves.

The man continued, "He understood that he had to really go out and diligently hustle, which he had not done. He then went in and out of every place searching for employment with the prayer of faith. He was praying and fasting that the Lord would deliver him up a job."

Brother Garcia then stood up himself and continued saying, "You may be surprised to know that the job that came to me was to mow lawns. 'I must sustain my family,' I said to myself." (Here was an engineer who took a job mowing the lawns of some rich man's property. He really had to humble himself to handle that, but he decided to do so.)

He then said, "One year has gone by, Brother Cook, and I'll tell you this glad news. I now have the major operation in this city for handling lawn maintenance. In fact, I was contracted by the municipality about six months after that experience with the bishop, and I now do all the lawns for the whole city. I now have twenty men working for me.

I then said to Brother Garcia, "What about engineering?"

He said, "Forget engineering. I'm making a lot more money now."

This experience taught me a great lesson about the way the Lord works. Why did all of this spiritually work for this good man? It is because:

- He humbled himself.
- He was willing to be diligent and sacrifice.
- He overcame his pride.
- He prayed in faith, and that which appeared to be his greatest trial turned out to be his greatest blessing.
- He followed the counsel of his priesthood leaders.

Cannot we all do likewise? When we humble ourselves and offer the required sacrifice (such as diligence and the prayer of faith), then the Lord acts. This bishop was an uneducated man and was not wise in the ways of the world. But he had been ordained as a bishop in the Church, and he understood that he had to pray to the Lord to obtain answers to help his people. Then in came the engineer who was making ten times what the bishop was making and who was better educated. But the bishop was the one who had the answer.

No one may know all of the answers to our temporal

problems, but the scriptures teach a number of principles
that are very clear. Here are a few of the keys:

1. *Rely upon God.* If you want to be blessed temporally,
follow the counsel given by the Lord in D&C 104:78–82,
including the instruction concerning debt.

The keys found in these verses are true and powerful.
Let us be sure to teach them to our children.

2. *Keep the Commandments.* The second principle in
solving our temporal problems is to keep the commandments. The scriptures are full of this injunction, and the
Lord has said many times that he will bless us temporally
and spiritually if we will be obedient.

Let me mention three commandments that relate specifically to temporal blessings:

*Tithing.* The Lord has promised tremendous blessings
to those who faithfully tithe. Did he except the widows?
No, he did not. As poor as they were, they also paid a tenth.
Does he except children? No, he does not. That's hard sometimes for very poor people to understand. Yet, when it dawns
in their minds what the truth is, they really resonate to it.

Some people have almost nothing, but just the same, we
teach them to pay a tenth of their income. I have heard some
of them say, "I don't have anything." But they do. Are they
making only fifty or a hundred dollars a month to sustain
their family? A tenth is still required. The Lord made no
exceptions. This is the way the Lord can bless us. This principle should be clearly taught to all of our children as part of
the answer to temporal problems (see Malachi 3:8–11; D&C
119).

*Fast offerings.* We've all heard many stories, and I can
bear personal testimony, as can you, to the blessings that
come from giving fast offerings. Let us teach our children the
same.

In Matthew 6:25–33, the Lord taught, "Take no thought
for your life, what ye shall eat, or what ye shall drink; nor
yet for your body, what ye shall put on."

What kinds of problems is he talking about? Temporal ones.

"Is not the life more than meat, and the body than raiment?"

He's again putting into perspective the spiritual and the temporal. Continuing on:

"Behold the fowls of the air: for they sow not, neither do they reap, nor gather into barns; yet your heavenly Father feedeth them. Are ye not much better than they?"

Think about that for a minute. Here are the Lord's fowls, and they do seem to be taken care of, don't they? And the Lord is saying, "Art thou not much better than they?" "How could I take care of them and not give some promise to you regarding your temporal welfare?"

"Which of you by taking thought can add one cubit unto his stature? And why take ye thought for raiment? Consider the lilies of the field, how they grow; they toil not, neither do they spin: And yet I say unto you, That even Solomon in all his glory was not arrayed like one of these."

Again, think about what he is telling us. He has provided the beauty of the fields and the flowers, and they don't even work for it. Aren't we much greater than the lilies? And then comes this great promise in verse 30: "Wherefore, if God so clothe the grass of the field, which to day is, and to morrow is cast into the oven, shall he not much more clothe you, O ye of little faith?"

What's the problem? Little faith.

"Therefore take no thought, saying, What shall we eat? or, What shall we drink? or, Wherewithal shall we be clothed? (For after all these things do the Gentiles seek:) for your heavenly Father knoweth that ye have need of all these things."

Many people have quoted this next verse but are not aware of the importance of all that preceded it: "But seek ye first the kingdom of God, and his righteousness; and all these things [the temporal things] shall be added unto you."

We are not to be too concerned about making a living.

Yes, it is a commandment to do so. But there is a great need for faith. The Lord promises us blessings economically and spiritually if we will put our faith in him.

My understanding, having lived in many of the Latin American nations, is that there is not an exception. I've been in hundreds and hundreds of homes and knelt on some mighty humble floors, in bamboo huts and all the rest. I've not seen an exception to the Lord's pouring out his blessings upon his people temporally if they would keep his commandments, if they would exercise faith in him and do those things he has commanded. Their problems get solved. They are not magically solved, but he gives them a step here and a step there. They begin to grow and develop and pull out of the serious economic problems they face. I bear testimony to the truthfulness of that fact.

*The Sabbath Day.* I believe there is a direct relationship between honoring the Sabbath Day and being blessed temporally as well as spiritually. We must teach our children this principle. The Old Testament is full of such references. You would do well to search for them in the Topical Guide. I will refer to one modern-day scripture in D&C 59:16–20. The Lord gives a promise with respect to keeping the Sabbath day holy. He says:

> Verily I say, that inasmuch as ye do this, the *fulness of the earth* is yours, the beasts of the field and the fowls of the air, and that which climbeth upon the trees and walketh upon the earth; yea, and the herb, and the good things which come of the earth, whether for *food* or for *raiment*, or for *houses*, or for barns, or for orchards, or for gardens, or for vineyards; yea, all things which come of the earth, in the season thereof, are made for the benefit and the use of man, both to please the eye and to gladden the heart; yea, for food and for raiment, for taste and for smell, to strengthen the body and to enliven the soul.
>
> And it pleaseth God that he hath given all these things unto man; for unto this end were they

made to be used, with judgment, not to excess, neither by extortion (italics added).

It's interesting that the fullness of the earth is given us for food, clothing, and even houses. In other words, if we will obey this law, the Lord will bless us temporally as well as spiritually.

I bear testimony that obedience to the Sabbath does have a direct impact upon our financial status as well as that of our children.

3. *Obey Principles of Economic Stability.* We will teach our children to be economically stable. This means that we will:

a. Avoid debt like the plague. We will do everything possible to not get into debt (with the exception of extraordinary long-term expenditures like a home or an education), or, if we are in debt, we will get out as soon as possible with all urgency. We will not purchase things on credit. We will not become involved in installment payments.

b. We will save part of our income from every check without fail. We will always "pay the Lord" first through our tithing. We will then "pay ourselves" through our savings.

c. We will clearly distinguish between needs and wants and satisfy only our needs. We will guard carefully against unduly trying to fulfill our wants as that will get us into financial difficulties.

d. We will always maintain a personal or family budget. We will not only record expenditures as spent but also plan in advance what ought to be spent and spend only that amount.

e. We will live within our means. It takes humility to so do, but it is without question against the commandments to live beyond our means. We will thus be frugal in all of our living.

If we faithfully teach these principles to our children and if they learn to live by them, most of their economic problems will be solved or prevented. The Lord is true to his promises. If we will learn the principles and live them, we will be blessed both spiritually and temporally.

Let us therefore teach our children the importance of working at home and in the workplace, and we will then properly prepare them for adulthood and for full and productive lives. May the Lord bless us to teach them the principles related to finances and the principles governing both spiritual and temporal blessings. The living and teaching of these principles in your family will be of great assistance to you in raising up your children to the Lord.

CHAPTER NINE

# TEACHING YOUR FAMILY THROUGH MEETINGS AND ACTIVITIES

At a stake conference in Lima, Peru, I met a young woman who was the only member of the Church in her family. Over the months since she had joined the Church, she had heard much counsel about holding family home evenings. She wanted to do so but wasn't sure how to go about it. She was only seventeen years old, and no one else in her family was interested.

One Sunday she heard a particularly strong testimony about family home evening and decided she had waited long enough—she would begin holding it. She went home that very day and in her living room began to sing a song, say a prayer, and have a lesson. Her family made fun of her, particularly her two older brothers. They laughed, jeered, asked what she was doing as a Mormon, and so on. In tears she fled to her bedroom, where she finished the lesson that night.

The following Monday, in spite of the resistance she had encountered from her family, she went ahead and had family home evening—and the next Monday as well. On the following Monday night as she began singing the opening song, there was a knock on her door. Her older brother said, "Mary, may I come in? I really would like to know what you are doing."

She said, "Well, yes, if you're not going to make fun of me." He said he wouldn't and came in. They sang, prayed, and learned together. The following week the second brother joined them.

As she bore testimony in stake conference that day, she said, "And here, Elder Cook," pointing to one of the front rows, "are my parents and both of those brothers. They are all members of the Church now."

What a tremendous blessing! This seventeen-year-old

girl, through obedience to the commandments, was the instrument by which her whole family was converted. Surely the Lord meant it when he said: "I, the Lord, am bound when ye do what I say; but when ye do not what I say, ye have no promise" (D&C 82:10).

Ought we not, then, to love our families more deeply and try harder to treat each family member as the Lord treats us? Home evening can have great impact on a family, whether they are members of the Church or not.

Family home evenings and family councils are *important* family meetings, and each family has to decide when and how they will hold them. Many have found it helpful to have a family devotional on Sunday in which they teach the doctrine of the Church, perhaps in place of scripture reading that day. Then they hold an activity on Monday night. The activity is often just something they do for fun and recreation. But many times families can go out and serve someone who may have a need. Family home evening can also include a family council in which the family counsels together to solve a problem the family is having or to plan out work or upcoming events.

The prophets have clearly taught the importance of family home evenings and family councils. President Marion G. Romney once said: "No greater service can be given to a family . . . than to motivate them with a vision of the benefits of a regular family home evening, and thereby strengthen family ties in this life and prepare for the continuation of this sacred relationship in the life to come."

President David O. McKay said: "Families who prayerfully prepare and consistently hold their weekly home evenings, and who work together during the week to apply the lessons in their lives, will be blessed."

And Elder Boyd K. Packer has said: "Family home evening can inspire that turning of the hearts. The purpose of the family home evening is to draw families together in love and sweet association, to open the doors of communication between parents and children, to make them happy they live together and belong to one another—eternally."

Sometimes the fruits of family home evening can be a bit humorous. When our first three boys were quite young, I lined them up along the fireplace and taught what I thought was an excellent lesson on why young men should go on missions. After finishing the lesson, I asked the oldest boy, "Son, are you going on a mission?"

He said, "Nope!"

I was surprised, as was his mom.

I then ventured the next question: "Why not?"

He looked up and said, "I can't, Dad. I'm still in my pajamas!"

You can imagine how inadequate I felt in not being able to relate to my "students."

When I was called as a General Authority, we tried to teach our young children what that meant. Shortly thereafter, our seven-year-old son bore his testimony in sacrament meeting. He had forgotten a little what a General Authority is. He couldn't even remember those words. All he could say was, "My dad has been called to be a . . . , to be a . . . , to be one of those men who works with Jesus." He couldn't remember the term, but he knew the feeling. Family home evening is a real blessing to families.

George Durrant said it this way: "Parents who harbor a dream for their children's destiny know that the Lord's family home evening program is like a gift from heaven. It is not something that we have to do. It is something that we get to do. . . . The prophets have said, 'Children coming from such homes will not go astray.' You can have sons and daughters who are responsible, who desire service, who love virtue, who are strong in testimony, who love and are loved because you have family home evening and share this spirit in your home continually" ("A Gift from Heaven," *Ensign*, March 1971, pp. 6–7).

## PLANNING FAMILY MEETINGS

One important element of directing family home evenings and family councils is to plan ahead. Parents will have to do some of that. Then, as their children get older, much of the planning can be handled by them.

To help us plan our family home evenings, we have used various lists and assignment wheels that told us whose turn it was to conduct, to lead the singing, to pray, to give the lesson, to prepare refreshments, and so on.

### COOK FAMILY
### HOME EVENING ASSIGNMENTS

| ASSIGNMENTS | 1/1/80 | 1/8/80 | 1/15/80 | 1/22/80 | 1/29/80 |
|---|---|---|---|---|---|
| Conducting | Son | | | | |
| Pianist | Dad | | | | |
| Chorister | Daughter | | | | |
| Talk | Son | | | | |
| Special Number | Mom | | | | |
| Lesson | Daughter | | | | |
| Testimonies | Son | | | | |

### COOK FAMILY COUNCIL AGENDA

Date: _____

Opening Prayer: _____

LISTEN AND SOLVE INDIVIDUAL DIFFICULTIES:

| Problems | Solutions |
|---|---|
| 1. _____ | 1. _____ |
| _____ | _____ |
| _____ | _____ |
| _____ | _____ |
| 2. _____ | 2. _____ |
| _____ | _____ |
| _____ | _____ |
| _____ | _____ |

Closing Prayer: _____

## COOK FAMILY
## DEVOTIONAL AGENDA

Date:_____

Presiding:_____

Conducting: _____

Opening Hymn:_____

Chorister: _____

Pianist:_____

Opening Prayer:_____

Memorized Scripture/Article of Faith:_____
_____

Talk:_____

Special Number: _____

Lesson (review last week's lesson results/family council results)
_____

Testimonies:_____
_____

Family Council: (1st Sunday and /or need basis)_____
_____

Plan Family Home Evening Activity:_____
_____

Assignments for Next Week: _____
_____
_____

Closing Hymn:_____

Closing Prayer:_____

Interviews: _____

Even little children who can't read can conduct family meetings. Parents can discuss with them what is to happen and in what order. Then they can make an agenda with pictures instead of words that the children can follow. It's a lot of fun to watch children conduct family home evening. It also builds their self-confidence and makes them feel like an important part of the family.

Later in our marriage, we no longer needed an agenda;

our family had simply learned how to conduct the meetings. Now we just assign someone each week to teach family home evening.

The main thing is to organize things, without being too formal, so that good things can occur in your family. The goal is to have a happy, satisfied, fulfilled, excited, developing, growing family.

Family councils can often be incorporated into family home evenings, giving family members an opportunity to discuss personal or family problems. We have found them very helpful in coming to agreements on discipline, rules, and so on. We have tried to conduct much of our family business, such as budgeting and scheduling, in these meetings. We have also used these meetings to reach agreements on family decisions that have had far-reaching effects.

One evening when I arrived home from a stake conference trip, my wife said, "I have just found out that one of our relatives is in prison." She then said with a twinkle in her eye, "Furthermore, it's one of *your* relatives."

A distant cousin of mine, whom I will call John, had called from the local prison. We had never met him, but we knew his father. He had told my wife that if he could spend time with a good family, it would shorten his time in prison.

She asked me what I thought about letting him visit us. I responded rather negatively, perhaps because I was tired, saying, "Well, you know, we've responded to a lot of people here and there, and I'm not so sure we need to respond to something like this. Let's talk more about it later." Time passed. We did not talk about it.

I returned from another trip a week or so later, and my wife said John had called again. I again responded rather negatively, saying it probably wouldn't be wise to have him in our home when I was traveling so much. Thus, once again I dissuaded my good wife from her righteous desires.

A few weeks later, my wife approached me early in the morning when I was reading and said, "You know, honey, I've mentioned two or three times about our trying to be of assistance to John. Each time you've responded rather negatively. I just want you to know how strongly I feel that we really ought to minister to him, that we really ought to help him and do what he's asked of us. However, I'm not going to bring it up again. I just thought you ought to know of my strong feeling." She then walked out of the room and left me alone.

Feeling bad about my negative responses, I sought her out and said I didn't think we should make a decision like that on our own but that we ought to bring together the family council to decide it. We called all ten members of the family together, explained the situation, and took a vote; nine in favor, one against. Then I stressed some more the possible danger of having a prisoner in our home when I was not present. (I knew what his crime had been.) A couple of the youngest children then changed their vote because they were persuaded by their father, and the vote was seven to three.

After still more discussion, one of my sons said, "Why are we talking about this any further, Dad? Why don't we just kneel down and confirm it?"

I said, "What?"

He said, "Yes, why don't we just kneel down and confirm it? The Lord knows whether we should or whether we shouldn't."

I was very much taken aback by his inspired statement, and I felt repentant and humbled for not having directed the family to seek an answer from the Lord. We all immediately knelt down, and that son and I prayed. After the prayers, the vote was ten in favor. I immediately called the prison.

When John heard my voice, he just wept. "Thank you. Thank you for calling," he said. "Thank you, thank you so much." I told him that we would be going to church in a few hours and then coming home for dinner, and that we would like to have him spend the whole day with us. He was most pleased at the prospects.

John wept through the church meetings for almost three

full hours. I was quite surprised and touched by his humility. However, I was still a little worried about how he might respond to the children when we returned home. My fears were not realized, as within five or ten minutes of being in our home, he had every one of the children eating out of his hand. He knew some magic tricks. He knew how to joke with the children. He *knew* how to deal with children. In fact, it appeared to us that he really had a gift. We had a delightful Sunday afternoon and evening together. When we took him back to the prison that night as a family, once again we felt spiritually different, and we knew that he did as well.

John came to our home a number of times over the next few months until finally he was released from prison. We heard later that he was married and was moving forward with his life. How the Lord blesses all of us if we attempt to reach out to the needy! I'm not suggesting that we should respond to everyone in prison, on the street, or anywhere else. I am suggesting that the Lord can surely direct us in whom we should help, and one way he can do that is through family councils. I'm surely thankful for the family council we held on this matter, as much good came of it. Truly, as the psalmist wrote, "Children are an heritage of the Lord: and the fruit of the womb is his reward. As arrows are in the hand of a mighty man; so are children of the youth. Happy is the man that hath his quiver full of them: they shall not be ashamed, but they shall speak with the enemies in the gate" (Psalm 127:3, 5).

May the Lord bless all of us to be more giving and to encircle the needy with the love of our families. Family home evenings ought to deal with the feelings of the heart and not so much with instruction, although that can be a part. Let us hold more effective family home evenings and family council meetings and thereby raise up our children faithfully to the Lord.

## PLANNING FOR FAMILY EVENTS

To be most effective, family councils, home evenings, and other events and activities should be planned ahead of time. In fact, when parents are planning their schedules, they should put family matters first. For example, if you want to hold a weekly family home evening, would it not be wise to put that on your calendar every week? Plan out birthdays and other special times in advance. Mark the days on which the children will be out of school so you can plan work around them and, if possible, be home then. By obtaining a calendar from school, you can check for such things before planning activities at work or at church and thus be able to maximize family time.

Plan some quality family home evenings or devotionals. At times these can be held in a relaxed atmosphere, but at other times, when important subjects are to be discussed, they should be planned with the same effort and care given to a quality presentation at work.

Family activities as well can sometimes be spontaneous, but at other times they should be planned out in advance: trips to a museum, a family history center, a temple (to do baptisms for the dead), an amusement park, and so on can provide many positive experiences. The key is to do a variety of things and have a fun time together.

Having fun together provides an important part of the growth and development of a family. Children need to just enjoy being with their family, and activities can provide that important ingredient of family life.

Planning fun events in advance creates anticipation in the family. Thinking about an outing over the days or weeks before it actually happens sometimes brings as much satisfaction as the event itself. The anticipation can also help children get through some tough moments at school or at work.

In spite of all of the planning you might do, be aware of the promptings that come in the very moment a family member has a special need. In such cases, family plans should be set aside to meet that need.

Plan your affairs each day so that you are up first in the morning and can be prepared to minister to your children as they arise. Above all, remember that your children are with you for just a short time, and you must do all you can to prepare them for life and to give them all the time you can.

## BEING INVOLVED
## WITH YOUR CHILDREN

Take time to be really involved with your children. Pray with them, play with them, work with them, worship with them.

Take the responsibility to leave your family happy in the mornings. Before going to work, do all you can to help set a happy spiritual environment every day, and thus you will send your children off to begin their day on a spiritual basis.

Spend time with your children. Perhaps that is the greatest gift you can give them. You will not be able to affect them much unless you hear and feel what they are hearing and feeling in their lives. Only then will you be able to counsel them and help them learn how to face life and overcome their challenges. Above all, listen, listen, listen.

Leave your briefcase at work. Parents who bring their work home almost always rob their children of "family time." If you do bring work home, perhaps it ought to be done early in the morning or late at night when the children are in bed.

I believe that parents should avoid reading the newspaper or watching TV when their children are around. Such activities, again, are better left until the children are in bed or doing their homework. Again, time with your children is your most valuable gift to them.

If you have a larger family, be careful to spend as much time with the younger children as with the older ones, who tend to be more dominant, have more challenges, and require more attention. Unless parents are careful, they may neglect the needs of younger children.

Lighten up! Increase love among family members by sticking little notes around the house that say "I love you" or that mention something special you have seen one of your children do.

Play games together, take walks together, and do all you can as a family. If you do, you will find that love will increase in your family.

I believe it is essential that families eat together. Doing so provides extra time every day. Families that eat together talk together. Families that talk together stay together. Use mealtime to talk about schoolwork, review news events, tell some jokes, and relate experiences.

Don't let family life center around the television. Some families think watching TV is being "together," but usually there is not much value in that kind of togetherness. It is sad to see families spend so much time in front of the television when there is so much else to know, feel, and do together.

Be sure to spend adequate time with each individual child. All children need to know they are special and that they will have your undivided attention sometime during each week.

Remember that children often need talk at inconvenient moments. They may come when you are busy, when you are already committed, when you are reading, when you would really like to go to bed. Remember that you can't dictate what they are feeling, and if they have a need, you should try to respond to it.

Pass on to your children some of the skills you have learned. Although families live together, the parents often fail to share what they know about prayer, scripture reading, human relations, planning, getting a job, and so on. The time spent in passing along such skills and information will have much greater payoff than watching television.

At night, be sure not to miss that last hug, a story to a

little one, or a goodnight kiss. Even though these things can become routine, it is a powerful routine that can greatly benefit family members.

Be sure to decide most issues together in family council. There are some personal things the parents will decide, but most issues, we have found, can best be handled by family discussions. Then the whole family feels like a part of things, and all are authors of the "family plan."

Seek out service opportunities to do with your family. These will bring some of the greatest rewards of all. Memories of serving others together will endure forever and help your family to follow the example of the Savior.

## RECEIVING DIRECTION
## FROM THE LORD

Be sure to pray specifically for your family and attempt to receive direction from the Lord regularly about the needs of the individuals in your family and your family as a whole.

Don't be too worried about children making mistakes. They all do that, as do adults. But watch for *patterns* of errors that are being developed. There is a great difference between making a mistake and developing a pattern of mistakes. Try to correct most of the patterns and let some of the smaller errors pass by. If you take care of the little problems and little attitudes that are out of order, there may never be any big ones.

Pray with your children alone—just father and son or daughter, or mother and son or daughter.

When your children have a problem, do your best to read a passage from the scriptures to give them direction from the Lord. Not only will the counsel be correct but it will also teach your children to rely upon the scriptures in obtaining answers to their problems.

Unless unusual circumstances exist, a wife ought to be at home with her children. Don't ever trust the teaching of your children to others or feel that the Church will teach them. The Church's role is to help parents teach. The true responsibility rests with them.

Be loyal to your family above all the world's concerns. If you will be true to them and to the Spirit of the Lord, all your other priorities will fall into place.

## GAUGING YOUR PROGRESS

Your progress as a parent can be measured somewhat by how well you are able to take a reading of the intimate feelings of your children's hearts. Will they share with you? Will they seek counsel from you? Learn to take the "temperature" of your children regularly to see where they are. If you feel they may be a little off, you will then be able to take some action.

Perhaps nothing will cover the errors parents make better than simply loving their children. Hug them physically. Speak kindly to them and be supportive of them. The same kind of response will come back to you many times over; then you will know how you are doing as a parent.

Another way to know how you are doing is to determine if your children really want to be home with you. And do you want to be home with them? Of all the places I have been in the world, there is no place I would rather be than at home with my family.

Perhaps these four items best summarize the role of good parents:

1. They lead their children to the Lord.

2. They love their children, cheer them up, encourage them, and support them.

3. They spend time with their children, teach them, have an enjoyable time with them, and help them develop their talents and gifts.

4. They spiritually prepare their children for life by fortifying them with good attitudes and beliefs. They teach them how to work, how to play, how to serve, and how to draw close to the Lord.

5. They remember that no other success will compensate for failure in the home.

## CHARACTERISTICS OF
## EFFECTIVE MORMON FAMILIES

Some years ago a study was conducted by the Department of Sociology at Brigham Young University to try to determine the characteristics of effective Mormon families. The study gathered information from more than two hundred of these families to find out what made them effective. The researchers wrote to me about their conclusions:

> Dear Elder Cook:
> With the strong emphasis in the Church for building good families, you may be interested in the results of our research of the characteristics of effective Mormon families. We asked Stake Presidents from different states to identify the 15 strongest families in their stakes. Then we gathered data from some 200 families to find out what made their families so effective. We compared these findings with some less effective families as well. Here are some of the things we discovered.
>
> 1. Almost 100% of these families are full tithe payers, attend all of their meetings regularly and always accept a job or position in the Church.
>
> 2. These families have very clear goals as to what they want for their children. Virtually 100% said their goals include: having their children marry in the temple, get a good education, develop a strong self concept, be active in the Church, develop a strong sense of family unity and have children go on a mission. (We also found that the less effective families did not have these clear goals for their children.)
>
> 3. In effective families, 73% said they always or usually held daily family prayer.
>
> 4. Two thirds of these families said they always or usually held regular weekly family home evening. The other one third also held family home evening, but not as regularly.
>
> 5. These families did not identify movie stars or

sports figures as family heroes. They most often said the heroes in their families were church leaders or other older family members.

6. Husbands and wives work at having a good personal relationship in their marriages. On a scale of 1 to 10, the average family was at 8.5 in terms of feeling the marriage was strong and good.

7. Ninety-six percent said they most often would do things together as a family. 92% said they always went as a family to activities where another family member performed or was in a game or activity.

8. These families are not free from adversity. 80% said they had some real adversities in their lives (illness, death, problems with children etc.) but they worked as a family to deal with problems. The family was the first line of defense in times of adversity. They worked things out together as much as possible.

9. Over 80% said they *daily* express affection physically to other family members.

10. These families on the average watch TV only 1/3 as much as the average family in America.

11. Effective families tend to see themselves as somewhat stricter than other families. They had rather few rules but very high expectations. They expect a lot from their children.

12. They tend to reward their children more by giving praise or some special treat, rather than giving money.

13. These families spend a great deal of time talking together. Almost 100% said they talk regularly as a family and also to each child individually on a regular, almost daily, basis.

We hope this information will be useful to you. It should help to show what families should do if they want to become more effective.

Sincerely,

William G. Dyer
Phillip R. Kunz

Notice that these effective families held family prayer, scripture reading, family home evenings, and other spiritual activities discussed in this book. Also, items 7, 10, and 13 relate directly to spending time in activities together.

Activities are a real blessing to a family. They provide a way to have fun together, relieve tensions, and develop relationships on new levels with one another. Activities are especially exciting for younger children. Activities are an integral part of the teaching and training of the family. At the same time a family is having a fun time together, parents have an opportunity to teach about many things.

Unfortunately, some members of the Church and of the community in general have determined that activities should be left to the school or to the Church. They feel that it is the role of these organizations to entertain their children and provide appropriate activities for them. Some members of the Church are even tempted to leave activities to seminary or to the Young Women or Aaronic Priesthood programs. If that direction is followed, families can inadvertently lose out on some crucial time together and at the same time inadvertently weaken their family.

There seems to be no question that the "chairman of the activities committee" in your family is you as a parent. You will want to have your children help you, but you will take the lead in planning different activities in which your family might be involved. That leadership should not be left to anyone else. Part of the bonding that occurs between parents and children comes from having a fun time together. One of your major objectives must be to become their best friend, and part of a friendship is having fun, as well as learning together and doing the many other things mentioned in this book.

Parents will want to include in their schedule an appropriate sequence of activities for the family. The family's activities ought to be jointly decided by all family members and thus be able to compete to some degree with some of the more exotic or well-planned activities put on by the school and the Church.

## BALANCING ACTIVITIES BETWEEN HOME, CHURCH, AND SCHOOL

"How can I provide all of these family activities," some parents might ask, "when my children have so many other activities outside the home?" And that is a valid question indeed. A greater focus on home-centered activities would reduce the number of demands on active families but still reach the less active who have more of a need for help from the Church.

Perhaps our family has a different perspective than most because we have lived outside the United States for so many years. In some of the countries in Latin America, there are almost no school or other activities to which the children could go that were not very worldly and that didn't involve the use of tobacco and alcohol. The Church in those countries was in a basic developmental stage and thus offered few activities. My wife and I soon saw that we would have to be the "activities committee" for our family.

When we arrived home in Utah, we returned to a very active ward. In fact, in our first three months, we counted thirty-nine activities to which we were invited as a family or as individuals—Young Women's activities, the annual Relief Society anniversary, the high priests' ice-cream social, Scouting affairs, and on and on. If I'm not mistaken, we went to about three of those activities as a family, and some of the children attended a few more.

Soon after that, our good bishop told me he was worried about my family. I said, "If you know something I don't, I'd be very anxious to know. Please tell me."

"Well," he said, "I have a feeling that your family isn't as supportive of the Church as they ought to be. For example, last Sunday night we had a Scouting meeting for all the Scouts and their families in the stake. At the meeting, they counted the number of people in each ward. The ward having the most people present won a prize. Because your large family was not there, we didn't feel you were supporting the Church as much as you should." (He said all of that very carefully, lovingly, and with good spirit.)

I said to him, "Well, I might be mistaken, Bishop, but my understanding is that the Church is supposed to support the family. If we had been to that social meeting that night, we would have missed the tremendous family devotional we had in our home." I asked him if he'd ever seen our children miss priesthood meeting, sacrament meeting, Sunday School, or Mutual. He said he had not. I continued, "I understood that all those other things were electives, that they were optional, and that we could choose which ones we wanted to attend. Is that not true?" He wasn't too sure.

Then I said to this good bishop, "Do you know what my biggest problem has been since I returned home from Latin America?"

He said, "No, what is it, Brother Cook?"

I said, "It's been the Church itself, and perhaps the school here to some extent."

He said, "What do you mean?"

I said, "Because I travel a lot on the weekends, the week nights are very important to me, as are Saturday and Sunday if I'm home. I must have that time with my own family. In Latin America we had family home evening almost every night. I don't mean a lesson; I mean just a fun time.

"Sometimes we carved things. Sometimes we built things. Sometimes we took walks around the block. Sometimes we helped the widows or ministered to others in need. Sometimes we had lots of fun with other families. But since I've come home it's been difficult because some group has my children on Tuesday night, another group on Wednesday, and somebody else on Thursday, and they are with their friends on Friday night. My biggest challenge has been all of these activities going on outside the home."

This faithful bishop was quite shocked at my response but I'm sure he understood. I suggested there might be wisdom in having the family heads in the ward determine how many activities there ought to be, and then in helping parents understand that they—not the Church or the school— were primarily in charge of the activities in their family.

In the following months, with the planning and involvement of parents, this good bishop greatly reduced the number of activities in our ward. He also retaught the principle that parents were to hold activities with their own children, and that in its support role the Church would sponsor some group activities as well. (It should also be mentioned that he knew, as did we, that he had to provide more activities than "the ideal" to help families who had greater needs than we did.)

President Harold B. Lee said: "It seems clear to me that the Church has no choice—and never has had—but to do more to assist the family in carrying out its divine mission . . . to help improve the quality of life in the Latter-day Saint homes. As important as our many programs and organizational efforts are, these should not supplant the home; they should support the home" ("Preparing Our Youth," *Ensign*, March 1971, p. 3).

## ACTIVITIES WITH GRANDPARENTS

In planning activities with your family, please don't forget some of the most important members of your family— grandparents. Grandparents can be of great assistance in raising a family, particularly if they live nearby. Make a special effort to involve grandparents in as many family activities as possible. They can provide excellent gospel instruction if they are faithful members of the Church, especially in home evenings and during scripture reading. At times when children are having a difficult time, grandparents or other family members such as uncles and aunts can be of great assistance in times of need. At times like these, worthy grandparents can become children's heroes.

In the gospel we know families are multi-generational.

I believe that the Lord meant families to include aunts, uncles, cousins, grandparents, and beyond.

At times grandparents have the idea that they have raised their children, that their turn is over and now they can go and do as they please. Some in the world have said their obligation to society has been completed. We know better. We should make every effort to strengthen and include the extended family in our lives.

Grandparents normally have free time to spend with children because they do not have the immediate demands of a family. Thus, they may be of great assistance to their children who will appropriately involve them. Even grandparents who live a long distance away can be of help by telephone, letter, and occasional visits. Nonmember grandparents can also help in teaching, sharing, and loving their grandchildren.

Good grandparents will have the vision of trying to draw their whole family together and will provide a righteous influence that could not otherwise be provided.

## FAMILY ACTIVITIES

One of the real challenges families have is deciding what to do for activities. Many of those outside of the home cost money, and thus it's difficult for a family to do many of those. However, they can do many other activities with no cost at all. Following is a list of activities we have found to be fun and helpful to our family:

1. Visit a local museum.
2. Go to a planetarium.
3. Do research at a family history library.
4. Do baptisms for the dead.
5. Go hiking.
6. Visit Church historical sites.
7. Tour a printing plant.
8. See a T.V. station.
9. Watch a jury trial.

10. Visit a Catholic or Protestant church.
11. Go to a candy factory.
12. Tour a fire station.
13. Enjoy a Church visitors' center.
14. Work out at a gymnasium.
15. Go swimming.
16. Surprise another family.
17. Play at a city park.
18. Visit grandparents.
19. Visit a sheepherder and his sheep.
20. Explore an unusual place near home.

All of these activities can be done with little or no cost, and some are educational.

Other activities that might require a full day to finish:

1. Skiing.
2. Boating.
3. Swimming at a nearby lake.
4. Camping.
5. Hiking to a distant cave.
6. Going to a nearby national park.
7. Having fun at a water resort.
8. Staying at a cabin.
9. Going on a picnic.

Other, more commercial activities include:

1. Ice skating.
2. Roller skating.
3. Going to the movies.
4. Going to the zoo.
5. Buying an ice cream cone.
6. Visiting an entertainment park.

There are many such activities that will, of course, vary according to where the family lives.

## ACTIVITIES FOR YOUNGER CHILDREN

Families with younger children can have fun by:

1. Marching around the house to a song, crawling under the bed, and wrestling.

2. Having them run to get a pair of socks, turn on the heater, get a drink, climb three stairs, come back, jump over a chair, come back, and give a hug: "That's the assignment—go!"

3. Playing a game of "I'm going to tell you your future." Then hold their hand and pretend to tell them how you're going to feel the day they go on their mission, get married in the temple, and so on.

4. Giving each child a nickname, something that is positive and uplifting. It may be that they've been named after a grandparent or other faithful person, and thus you can magnify that role model. For example, one of our children has the nickname "Claranzo," a take-off on a grandfather's name. One of our daughters "fell into" the funny name of

"Jelly Beans." A fun, positive nickname can make a child feel special.

5. Reading to your children. Children get excited about a good story, and so does the reader.

6. Playing a game where you can say good things about each other. You can say at dinner, "It's so and so's turn," which means that everyone says something he or she really loves about that person. This brings a lot of love into the family.

7. Role playing. Try using stories from the Old Testament, such as the story of Moses or Joseph in Egypt.

8. Using more humor in the home by telling jokes and having a fun time together.

9. Having children start their diaries or begin their individual and family history; reading to them from Church pamphlets and magazines, and so on.

10. Playing Twenty Questions. You think of some gospel character and the children try to guess who it is by asking yes or no questions. Or you ask gospel questions and have a contest between teams in the family, fun questions that are alive, quick, and fast moving.

11. Telling your children about your younger life, your mission, your marriage, and your other experiences. They love hearing missionary stories or stories about the time you were married.

12. At times being totally unpredictable about what you're going to do on an activity. Just surprise everyone.

Let the older children help plan what to do. That will increase their love for their younger brothers and sisters. Remember too that older children often need one-on-one time with a parent, swimming, bowling, playing racquetball, or taking a walk. Our daughters have always liked special daddy-daughter dates. Don't forget that these fun activities can be turned into good teaching moments as well. Remember above all else that heaven is to some degree just a continuation of an ideal home. Nothing else is more important.

## FAMILY GAMES

There are also lots of fun games families can play. If your family is not accustomed to playing games, you might turn to the Church's *Family Resource Book,* which contains excellent games to help stir the creativity of parents and children alike. Following are some games we have enjoyed over the years:

Blindfold
Spin the bottle
Tell the truth
Charades
Ping Pong
The gossip game
Computer games
Checkers
Celestial Pursuit
Chess
The deer hunter game
"Do you love your neighbor?"
Poor pussy
Kick the can
Impersonations
Basketball
Baseball
Volleyball

We've also had fun doing exercises as a family.

Of course, each family should select games and other activities that are fun for them.

## QUIZZES AND TESTS

We've often had a good time with quizzes or tests that we have made up or taken from various books and magazines.

We have used the following quiz at Christmastime:

Name the carol whose opposite is given here:

1. Here in a House
2. See the Denouncing Demons Shout
3. Sadness to Mars
4. Close, Close to Here in Sun Valley
5. Noisy Morning
6. Go Away, Ye Faithless
7. Down on the Lawn
8. O Fiendish Morning
9. Walking over the Grass
10. The Last Christmas
11. I Saw the Gongs on Valentine's Night
12. Walnuts Baking in a Closed Oven
13. Summer Sea of Knowledge
14. Golden Gongs
15. I'll Stay Here for the Fourth of July
16. The Big Hammer Girl

*Answers:*

1. Away in a Manger
2. Hark! the Herald Angels Sing
3. Joy to the World
4. Far, Far Away on Judea's Plains
5. Silent Night
6. Oh, Come, All Ye Faithful
7. Up on the House Top
8. O Holy Night
9. Dashing through the Snow
10. The First Noel
11. I Heard the Bells on Christmas Day
12. Chestnuts Roasting on an Open Fire
13. Winter Wonderland
14. Silver Bells
15. I'll Be Home for Christmas
16. The Little Drummer Boy

## HEIGHT AND WEIGHT CHART

We've also had fun over the years keeping track of the children's height and weight. We would have them measure or "weigh in" every six months, and we would record the results on a separate sheet for each child. They enjoyed seeing they were growing in both height and weight. It made growing up fun for them and allowed them to get a better feeling for how they were maturing. In time they all enjoyed passing up their mother.

## CAREER VISITS

We have had a fun time with our children when we have used some of our activity nights to learn about various careers. It has allowed them to see what kinds of jobs are available and to think about whether or not they might like them. We've visited places like these:

> Fire station
> Police station
> Steel plant
> Candy plant
> Architectural office
> Engineering office
> Dairy
> Farm
> Garbage dump
> Fish farm
> Forestry
> Sewage plant
> Car dealership
> Electrical company
> Business office
> Bank
> Telephone company
> Department store
> Computer plant
> Printing press
> Beauty shop
> Newspaper office
> Courthouse
> Municipality
> Employment center
> University

Copper mine
Art museum
Bishop's storehouse
Deseret Industries
Cemetery
City library
Family history center
Extraction center

## FAMILY MUSIC

Many families enjoy singing and listening to good music together. We have a number of tapes that we sing along with in the car or sometimes just for a fun evening. We have both sacred music and fun music such as cowboy songs, romantic songs, and so on. Families can also sing from the Primary songbook or the hymnbook. We particularly enjoy singing at the piano, with the guitar, or with the flute. Music brings a wonderful spirit into the home. The Spirit truly comes as families sing fun and religious songs together.

## DECIDING ON THE ACTIVITY

While there are plenty of activities for families to enjoy, they sometimes have trouble deciding which ones to do and when. If a family will plan out their activities on paper or on a calendar, they will find it easier to put some variety into them. In a family council, we would usually plan four weeks' activities at a time. Just take a piece of paper and make a list like the following:

| Date | Event | Participants |
|---|---|---|
| July 15 | Fire station | The whole family |
| July 28 | Waterskiing for the full day | All but one son who has to work |
| August 10 | Games at home | Older daughter in charge |
| August 17 | Dinner in the canyon | The whole family |

Having made these decisions in advance helped us be

more faithful in fulfilling our responsibilities relative to family activities.

If families are going to "compete" with school or church activities, they'll have to do some fun things. If families plan these things together, their enjoyment will be increased, and they will also increase love among family members. These activities also provide a chance to "cleanse" your children every few days from what they may have picked up from the world. Just being together and talking allows a tremendous "cleansing process" to go on.

Sometimes, because of the various ages of the children, it might be fun to split up activities. One parent can go with the older children and one with the younger ones.

## REFRESHMENTS

Above all, don't forget the refreshments! All family members love refreshments. They can be things you buy at the store or things you make at home. Our family most enjoys donuts, ice cream, bottled fruit, taffy, baked apples, cold cereal, hot chocolate, fruit leather, marshmallows, popcorn, and cookies.

## CONSTRUCTIVE FAMILY PROJECTS

There is real value in involving children in constructive projects around the home where they can develop skills, hobbies, and talents. Many times children are bored at home and just want to be with their friends or perhaps to do activities with little value. Or they may want to watch television or videos evening after evening or all day on Saturday.

Some of the Brethren have taught that some families are *too activity oriented* and are just doing "fun things." They've suggested that great strength can come from doing family projects, things that are a bit more constructive but still fun.

Family projects have allowed us to have a "family home evening" every night, with each family member working on some constructive project, many times with a parent or a brother or sister. These projects have included:

Planting a garden
Quilting
Learning to cook
Writing in a journal
Learning to sew
Writing personal and family histories
Learning how to repair things around the house
Writing letters to family members
Organizing individual and family photo albums
Painting a picture
Balancing the family budget
Drawing
Preparing a year's supply
Preparing seventy-two-hour emergency kits
Developing weekly menus
Baking bread
Studying phonics
Holding a read-a-thon
Working on merit badges
Studying Spanish
Exercising
Doing math
Dancing
Looking things up in the encyclopedia
Carving wood
Singing
Carving soap
Improving handwriting
Holding a spelling bee
Taking typing lessons
Taking music lessons
Learning missionary lessons
Having a scripture chase
Holding a sports night

Holding a drama night
Holding a book of remembrance night
Learning to iron
Learning to work on the computer
Learning about manners and etiquette
Working on the Young Women's "Personal
    Progress" program

These projects, while enjoyable, add to the skill and talent of each family member. They also give great satisfaction to family members—much more than do games and similar activities.

## FAMILY CALLINGS

Just as we have callings in the Church, so we extend callings to our children in the family. The children handle these assignments on their own or with assistance from a parent or brother or sister.

One child has taken the lead in missionary work—putting our family picture and testimony in copies of the Book of Mormon and making contacts with neighbors. Another child has taken the lead in putting our family history information into the computer, arranging to go to the Family History Library to do research, and organizing the family to be baptized for the dead.

Another child is in charge of helping the needy. We have maintained a list of people in the neighborhood who need help, and this child makes sure that we respond individually or as a family.

One of our other children helps us keep track of our food storage, telling us what we need to purchase when we are getting low.

Yet another child takes the responsibility to plan a weekly activity for family home evening. Another encourages us in family scripture reading, family home evening, and family prayer.

All of these activities help involve children in productive things.

We have an annual family activity where we write New Year's resolutions. If they are not too private, we share them with the family. Then we ask if anyone can think of any others they would add to the list. Invariably, there are a few, and that gives us an opportunity to help each child set some long-range goals. Typically, the resolutions have been in five areas: spiritual, educational, physical, financial, and social. After that, we agree on two or three family resolutions in those same categories.

Every other month or so, we review those resolutions as a family. We have encouraged the children to put them on a note card on their dresser where they can review them frequently. This has particularly helped our girls in setting goals for Personal Progress.

## CHILDREN CAN STRENGTHEN THE FAMILY

Once we were talking during supper about how the children could better strengthen the family. We were centering on what it is that makes a family successful. After some discussion, we came up with what we called "The Family: Ten Commandments for Children":

1. Elijah shall "turn the heart of the *fathers* to the *children*, and the heart of the *children* to their *fathers*" (D&C 128:17; italics added).
2. Follow your parents, avoid peer pressure and the teachings of friends. Priorities: (1) The Lord; (2) family; (3) friends (see D&C 68:25).
3. Be obedient, trust your parents, keep the (their) commandments (see 1 Nephi 8:37; 2 Nephi 4:6).
4. Strengthen your brothers and sisters, do not quarrel, serve them, be an example, be positive, build your family (see Mosiah 4:14–15; Alma 39:1, 10).
5. Love your family physically—throw your arms around them. Give lots of hugs (see D&C 88:123; Jacob 3:7).

6. Encourage family scripture reading (see Luke 24:27, 32).
7. Encourage family prayer (see 3 Nephi 18:21).
8. Encourage family home evening (see Deuteronomy 6:4–9).
9. Encourage wholesome family activities (see D&C 95:13).
10. Prepare yourself for parenthood (see Exodus 20:12; Proverbs 6:20; D&C 1:3).

Children really can support and strengthen their family and make it stronger. You will notice that besides spiritual things, these "commandments" include time for love, activities, and fun together. That balanced approach to family life seems to bring the most success.

## SUMMER PROJECTS

We've found it very helpful, during the summer especially, when the children are always saying, "Mom, what can I do?" to have planned out some projects for them to accomplish within a certain time frame, such as the summer months. The following activities helped us develop our skills, talents, and abilities:

| Dad | Mom | 15-year-old girl | 13-year-old boy | 10-year-old boy |
|---|---|---|---|---|
| guitar | piano | cooking | trumpet | piano |
| piano | flute | flute | piano | Spanish |
| computer | Spanish | piano | Spanish | computer |
| singing | reading | singing | computer | guitar |
| Spanish | exercise | computer | puzzle | |
| memorizing scriptures | computer | Spanish | model-making | |
| | | haircut (learn to give) | cooking | |
| | | | guitar | |

| 6-year-old girl | Family Projects | Joint Projects |
|---|---|---|
| reading | exploring | Mom/a daughter on the flute |
| writing | Spanish | Dad/a son on the guitar |
| Spanish | family games | Dad/a daughter and a son learning computer |
| swimming | sing with guitar/piano | 2 daughters on piano and flute |
| singing | encyclopedia search | |
| | scripture chase | |
| | service project | |

In these projects, Mom was to teach flute. Dad was to teach piano, guitar, and computer. Our older daughter was to teach piano and flute. We have also found reading to be an extremely useful activity, not only as a summer project but as something that can be done year round. Frequent visits to the library to obtain appropriate reading material for all the children has been a continuing activity. Children can be introduced to great heroes through reading the classics or just enjoy fun, wholesome reading. It also allows the older children to help the younger ones read. The involvement among family members in teaching one another a variety of skills has really increased the love in the family. Also, developing their talents and abilities has given our children additional self-confidence and a level of maturity that they would not have otherwise achieved.

## HOLIDAYS AND BIRTHDAYS

Families can take advantage of all the holidays that occur during the year in the country where they live. These might include religious holidays like Christmas or the restoration of the priesthood, or they might just be fun government or traditional holidays. Birthdays also provide great opportunities for family celebrations. As our family has matured, we have become more and more adept at having fun on birthdays. It's easy when children are little to have birthday parties with cake and ice cream. But as the years pass, it becomes a little more challenging to plan a fun birthday.

We have found it most edifying in our family to spend time before the birthday to plan some things that we know the person really likes. All in all, it's a great time to honor an individual in the family. We've always written little notes to each other and read them aloud to the family. That has made the person being recognized feel additional love and attention from all family members. We make that person the king or queen for the day.

On Christmas, we have tried to teach our children the

Christmas Story with a little program based on the scriptures that illustrates the life of Jesus. Each family member plays a role from the scriptures:

## CHRISTMAS PROGRAM

Opening hymn: _____
Chorister: _____
Pianist:_____
Invocation: _____
Opening testimony about Christmas: _____

| SCRIPTURE REFERENCE | NAME OF FAMILY MEMBER |
| --- | --- |
| 1. Moses 4:1–2 | Satan: |
|  | Jesus: |
| 2. 2 Nephi 17:14, 19:6 | Reader: |
| 3. Matthew 1:18–25 | Joseph: |
|  | Mary: |
|  | Angel: |
| 4. Luke 1:26–38 | Mary: |
|  | Angel: |
|  | Jesus: |
| 5. Luke 2:1–20 | Joseph: |
|  | Mary: |
|  | Mule: |
|  | Angel: |
|  | Jesus: |
|  | Shepherds: |
| 6. Matthew 2:1–12 | Joseph: |
|  | Mary: |
|  | Jesus: |
|  | Wise Men: |
|  | Herod: |
| 7. Luke 1:80, 2:40–52 | Jesus: |
|  | Wicked men: |
| 8. Moses 3:7, 9–10 2 Nephi 19:9 | Jesus: |
| 9. Acts 1:6–11 | Two men in white: |
|  | Jesus: |
|  | Apostles: |
| 10. Mark 14:20–25 | Reader: |

Sacrament teachings:_____
Sing sacrament hymn:_____
Concluding testimony: _____
Hymn: _____
Benediction: _____

Of course the same kind of program could be developed around other holidays as well.

Once while living in Peru, we decided to have a different kind of Christmas. It consisted of two parts. First, we would contribute what we would have spent on our family, all but one purchased gift for each person, to someone in real need. Second, whatever else we gave each other had to be made with our own hands. It could not be purchased from a store but was to made with items we already had at home. Thus we'd have to improvise and give of our time, our talents, and ourselves.

One of our sons decided to make a key holder for his mother's keys. We had fifty or so house keys but nowhere to put them, and they frequently got mixed up. He decided a key holder would make an excellent gift.

We looked for a piece of wood to make it. I wanted to buy it, but my son reminded me that we couldn't. We spent an hour getting a little piece of wood ready that would have taken us minutes to buy. When we tried to sand it, we realized we didn't have anything to sand it with, so we scraped off the rough edges with a rough board. We soon came up against the problem of painting it. Fortunately, we had a little yellow paint, but we had no paintbrush.

Again I thought about going to the store, but my son said: "Dad, someone had to invent the paintbrush. How did he do it?" We made a brush by pulling some straw out of my wife's broom, and though I had my doubts about how it would work, we made a brush as good as one from the store. We then had a problem with what to use for the hooks for the keys. We solved that problem by bending nails into shape, doing each with love and lots of patience. On Christmas morning, this boy had a delightful experience as he gave his mother a true gift from his heart. We still have that key holder after all these years.

One young daughter found a good-sized rock, painted it with the same yellow paint (since it was all we had), and wrote on it, "Mom, I love you." We still have it—a rock prepared with loving hands and a pure heart.

Another son made a llama from straw pulled from the broom. (Poor broom, it had almost disappeared.) Since he was the oldest, this boy really created a quality item. It probably would have sold well in any store in Peru. That, too, is still part of our family collection.

## PERSONAL GIFT CERTIFICATES

The giving of self for Christmas and birthdays brings an added measure of the Spirit. We have often given personal gift certificates anonymously to our neighbors that say things like "The snow in the front of your house will be shoveled. One of these days some neighborhood 'angels' will do it."

What happens in the heart of the giver is much more important than what is received. We have also given similar certificates to family members. They say things like "I will make your bed seven times" and "I will do your dishes three times." My wife likes this one: "Six hours of peace and harmony."

And to one of our mothers who lived far away, a certificate promising to send twelve letters, one letter each month of the year. This gift was better than anything we could have bought in a store because it showed more profound love, more giving of self. As we have considered what Christ gave, each time we have come to the conclusion that he really gave of himself, time and time again.

One time during the Christmas season, with a certificate we gave to an older couple, we included this little poem that we wrote:

> This gift to you is something special,
> It represents the true spirit of giving,
>     the Christmas vessel.
> The giving of knick-knack, trinket, or doll
> Is not long lasting, and into this pattern we
>     choose not to fall.

> For the memories of presents quickly pass,
> So we have desired something that will last.
> It's time together that really will count;
> As we build family ties, our love will mount.
> The days together in a year are a few but they
>     inspire.
> Thus this gift can be spent together any day you
>     desire.
> The gift we offer is a dinner together out to eat,
> And the cost will be our Christmas treat.
> Time together should build our understanding,
>     love and rapport,
> And will strengthen our love to the eternal core.

Involving the family in many wholesome activities is an enriching experience. It adds fun, zest, and spark to family life. Be sure that children are full participants in deciding what to do, and you will have much more success with your activities.

Let it not be misunderstood that families should not be involved in school or church activities, but let it be understood that those must be secondary to family activities. I pray the Lord will bless all of us to work a little harder to have more fun times together as a family and thus create memories to laugh about and talk about for years to come.

# TEACHING YOUR FAMILY LOVE AND SERVICE

Some time ago I was in the practice of making bread on Monday, my day off (my wife had taught me), and then as a family we would take a loaf or two to someone in our neighborhood who was in need. On one particular evening we thought we would visit a certain widow and give her a loaf to cheer her up. We went down the hill to her house, but she was not there. We thought we would then go by and visit another person, but she was not home either.

Some of us were kidding each other that maybe we weren't very inspired about where to go. We had offered a prayer earlier that we would be inspired to know to whom to give the bread. We were jokingly saying things like, "Maybe we should just take it home and eat it ourselves."

We started heading toward home thinking, "Well, we tried to give the bread to someone," but then one of us felt impressed to say, "Let's go see Brother Jones. He's been a widower for about a year and must surely be lonely. Maybe he'd like to have a loaf of bread." As we went up his walkway, I told the children we ought to sing to him. They resisted saying, "No, let's not do that."

When he opened the door and saw our whole family standing there, he was really taken aback as to what it all meant. We told him we had just come by to wish him well and express our love to him. We went into the living room and visited with him a few minutes.

Then I said, "Why don't we sing to Brother Jones?" The children didn't want to very much. My wife thought of a number of songs we could sing but finally suggested "You Are My Sunshine." As we sang, we could tell he was a little embarrassed at first, but then came some real emotion and gratitude.

He expressed his love to us and said, "Today, this very day, is my forty-fifth wedding anniversary. No one knew that, and no one remembered me on this day. To have you come tonight and sing this song touches me deeply in my heart. I want you to know how much I appreciate your coming. I'll enjoy this bread, but more than that, I'll never forget the gift of love you gave me in coming to see me tonight."

How true it is that it is more blessed to give than to receive. As important as it was to him, I don't think Brother Jones received as much from the visit as we did. As we walked down the walk from his house, we knew something special had happened. It was hard to describe the joy we felt as we left his home that night. Our love for him was even deeper. When he passed away a few months later, we were grateful to have had that experience with him and to know we had added a bit to his happiness.

We have always been amazed that we can never give to someone else with the Spirit of the Lord and not be blessed a hundredfold in return. Jesus told his disciples, "A new commandment I give unto you, that ye love one another; as I have loved you, that ye also love one another. By this shall all men know that ye are my disciples, if ye have love one to another" (John 13:34–35).

In other words if we truly love the Lord we will desire to love one another, both in the family and beyond the family.

The Lord also says, "If ye love me, keep my commandments" (John 14:15). Besides loving our families and those around us, we show our love to the Lord by keeping his commandments, especially faith, repentance, and the basic ordinances and covenants of the gospel.

In fact, the Lord clearly explained that love for him and for others are the two great commandments:

"A lawyer, asked him a question, tempting him, and saying, Master, which is the great commandment in the law?

"Jesus said unto him, Thou shalt love the Lord thy God with all thy heart, and with all thy soul, and with all thy mind. This is the first and great commandment. And the second is like unto it, Thou shalt love thy neighbor as thyself. On these two commandments hang all the law and the prophets" (Matthew 22:35–40).

Clearly, if we are obedient in loving God and in loving one another inside and outside our families, we will, because the whole law hangs upon these principles, be able to raise up our families to the Lord.

## MARRIAGE, A PARTNERSHIP OF THREE

In any righteous family, the marriage does not consist of just the husband and the wife who are sealed together for time and eternity in the temple of the Lord. The marriage also includes the Lord as a third partner. The best way to increase your love for your spouse and your spouse's love for you is to increase your love for the Lord. If you increase your love for the Lord, you will have greater love for one another.

My wife has known from the beginning of our marriage that I love the Lord more than I love her, and I have also understood that she loves the Lord more than she loves me. Because of that commitment to God, the love between us has been tremendously increased. President Joseph F. Smith said, "A home is not a home in the eye of the gospel, unless there dwell perfect confidence and love between the husband and the wife. Home is a place of order, love, union, rest, confidence, and absolute trust; where the breath of suspicion of infidelity can not enter; where the woman and the man each have implicit confidence in each other's honor and virtue" (*Gospel Doctrine*, p. 302).

The same is true of love for our children. As King Benjamin said, "Ye will teach them to walk in the ways of truth and soberness; ye will teach them to love one another, and to serve one another" (Mosiah 4:15).

## AVOIDING CONTENTION AND
## MAINTAINING PEACE AT HOME

Just as the Lord has commanded us to love one another, he has also commanded us not to contend with one another. The Lord has spelled out clearly who the author of contention is and why we must guard against it: "He that hath the spirit of contention is not of me, but is of the devil, who is the father of contention, and he stirreth up the hearts of men to contend with anger, one with another. Behold, this is not my doctrine, to stir up the hearts of men with anger, one against another; but this is my doctrine, that such things should be done away" (3 Nephi 11:29–30).

If we allow contention in our family, then we as parents are at fault. There is no place in a family for teasing or quarreling or anything else that stirs up contention among family members. The same is true if we allow our children to compete negatively against one another. That can only bring hurt feelings and anger into the home. The same is true of allowing children to be overly physical. Sometimes one of the children who is stronger than the others will exert physical force on the others. We ought not to tolerate such behavior, as, again, it brings contention.

If we continue working to bring the Spirit into our homes, over time we should see very little contention. Parents must especially be sure that their children do not fight with one another: "Ye will not suffer your children . . . [to] fight and quarrel one with another, and serve the devil, who is the master of sin, or who is the evil spirit which hath been spoken of by our fathers, he being an enemy to all righteousness" (Mosiah 4:14).

Elder F. Enzio Busche, in general conference of April 1982, explained that one of the best ways to remove contention is to pray: "I fervently prayed to my Heavenly Father to help me to handle the situation [a problem with a son]. Peace came over me. I was no longer angry. . . . As I expressed my confidence in him, he broke into tears, confessing his unworthiness and condemning himself beyond measure" ("Love Is the Power That Will Cure the Family," *Ensign*, May 1982, p. 70).

Just as King Benjamin told us we should not suffer our children to fight, he also told us how to solve the problem: "Ye will teach them to walk in the ways of truth and soberness; ye will teach them to love one another, and to serve one another" (Mosiah 4:15).

We have truly found that counsel of great benefit in our family. The devil is the source of contention, and it does not seem to matter whether you are the innocent party or not. If you participate in or aggravate the contention, then you are to blame.

While I was flying on a plane from Salt Lake City to Houston, Texas, some years ago, my seat had not been pre-assigned and I ended up having to sit in the smoking section.

No one was smoking next to me, so I felt quite comfortable. However, the fellow across the way and up one seat began smoking, and the smoke drifted back. He was sitting in the nonsmoking section.

I finally asked the flight attendant to ask him not to smoke. She was a little embarrassed and said, "Why don't you just change seats so he will be in the smoking section and you won't?" I agreed to that. Everyone in the smoking section pretty much heard the conversation, and I felt a little embarrassed.

As soon as I sat down in my new seat, the couple directly behind me began smoking and blowing their smoke my way. The more I sat there, the angrier I felt inside, especially as I had recently read articles about second-hand smoke causing cancer. The smoke kept coming over the seat. I thought, "Why do I have to tolerate this? Why can't I breathe fresh air? Why can't these people be more disciplined and not smoke?"

Finally, I turned all my air vents straight back so they would blow on them. The man was a little irritated and said to me, "What's the idea of doing that? It's already freezing, and my wife's getting cold."

I turned around and said, "Well, when you stop smoking, I'll turn the air off. I don't want to breathe your smoke." There was some contention between us, and I could tell he was really mad.

I turned back around in my seat, and then a moment of inspiration came. My eyes fell upon the verses I had just been reading, 3 Nephi 11:29–30 which say that the devil is the father of contention. And here I was causing the contention, even if I was right and even if the smoke was harmful. I began to have feelings come to me like these: "Contention is not of me. You ought not create it or, if it exists, augment it. You're being a party to creating contention." Feeling repentant, I turned around and told the man, "I'll turn off the air. I don't want to breathe your smoke, but I'll turn off the air so you won't be cold. I'm sorry for speaking so sharply."

He immediately said, "No, I'm the one at fault. I know I shouldn't even smoke. I'm sorry."

Interestingly, as soon as I took the contention out of the situation, he also calmed down, and I know I did too. He and his wife immediately stopped smoking, and I don't believe they smoked again until we arrived in Houston.

I realized it is not right to be the source of any contention. Mormon wrote to Moroni, "My son, I fear lest the Lamanites shall destroy this people; for they do not repent, and Satan stirreth them up continually to anger one with another" (Moroni 9:3).

Contention is definitely of the devil, and it causes anger to rise in people's hearts. I was probably the innocent party in this encounter but I was the source of harsh words between us. Thus, I ended up being the source of contention. I felt particularly bad about this because I had been reading the scriptures at the time.

When we're dealing with contention in our families, husband and wife need to start with the premise that there simply will be none. If children clearly understand that you really mean that—that there won't be any harsh words or put-downs or language like that—they will abide by it. If they don't, then some discipline must be put into effect.

I remember one little boy who, when told he wasn't so smart, said, "Oh, yeah? Then I'll give you the alphabet backward." We all knew he could do it frontward but were certain he wouldn't be able to do it backward. He flipped around, put his back to us, and then said the alphabet. We all laughed, and it reduced the tension of the moment.

We must be sure never to let one little incident blow everything out of proportion. We must not treat something like a Supreme Court case when it is really just a minor traffic violation. At times, if we're caught up in our own problems or emotions, that's exactly what can happen. Some principles we might want to keep in mind about contention are:

1. Contention brings discord and disharmony to the family.
2. Don't engage in contention with the one contending or the problem will be magnified.
3. Love and peace are the foundation of a righteous home. Contention is not to be allowed.
4. The one contending should be immediately dismissed from your presence so that you will not become involved in the contention.

One day, after seeing the report card of one of my sons, I told him that if he couldn't take control of what was going on in school, then I would. Of course, that greatly offended him. I was angry and he was angry, and there was some loud talk between us and some demands and ultimatums. As a result, he ended up going to school unhappy and mad, and I ended up going to work in the same spirit.

On the way to work as I prayerfully pondered what had happened, there came into my mind the words from the Joseph Smith Translation of Luke 6:29–30, which my wife and I had just read in the scriptures:

"Unto him who smiteth thee on the cheek, offer also

the other; or, in other words, it is better to offer the other, than to revile again. And him who taketh away thy cloak, forbid not to take thy coat also.

"For it is better that thou suffer thine enemy to take these things, than to contend with him. Verily I say unto you, Your heavenly Father who seeth in secret, shall bring that wicked one into judgment" (JST Luke 6:29–30).

The Lord seems to be saying we should give another our cloak in order to avoid contention—that it is better to lose the coat than to contend over it. The Lord in that way showed his great dislike for contention.

When people become angry, they usually harden the hearts of others in stirring them up to anger. That is one of the great tools of the devil—to get us to contend one with another. The devil delights in that because it hardens our hearts toward what is good, toward other people, and toward the Lord himself. And when our hearts are hardened, it is increasingly difficult for the Spirit to get through to us to teach us and guide us.

The Savior taught that in the old days it was said people were not to commit adultery; he added that he that even looks at a woman to lust after her has committed adultery in his heart. He was teaching the law of Moses but adding to it the higher law of Christ. Similarly, in the old days it was said that one should not kill, but Jesus again added the higher law of Christ, saying that he that is even angry with his brother is in danger of hellfire. Those statements of the Lord teach us that anger is a serious spiritual ailment (see Matthew 5:21–28).

I apologized to my son the next morning during scripture reading, and also to another son with whom I had had a confrontation the same night, saying the problem was my fault in having stirred them up to anger.

There is a way to handle problems without becoming angry and hardening our hearts. If I had exercised better control, I would probably have influenced my son to do likewise.

He responded in kind to my anger because of his own lack of maturity. If I had been in control, he probably would have been. Had he not been, I could easily have said, "Go to your room and wait there and pray until your heart is in order. Then come back and we'll finish the discussion. We can't discuss it when we're angry. There's no place for anger in this home."

It is impossible to be in a contentious spirit and have the Spirit of the Lord. It takes great discipline to be in control so the devil does not have influence over us. He has influence over us only as we allow it. As the Lord says of the fall, "The devil tempted Adam, and he partook of the forbidden fruit and transgressed the commandment, wherein he became subject to the will of the devil, because he yielded unto temptation" (D&C 29:40). We will not be subject to the will of Satan unless we yield to temptation; otherwise he can have no power over us.

### AVOIDING CONTENTION: THE DIFFERENCE BETWEEN BOYS AND GIRLS

One morning one of our daughters missed scripture reading. At breakfast many times we talk a bit more about the most important thing we have learned in scripture reading that morning. We were doing that, and she was feeling a bit guilty. I cautiously asked her where she had been and why she hadn't come.

"I couldn't decide what to wear," she said.

I said, not too sensitively, "You mean for the whole twenty minutes?"

She said, "That's right. I was staring at the closet for twenty minutes and couldn't decide because my older sister wore what I was going to wear."

All the boys laughed, and I think it made her feel bad for a moment. But we helped her laugh with us, when I said, "I don't have much choice. I get to choose a black suit or a blue suit, period."

The two younger boys said, "We don't care. We just take what's next on the stack." To them, it didn't matter whether it matched or whether they had to get a favorite article out of the dirty clothes. Boys just wear what's "next on the stack."

We had a good laugh about that, my wife especially. The good humor defused an otherwise contentious moment. It ended up being a sweet experience, and at the same time taught us a little more about the difference between boys and girls.

That daughter later wrote me this letter:

> Dear Dad,
>    I haven't done this in a long time. I wish I could remember more often. I want to tell you how much you mean to me. How much you teach me. I am so thankful of how well you know the scriptures for you to teach us. I learn so much at scripture reading because of you. I really hope I can find a husband just like you. I love you so much. I hope you have a good trip. I love to hear about your trips. Bye!

We all need to be reminded that most of our problems are just little ones, many of which have the potential to become big problems unless we handle them correctly. Let us stay close to our children and teach them to avoid contention. Then there will be no contention but only love for one another.

## EXTENDING LOVE TO OTHERS

One of the great benefits of service is that it teaches people to reach beyond themselves, to not be selfish, to help others, and to give Christian service. We ought to seek out those in need. We ought to be quick to respond to family members or others who may have physical handicaps, infirmities, or special mental or emotional needs.

When we practice true principles of Christian service, our compassion expands beyond ourselves. Then our love for others increases, our love of God increases, and the love of others for God increases as well. In all of the New Testament, probably no other message comes through as powerfully as the love that Jesus had for all people. He always set the example of ministering to others no matter what else he was doing. If we will go and do likewise, ministering to others with love, people will sense the spirit of Christ in us. They will then be able to follow our leadership because of our great love for them.

While fun family activities are important, experiencing the love and joy of heaven can bring your family closer to the Lord than almost anything else. If families want to experience that love, they will cultivate the spirit of the following passages:

> The thing which will be of the most worth unto you will be to declare repentance unto his people, that you may bring souls unto me, that you may rest with them in the kingdom of my Father (D&C 15:6).

> How great is [the Lord's] joy in the soul that repenteth! Wherefore, you are called to cry repentance unto this people. And if it so be that you should labor all your days in crying repentance unto this people, and bring, save it be one soul unto me, how great shall be your joy with him in the kingdom of my Father! And now, if your joy will be great with one soul that you have brought unto me into the kingdom of my Father, how great will be your joy if you should bring many souls unto me! (D&C 18:13–16).

There is no greater joy than helping to save a soul. This isn't just bringing the gospel to a nonmember or helping perfect a Saint. Sometimes we can bring someone to Christ through a very small thing, such as encouraging someone, visiting someone who is sick, sharing a smile or an embrace, being a good listener, cheering up a child, and so on. Each little act of kindness, in my judgment, is part of bringing a soul to Christ.

As you act as Christ did in relation to other people, those people will see Christ in you and desire to follow your leadership and teachings. Truly there is no greater joy than bringing happiness to others and helping them save their own souls. This basic principle of love must be paramount in our teachings and our example to our children if we desire to raise them up to the Lord.

President David O. McKay taught that love made homes more permanent and enduring: "Homes are more permanent through love. Oh, then, let love abound. Though you fall short in some material matters, study and work and pray to hold your children's love. Establish and maintain your family hours always. Stay close to your children. Pray, play, work, and worship together. This is the counsel of the church" (*Family Home Evening Manual*, 1968–69, iii).

Yes, let love abound in our homes, and then let it overflow into our neighborhoods to bless our fellowmen.

## TEMPORAL GIFTS OF LOVE

The only way these attributes of love can be acquired is for children to experience them, and the best place for them to experience them is in the home under the direction of their parents. We have found over the years that setting some goals as to whom we might assist in our ward and neighborhood, and when, have been a great help to us. We have used many family home evening activity nights, as I'm sure you have, to go out and serve so we could experience more joy and maybe a little less entertainment. It has been great to be able to plan ahead about whom we might help and to feel the gratitude of others.

### SHOVELING SNOW

On a Thanksgiving some years ago when our children were young, there was quite a snowstorm in Utah, where we lived. I don't especially enjoy snow, particularly when it's in my driveway. That morning I looked out the window and saw about a foot of it. I gathered up two of my boys, who

were seven and five at the time, and convinced them how happy they would be helping their dad shovel all that snow. As you know, that takes some doing, but parents can make work fun. In fact, worthwhile work is one of the real sources of joy. I took them outside with me, and we shoveled the entire walk.

After we finished we were cold, and we were ready to go in. But I saw a teaching moment, and so I said "I wonder if we shouldn't go shovel Bill's walk." (Bill was our neighbor next door.)

I was pleased as one boy said, "That sounds good, Dad." The other boy said, "I'm cold."

Trying to take advantage of the moment to teach, I said, "I wonder how Bill would feel this morning if he opened his door and saw his entire walk all finished." Then the other boy caught the spirit of it and said, "He would really be happy, wouldn't he?"

The moment was right to say, "Well, what do you think, son, that Heavenly Father would have us do?"

He said, "I think we had better shovel the walk." By the time we were through, we were tired, and the youngest boy said, "Let's ring the doorbell now and tell Bill what we've done." He was going for some short-run pleasure, wasn't he?

Again there was a real teaching moment as I was able to say, "No, son, I think it would be best if we didn't tell him and left it as a surprise. Heavenly Father likes us to do things anonymously." I had to tell him what that big word meant—that we do things without anyone knowing we're doing them. The next thing I knew my other boy had caught the spirit of it and said, "Well, what about Smiths' walk?" Before we finished that morning, we had done three other walks.

We went home with great satisfaction to tell Mom all about it. We had hot chocolate and joked and kidded about what we had done, how tired we were, and how cold we were, but how good we felt inside.

Within the next hour we had two or three phone calls expressing thanks for what had been done. We particularly smiled at one caller who said, "I can't figure it out. This morning there were three angels in our neighborhood. I'm not sure what their names were, but they really were angels and did what the Lord would surely have done had he been here. If you happen to see those angels around, please give them our thanks."

There was great joy in our family that day as we experienced some of those feelings promised by the Lord for doing good. These boys experienced the joy that comes to the heart from doing good anonymously and then being found out. In a sense, shoveling those sidewalks was a small task for us. It was really just the kindness more than the shoveling that was greatly appreciated by our neighbors.

President Joseph F. Smith said:

> Let love, and peace, and the Spirit of the Lord, kindness, charity, sacrifice for others, abound in your families. Banish harsh words, envyings, hatreds, evil speaking, obscene language and innuendo, blasphemy, and let the Spirit of God take possession of your hearts. Teach to your children

these things, in spirit and power, sustained and strengthened by personal practice. Let them see that you are earnest, and practice what you preach. Do not let your children out to specialists in these things, but teach them by your own precept and example, by your own fireside. Be a specialist yourself in the truth (*Gospel Doctrine*, p. 302).

The real fun of teaching doctrine to your children is in the practicing of it. To see the growth, the development, and the excitement they feel as they are learning the principles you have learned is a great joy.

## A MEXICAN GOOD SAMARITAN

I know a good Samaritan who really went the second mile to assist a total stranger and thereby showed that he was a disciple of Christ. After all, by those acts of kindness others will come to know that fact. A mission president in Mexico recounted this experience to me:

Ricardo, my first counselor, owns a machine shop, which I knew was in poor financial health. Business was slow, interest rates were high, and he was really afflicted with the responsibilities of the business, expecting to be forced to declare bankruptcy. He had been trying for two years, unsuccessfully, to get work from a company that could give him a lot of work. Our conversation went something like this:

"President, I am so happy! I feel so good! I just can't explain how happy I am!"

"Ricardo, why do you say that?"

"Do you remember the man from that company I have been working with to try to get work?"

"Yes."

"He called the other day because his wife asked him how we were doing and he didn't know. I told him I hadn't called because I was very busy trying to find work. He then asked me if I needed work, and I said yes! Then the conversation turned to other things.

"President, he just called me back last week and gave me an order that will keep us busy working all crews twelve hours a day for three months. This is sort of a test to see if we can really handle the work. If we can, he has promised to keep one machine busy full time. President, my men have all agreed, and I know we can do it! The business truck that I sold the other day—I'll be able to replace it in this one order. I'm so happy, and I feel so good!"

Then he began to explain to me that he would have to drive to Mexico City that very night, arriving about two in the morning to make arrangements for the raw materials he would need. I cautioned him about the dangers of driving at night on these highways and the risk of falling asleep at the wheel. He assured me he would be all right. He said, "I have so much energy and excitement! I'll be fine."

Energy? This triggered a thought from an area council meeting we had attended the previous day in Mexico City. So I asked, "Ricardo, what is divine motivation? What makes the Lord available at any and every moment to listen and forgive?"

Without hesitation, he answered, "Service to others"—the exact words we had been taught in that spiritual meeting the day before. I was so shocked at the immediate and accurate reply that the only thing I could think of to say was, "Why do you say that?"

He then told me this story:

"I was so down, so dejected, so discouraged about business affairs, financial obligations, commitments, my family's needs, and the needs of my employees that I went to the Lord as never before. I humbled myself and really poured out my heart to him.

"I confessed my sins, expressing that I was really confessing nothing, because he knew them all, but I asked for forgiveness and made certain promises to him. I really had a thorough and rewarding experience with the Lord.

"A few days later as I was returning home, I saw some people who appeared to have a problem. I saw a small crowd and stopped to investigate. I found that a truck had run over a ten-year-old boy named Miguel while he and his family were gathering cartons and valuables from the trash cans.

"The whole family was there, but they didn't know the boy's condition. They just knew the Red Cross had taken him and that he was unconscious.

"Seeing that they had no means to go to their son, I loaded them in my truck and went to the Red Cross. They wouldn't admit us, but I wiggled my way into where I could inquire of the doctor. I heard them saying there was no hope: fractured skull, broken bones all over—virtually just crushed. The doctor said they could do nothing. I asked if anyone could do something. He said possibly the Social Security program of the government.

"I spent the rest of the day trying to get Social Security to take the case by allowing me to hire the father and pay his contributions—just any way to get them to take the boy. They refused all attempts. I asked the Social Security doctor if someone in private practice could help the boy. He said that possibly a certain neurosurgeon could do something for him if anyone could.

"I went to see the neurosurgeon, who said, 'This is very expensive. Are you the boy's uncle?'

"I said, 'No, I don't even know the boy, but I will pay whatever it costs. Just do what you can.'

"The doctor said, 'If that is the case, then we will handle it a certain way and it won't cost so much.'

"I did agree to pay the neurosurgeon, but I was spending money we didn't have. My wife asked what was going on. I told her the story. She understood and supported me all the way. I had to sell my truck and some other things, but President, he is going to make it! He is responding well to treatment. President, he is going to be okay!"

As I listened to him, I discovered once again that:

1. Our afflictions bring us to the dust in humility.
2. We then pour out our heart to the Lord.
3. He tries our faith.
4. He blesses us beyond all expectation.

Can you imagine? Here is a modern-day story of a good Samaritan—a man who finds a complete stranger on the road and sells his own truck to pay for the operation. From my own experience I know how the Lord blessed this man within a short time in his business and gave him the ability to purchase another truck. Truly this act of giving taught that boy's family and all who were involved about what it means to be a real disciple of Christ.

There are many temporal gifts of love. These might include cash, a special Christmas for a family in need, a hundred pounds of beans or wheat left on someone's doorstep, and so on.

My family, too, has often received loving service from others. I will never forget the time when someone unknown to me called a men's clothier and paid the cost of a new suit for me. I was fitted for the suit without ever knowing the identity of the gracious disciple of the Lord who had helped us in a time of need. May we always do our best to do likewise and thus be true disciples of Jesus Christ.

## SPIRITUAL GIFTS OF LOVE

We can also give other significant gifts that are spiritual in nature. They may come directly from the Lord, or we may be an instrument in the hands of the Lord to give the spiritual gift.

I was once the visiting General Authority at a stake conference in Montana. After our evening meetings and activities, the stake president and his wife and I just visited for about an hour or so. They were having some real challenges, especially financially, and were not certain about what to do.

We shared some scriptures, testimonies, and stories and had a good evening together.

As I retired, an interesting feeling came to me as I began my nightly prayer. I felt that this stake president should have a priesthood blessing. I considered whether to go out and give it to him right then while they were in the Spirit or to do it in the morning. I opted to do it in the morning and went to bed.

The next morning, I was still wondering about giving him a blessing. I wasn't sure he would want one, but the impression seemed strong that he really should have a blessing. I set aside what I had planned to do that morning, got dressed, and went out to find him in the kitchen with his family.

I got him alone and offered to give him a priesthood blessing. He seemed quite surprised. He was not resistant but seemed to be wondering if he really needed one. We called in the family, and he offered a word of prayer. Then I gave him a blessing of encouragement and comfort to help him sustain his family in the difficult times he was having.

After the blessing, his wife was in tears. I went to get my briefcase so we could go on to our meetings. When I came back out, he told me (she couldn't because of her emotions) that unbeknownst to me or her husband, she had been praying for a week that the General Authority would sense the need for a blessing and provide it to her husband.

She later said to me, "I would never think of asking or bothering a General Authority for a blessing for me or my husband. I didn't even want to bother my husband to suggest to him that he should have a blessing. But I just prayed to the Lord that if it were right, that the General Authority would sense the need and give a blessing to my husband."

We then went off to the Sunday meeting. I called on a number of people from the congregation to bear testimony. As we were finishing calling on the people, I asked the stake president if his wife had borne her testimony in conference recently. He informed me that she never had. We then called on her, and she bore a beautiful testimony that touched all the people in the conference.

As the president was taking me to the airport that afternoon, he said, "My wife wouldn't tell you this, but you ought to know that my wife told me three days ago that she felt she was going to be called on to speak in conference. I surely have a faithful wife. It's also clear that the Lord works through his servants."

There was a great deal of love in this stake from these people and especially from the president, his wife, and their family. It's amazing to me how the Lord will prompt his people and his servants to respond to real needs.

What a great gift of faith this wife gave her husband! He had a real need. He didn't know that he did, or perhaps he didn't want to be humble enough to ask for help. His wife was able, through her righteousness, to influence both her husband and me. Some wise individual said, "As strong as the mother is spiritually in the family, so shall be the family." This certainly seemed to be the case with this good woman.

One can see that if parents like these teach their children about the powerful effects of love, they will quickly learn from the example of their parents.

## THE LORD'S GIFT: A HEALING TO A FAITHFUL MAN

Sometimes the Lord will minister to his people through one of his servants even though the servant doesn't know it. Just the same, the Lord will bless the one in need in the way he chooses to bless him.

A few years ago, Sister Cook and I attended a stake conference in a city in Guatemala. At the time, I had three broken ribs. During the meeting the stake president told the people about my condition and asked them to let me leave after the meeting without the customary handshaking and abrazos (hugs). They were very considerate and did as he requested.

As I was about to leave the chapel, however, at the suggestion of Sister Cook, I turned around and went back to the front of the chapel. I walked up to the brother who had led the choir, shook his hand, and thanked him for the music. There were some real tears shed. We greeted each other with an abrazo, and then I left.

A year later, we again attended a stake conference in the same city. This same brother came up to me and told me how that short encounter a year ago had changed his life. At that first stake conference, he was suffering from a spinal disease that created a paralytic condition. He was unable to walk more than a step or two without crutches, and then only with excruciating pain. In fact, he was on crutches while leading the choir. When we shook hands, he felt the Spirit of the Lord go through him. He was filled with a wonderful, warm feeling.

This brother went on to tell me that he had walked out of the chapel and into the hallway, where he met the mission president. It was only then that he realized he had walked that distance without his crutches. Previously, he had not been able to take even a step or two without great pain. Not only had he walked without his crutches, but he had also walked without pain.

He said in astonishment, "I've left my crutches!"

The mission president said, "Well, if you have come this far without them, drop them; you don't need them."

This good brother said to me that somehow when we had shaken hands a year earlier, the Lord had healed him, and he had never needed his crutches since. He was very emotional as he related this story, and he bore witness to me that the healing had come from the Lord.

Truly the Lord bestows his love upon whom he will. This man must have been sufficiently worthy and had sufficient need that the Lord healed him in an instant in a rather unusual experience. I would ask again, has not the Lord ministered great gifts of love to each of us, and ought we not to do the same to others?

## A LONELY MAN IN MEXICO

When we lived in Mexico, we came to know a man I will call Brother Clark. He was an American who had lived in Mexico for many years and was more than eighty years of age. Perhaps because he had no family or loved ones around him, he had become a bit cranky and hard for some to get along with. Perhaps because of the love of my wife, she was able to overcome that, and after a number of visits she finally invited him to come to our home for dinner.

He was delighted to accept, with the condition that he could bring his chess board and play my sons and me. We had a pleasant dinner with him that night and enjoyed visiting with him. He'd had some tremendous challenges over his life, and he shared a few of those with us that first evening. After supper, he played chess with me on one board and with one of my older sons on another, both at the same time. He beat us both. There was no question that Brother Clark's mind was still very alert. We sang. We talked. We prayed with him. We just had a fun night.

After we took him home that evening, he called us. He said, "Brother Cook, I want you to know that is the best evening I have had with a family in my life. I had forgotten there were families like that. I want you to know I will never forget tonight." As I hung up the telephone and shared his comments with my family, we were all very moved. We had loved Brother Clark before, but we loved him even more now.

It made us sad that he thought that simple evening had been one of the greatest nights of his life. Perhaps that helped move us try to draw closer to him over the coming weeks and months.

He came to dinner and visited with us a number of times. During this time he would not come to church but he allowed the priests and deacons to bring him the sacrament in his home.

Finally, the time came for us to move back to the United States. Shortly thereafter, we received word that Brother

Clark was now attending church. A month or so later we heard that Brother Clark was to be the main speaker in sacrament meeting. Finally he had become a member in good standing in the Church.

Some months later, we were saddened to hear that Brother Clark had passed away. But how happy we were to know that with assistance from us and other good Saints who loved him, he was humbled and turned to the Lord. He counted his blessings, and we counted ours for the love of God extended to all of us.

## A GIFT OF LOVE AND PEACE
## THROUGH AN EMBRACE

I will never forget another experience that occurred in Mexico. I had gone to a stake conference and held the usual meetings. In the general session Sunday morning, the young Mexican stake president stood up to speak, and he said, "I want to tell you the greatest lesson I have learned from Elder Cook."

My mind raced ahead, wondering what he was going to say. I thought, "What did he learn? Faith? Repentance? Service? Doctrine?"

He said, "I had heard that Elder Cook likes things to be done in exactness and good order. I knew that he wanted to see the results of our having increased attendance in meetings, sent youth on missions, helped people pay a full tithing, and so on. I was quite concerned and worried about it this whole weekend of conference. I had 'stewed over' it for four or five nights and did not sleep very well. I wanted everything to be just right.

"That Saturday afternoon as this General Authority came into our building and started down the hall toward me, my anxiety increased a hundredfold. I was a basket case by the time he reached me, although I am sure that he didn't realize it. He shook my hand and greeted me. Then he turned away for a moment, put his briefcase down, and came back and just threw his arms around me. He gave me a divine abrazo.

"I bear testimony that all my anxiety left me. The Spirit of the Lord filled me. I felt the love of the Lord for me and the love of this good brother for me. I bear witness that perhaps the greatest good we can do for one another is to minister love to them." This good stake president then went on to teach a powerful lesson about loving and ministering to others."

How kind the Lord was to him and to me to allow us to experience love in action together. May each of us do our best to do likewise, to administer gifts of spiritual love to the people.

## A GIFT OF LOVE TO A SPIRITUALLY FALTERING FAMILY

A few years ago in Mexico City, the priesthood leaders had been visiting the homes of the less active and having some tremendous results. My wife, as an area general board member, also began teaching visiting teachers about how to be true shepherds and how to invite more of the Spirit of the Lord into their visits.

On a stake conference assignment with me, she accompanied a Relief Society president on a number of visits, with tremendous success. The next morning at the Sunday session of conference, as a result of their visits, two less active families and one newly baptized family were in attendance. We were all overwhelmed in love to see the response of these Saints to the Lord and his servants, even these two good sisters, in making these visits.

Then about a year later, in a different part of the city, I was teaching a group of priesthood brethren how to make such visits. As the meeting ended and we left to make the visits, a man asked me, "Do you know me?"

I said, "I don't believe so, good brother."

He said, "No wonder. You never came to visit me." He smiled, and continued, "But your wife did."

I then recalled that he was the head of the newly converted family my wife had visited a year earlier.

He said, "May I tell you a secret? My wife and family and I had decided, the very week your wife came to visit, that we were leaving the Church. We had been offended in the ward. We were determined that we would depart from the faith and never return.

"I bear witness to you, Brother Cook, that your wife touched us with the Spirit of the Lord. We felt the love of God in her. We felt the Lord speak through her as she stirred us up in remembrance of God and our ordinances and our commitments to him. I would not be here today if it were not for her."

He then added with a smile, "You will be pleased to know that I was called just last week to be a member of a bishopric. That's why I'm in this meeting learning how to go out and visit the homes. How I wish now that I had observed more carefully how your wife ministered to us! I wish I knew better what she did to bring the Spirit so forcefully to me and my family."

## THE NEEDS OF THE ELDERLY

As a family, we decided some time ago that we would spend many of our family home evenings in service to others. One night we visited an old folks' home near our neighborhood. We talked to the head nurse and asked if there was anybody who had not had a visit for a long time. We could see by her face that she was thinking, "There are about a hundred. Which do you want?" But she did give us the names of two or three people.

We visited a woman named Joyce and a German woman named Louise. They were both in their seventies. Joyce could hardly lift her head from her pillow.

We shook hands with them and could see that though they were surprised at our visit, they were very pleased we were there. We told them we had just come to tell them we loved them and to see if we might be of any service to them that night.

Joyce told us of her problems—of the difficulties she was having with her back. Louise told us of her children and showed us a picture of them. We were prayerfully considering what to do, and after we had talked a while, I suggested we might sing a song before leaving. My wife with inspiration said, "Let's sing 'You Are My Sunshine.' " As the whole family began to sing, these two women just started weeping. I don't think anyone had told them for a long time they were anybody's sunshine.

Joyce was so touched that she sat up in her bed. They were delighted to have us sing. Others in the hallway looked in to see what was happening. Louise was particularly touched. I asked her, "Do you know a song we could sing?"

She said, "I know a German lullaby." Then she sang a beautiful lullaby to us in German. She had a beautiful voice. Needless to say, not only were they touched but we were very touched by the Spirit. Mostly I felt something happen in the hearts of my children and my wife, and in my own heart.

As the rest of the family went down the hall, one of my sons and I went into another room and visited a woman who was seated in a wheelchair. I took hold of her hand, greeted her, and told her we had just come by to say hello. She held my hand tightly and would not let go. She asked me why we were there and if we really loved her. We told her that we did and that she looked very pretty.

Another woman in the room began talking to us while she combed her hair. These lonely women just couldn't get over the fact that we would come and visit them. While we were visiting, I kind of fooled my son by pressing his hand into the hand of the woman in the wheelchair. She then grabbed hold of him and I was free. He stood there pinned by this woman who wouldn't let go of his hand. We all laughed. They just didn't want us to leave. My son looked to me for help, but I just smiled.

As we went back into the hallway, another woman was whistling. We said, "My, you have a beautiful whistle. Whistle us a song." So she whistled several songs beautifully. She whistled better than any of us.

I was touched to see my wife kneeling next to a woman in a wheelchair who could not speak. She was holding and caressing the woman's hand and talking to her. The woman was so touched that even though she couldn't speak back to her, it was evident she was receiving my wife's love. I thought to myself, "I have just seen an angel. There's a real angel kneeling alongside that woman in need. My wife is truly a Christ-like person."

On a previous visit to this old folks' home, as we were leaving the building I saw a woman in a wheelchair. I said to one of my boys, "Come on, Son, let's just go say good-bye to that lady." She was in a dark corner, and we hadn't noticed her. We went over and took her by the hand. I told her we just wanted to say we loved her and asked if we could be of any help to her.

She said, "Oh, thank you for noticing me. Thank you for noticing me. Thank you for noticing me"—three times in a row. She said, "I'm stone deaf and I cannot hear a word you are saying, but thank you for noticing me." I think just the touch of her hand made us feel that we were doing what the Savior would have done had he been there.

May the Lord bless each of us to be more committed in our own hearts to give more, to forget about self, to extend to others the hallowed, saintly, sacred gifts that Christ gave. May we keep his example in our minds. May we teach with power and conviction, not only in our words but also in the powerful example we set wherever we go.

I cannot stress too strongly the need for parents to set the example for their children in these matters, and then for the parents and children together to set the example for other families in their neighborhood. All of us, children and parents alike, learn best by example.

I bear witness that the principles of the gospel, the principles of love, are true. I think we are all struggling to know how to apply these principles. No one seems to have all the answers, but keep in mind that great pattern that Jesus gave us by what he did. If you search after that, you will find the answers of what to do.

Many times our greatest difficulty in serving others is as simple as just deciding when and to whom to go. You might find it helpful to give a calling to one of your children for a few weeks or months to be the coordinator of service projects for your family. We may know the needs better than that child, but the child can still help us plan things so we do provide the service.

Experiences in serving others will help young men and young women prepare for the significant service they will render in the future, especially in serving as full-time missionaries. In addition, these experiences will bring more love into your own family. Jealousy, negativism, and criticism will be set aside, and love will reign in your home as your children learn to serve not only people outside the home but each other as well.

President Joseph F. Smith said:

> I would have it understood that I believe that the greatest law and commandment of God is to love the Lord our God with all our mind, might and strength and our neighbors as ourselves, and if this principle is observed at home the brothers and sisters will love one another; they will be kind and helpful to one another, showing forth the principle of kindness and being solicitous for one another's good. Under these circumstances the home comes nearer being a heaven on earth, and children brought up under these influences will never forget them, and though they may be in trying places, their memories will revert to the homes where they enjoyed such hallowed influences, and their better natures will assert themselves no matter what the trials or temptations may be (*Gospel Doctrine*, p. 295).

If we teach our children to love one another, they will never forget those teachings. The memories of serving one another will stay with them, no matter what trials or temptations they may face in the future.

In conclusion, let us go about ministering to others, doing our best to do good for all mankind. Let us teach our families to enjoy doing good, to give love for the fun of doing it, and not just from a sense of duty. If we will all give love freely and anonymously, the Lord will greatly bless us and those to whom we minister.

I believe that in the end, the thing that will matter most will be the service we have given to others.

> When the Son of man shall come in his glory, and all the holy angels with him, then shall he sit upon the throne of his glory: and before him shall be gathered all nations: and he shall separate them one from another, as a shepherd divideth his sheep from the goats: and he shall set the sheep on his right hand, but the goats on the left.
>
> Then shall the King say unto them on his right hand, Come, ye blessed of my Father, inherit the kingdom prepared for you from the foundation of the world: for I was an hungered, and ye gave me meat: I was thirsty, and ye gave me drink: I was a stranger, and ye took me in: naked, and ye clothed me: I was sick, and ye visited me: I was in prison, and ye came unto me.
>
> Then shall the righteous answer him, saying, Lord, when saw we thee an hungered, and fed thee? or thirsty, and gave thee drink? When saw we thee a stranger, and took thee in? or naked, and clothed thee? Or when saw we thee sick, or in prison, and came unto thee?
>
> And the King shall answer and say unto them, Verily I say unto you, inasmuch as ye have done it unto one of the least of these my brethren, ye have done it unto me (Matthew 25:31–40).

May the Lord bless us to follow the great example of Christ in ministering to all in need, and in so doing teach our children how to follow Jesus by more fully loving God and our fellowman. May he say to us and our families, "Inasmuch as ye have done it unto one of the least of these my brethren, ye have done it unto me."

# NO EMPTY CHAIRS

President Ezra Taft Benson often said that his greatest objective in life was to raise up his family to the Lord. He wanted to be sure that when he passed away and his family later followed him, there would be "no empty chairs" in his heavenly home. He meant, of course, that he did not want to lose even one of his children. He meant that he would do all in his power to help save all of his children that they might have eternal life. It seems to me that this should be a worthy objective of every faithful father and mother. We ought to do all in our power to make sure there are "no empty chairs" in heaven.

When we return home to our Heavenly Father, all of us would like to hear words like these: "Well done, my good and faithful servant. Enter into your rest. You truly have been faithful in all things and now will be crowned with glory, immortality, and eternal life. You have kept the commandments, you have passed the test, you have finally returned home. "

But wouldn't we also love to hear words like these? "All of your children walk in truth. You have taught them well. You have taught them of faith in the Lord Jesus Christ, of repentance, of the ordinances and covenants, of prayer, of studying my holy words, and all the other essential principles and ordinances of my gospel. You have taught them of the atonement of Jesus Christ, of how to obtain the grace and forgiveness of the Lord.

"Be comforted and know that because of your love and faithful teachings and patience with each of them, there will not be one lost. In due time they will all be with you in the eternal home that you started, strengthened, and nurtured upon the earth. They will all live again here with us in the eternities. There will not be one empty chair in your family. We love you for having loved your children and my children so much. They will all be crowned with you, with glory, immortality, and eternal lives."

Can you imagine the joy and satisfaction you would feel to hear those words? That joy would be nearly impossible to describe.

In summary, how can we as parents raise up our family to the Lord? We ourselves must turn to God and turn all of our children to God. We must help them soften their hearts and teach them by the Spirit of the Lord. We must teach them to keep all the commandments. We must teach them, by our example, to follow the promptings of the Spirit of the Lord until they reach their eternal home once again. We must teach them the doctrine of the kingdom. Above all else, we must love them with all our hearts.

Parents can become discouraged or wonder if all the effort is worth it. Some parents wonder what hope they can have for a child who is not living the gospel. But there are great blessings that come from having been born under the covenant or sealed to parents as a child, as well as from the sealings that occur between husband and wife. Elder Orson F. Whitney said:

> The Prophet Joseph Smith declared—and he never taught a more comforting doctrine—that the eternal sealings of faithful parents and the divine promises made to them for valiant service in the Cause of Truth, would save not only themselves, but likewise their posterity. Though some of the sheep may wander, the eye of the Shepherd is upon them, and sooner or later they will feel the tentacles of Divine Providence reaching out after them and drawing them back to the fold. Either in this life or the life to come, they will return.
>
> They will have to pay their debt to justice; they will suffer for their sins; and may tread a thorny path; but if it leads them at last, like the penitent Prodigal, to a loving and forgiving father's heart and home, the painful experience will not have

been in vain. Pray for your careless and disobedi-
ent children; hold on to them with your faith.
Hope on, trust on, till you see the salvation of God
(*Conference Report*, April 1929, p. 110).

President Brigham Young by revelation said the following, emphasizing the value of temple marriage, worthiness,
and the binding power of the sealing ordinances in the temple:

Let the father and mother, who are members
of this Church and Kingdom, take a righteous
course, and strive with all their might never to do
a wrong, but to do good all their lives; if they have
one child or one hundred children, if they conduct
themselves towards them as they should, binding
them to the Lord by their faith and prayers, I care
not where those children go, they are bound up to
their parents by an everlasting tie, and no power of
earth or hell can separate them from their parents
in eternity; they will return again to the fountain
from whence they sprang (Joseph Fielding Smith,
*Doctrines of Salvation*, 2:90–91).

May the Lord bless us to give our very best effort to raising up our families to the Lord. I think in some respects we
do not understand clearly who the generation is that we are
raising up to the Lord. Many of us have children who may
well be present when the Lord comes. May this desire of
Alma and of John for their children be true of us as well:

My son, I trust that I shall have great joy in you,
because of your steadiness and your faithfulness
unto God; . . . I say unto you, my son, that I have
had great joy in thee already, because of thy faithfulness (Alma 38:2–3).

I have no greater joy than to hear that my children walk in truth (3 John 1:4).

May the Lord bless us to lead our children to the Lord, to
love them, to cheer them up, to encourage them, and to support them. May he bless us to spend time with them, to

teach them and prepare them for this life and, more important, for the life to come.

May the Lord bless us with the gift of sensing the thoughts and intents of our children's hearts, to be able to feel what they are feeling. May we be blessed to sense anything that may be out of order in their lives and then assist them, through the Spirit of the Lord, in putting it back in order. Above all else, may we be true to the Lord, working with him under the direction of his Spirit, to assist in the exaltation of all his children. May this promise from the Lord be true for us as parents: "For I will go before your face. I will be on your right hand and on your left, and my spirit shall be in your hearts, and my angels round about you, to bear you up."

May the Lord bless the great parents of Zion, including the single parents and all who are struggling so valiantly to raise up their families to the Lord. May this blessing be extended to you in such a way that as you pass through the veil, you will find no empty chairs in your family circle. May the Lord bless all of us to that end, I sincerely pray in the name of Jesus Christ, amen.

# INDEX

son throughout day, 130–31; son prays for father, 134; finding lost cables, 135–38; child brings umbrella to ward prayer for rain, 145; finding employment, 163–65; son protected from auto accident, 166; Christmas tree removal business, 240; ministering to prisoner, 269

Premortal family council, 3–6

Priesthood ordinances: inviting Spirit through, 67–71; healing achieved through, 167–69; preparing children to receive, 207

Prisoner, family ministers to, 268–70

Problems: letting children struggle with, 187–88, 191–92; seeking scriptural solutions to, 274

Projects, family, 290–92, 294–95

Prophets, living: counsel of, 29–30; praying for, 99–100; reading words of, as family, 124

Punishment: effective use of, 197–98; built into God's laws, 219

Questions, asking, while reading scriptures, 121

Quizzes, fun with, 286–87

Rabbit, boy turns loose, 192–93

Rain, prayer for, 145

Rats, family battles with, 151–52

Rebellious children, xiii–xvi, 71, 331–32

Refreshments, 290

Repentance: son learns principle of, 173–76; implies change of heart, 179; as goal of discipline, 194; teaching, to children, 222–24

Responsibility, learning, through work, 230

Responsiveness of children, 42

Revelation, personal, 109

Romney, Marion G., 38–39; on reading Book of Mormon as family, 115; reads to sick son, 123; on family home evening, 264

Rules, family: importance of enforcing, 192; as tool in discipline,

196–97. *See also* Discipline; Standards

Sabbath Day: conveying value of observing, 19–21; activities appropriate to, 213–14; scriptural injunctions regarding, 214–17; blessings of observing, 217; boy declines to work on, 245–46; honoring, temporal blessings accompanying, 260–61

Savings, 245, 250–52, 261

Scripture reading, family: high priority of, 18–19; benefits of, 103–4, 114-15; as model for personal study, 109–10; excuses for neglecting, 110–11; family makes decision to implement, 115–16; finding set time for, 116-18; choosing place for, 118–19; suggested methods for, 119–25; building variety into, 123–25; as teaching tool, 125–26; enhancing faith through, 129–30; overcoming negative feelings about, 130–32; family members testify of, 139–42; impact of, demonstrated in child's talk, 142–44

Scriptures: using, to teach family, 45–47; praying to understand, 48, 120; principles of prayer found in, 90–92; passages in, showing value of Lord's word, 104–6; importance of, quotations from President Benson on, 106–9; as key to personal revelation, 109; asking questions while reading, 121; peace found in, 132–33; passages in, on Sabbath Day, 214–18; helping children seek solutions in, 274

Sealing power, 331–32

Self-discipline, 189–91; learned through work, 230–31

Self-esteem, building, in children, 200–203

Service: seeking opportunities for, 274; blessings of, 301, 327–29; brings increased love, 309–10; setting example of, 326

Sex education, 221–22
Skills: developing, through work,
232–33; passing on, to children,
273
Sleep-overs, 156
Smith, Joseph, 129–30
Smith, Joseph F., 176–77, 302,
313–14, 327
Smoking, 219–20; on airplane, story
of, 304–5
Snow shoveling, 311–13
Spanking, 198
Spelling test, son confesses cheating
on, 217–19
Spirit: teaching by, 37–42; listening
with, 38–39; inviting, through
prayer, 43–45; using scriptures to
invite, 45–49; inviting, through
testifying, 49-53; using music to
invite, 53–57; inviting, through
expressing love, 57–62; inviting,
through priesthood ordinances,
67–71. *See also* Holy Ghost
Spiritual experiences: helping children have, 44; sharing, with family, 62-66; recording, 63, 171;
enhance gospel standards, 154;
recognizing, 171
Spiritual welfare: ideas for promot-
ing, 13–14; caring for, shows love,
317-19
Standards: setting, for family,
155–59; concerning dating, 159–
61 *See also* Rules, family
Summer projects, 294–95

Talents, developing, 232–42, 290–
95
Teaching: with the Spirit, 39–41, 42;
is parents' responsibility, 274–75,
313–14
Teasing, 180, 303
Television: worldly influence of, 161;
controlling use of, 211–12, 273
Temple president, President Kimball's counsel to, 148–49
Temporal welfare: ideas for promot-
ing, 14; spiritual connection to,
253-54; principles of, 258–62; car-

ing for, love shown through, 311–
17
Testimony: power of, 49–50; obtain-
ing one's own, 52–53; family dis-
cussion about, 112–13
Tests of faith, 137–38
Thermometer, broken, story of,
223–24
Time, gift of, 272
Tithing: teaching children to pay,
208–9; principle of, 258
Trust between parents and children,
188–89
Tuttle, A. Theodore, 24–25

Unemployed engineer, story of,
254–57

Vacation, family's trials during,
95–98
Values, spiritual, 19–21
Visits: to less active members,
323–24; to elderly, 324–26

Webb, Edward and Caroline Amelia
Owens, 204–5
Welfare, inspired principles of,
225–26
Whitney, Orson F., xv, 331–32
Wisdom, gaining, 40–41
Woodruff, Wilford, 235–36
Word of Wisdom, 29–30, 219–21
Work: commandments regarding,
226–27; teaching principles of, in
home, 227–30; spiritual benefits
of, 230–32; skills developed
through, 232–33; teaching,
through gardening, 233–35; outside the home, 235–36, 242, 249-
50; "entrepreneurial," stories
illustrating, 236–41; excuses for
avoiding, 242; finding, outside
home, 243–47; instilling desire
for, in children, 247–49
Worship, importance of, 36–37

Year's supply, 234–35
Young, Brigham, 207, 332
Youth, study of, in Church, 17–19